The Rapture Trap

D0454181

The Rapture Trap

A Catholic Response to "End Times" Fever

Paul Thigpen, Ph.D.

ASCENSION
P R E S S

Cover design: Kinsey Caruth
Printed in the United States of America
ISBN 0-9659228-2-0

Acknowledgments

Many thanks to . . .

- Matthew Pinto and his colleagues at Ascension Press. Matt conceived the idea for this book and labored with boundless energy and patience to see it brought to birth.
- Kinsey Caruth, for his fine cover design.
- Readers of the first draft, many of them also my good friends, whose thoughtful critiques improved the manuscript considerably: Kathy Andes, Mark Brumley, Brian Butler, Michael Fleury, Justin Foster, Barbara and Emily Griswold , Jeff and Lauren Morris, Mark Shea, Patrick Sullivan, and Scott Winchel.
- Lisa Lynch and Lucy Scholand, for their proofreading expertise.
- Carl Olson, who generously shared his personal experience and research on this topic. His book on similar issues should be out soon, and I look forward to it.

Contents

For my dear wife, Leisa,
and my delightful offspring,
Lydia and Elijah,
all blessed with hearts of infinite patience
and good humor.
They thought the Second Coming would probably
occur before I finally finished writing this book.

Foreword

In the mid-seventies, an engineering student I know experienced a powerful, life-changing adult re-conversion to Christ. He was "born again," in the popular language of evangelical Protestantism, and he grew intent on loving and serving the Lord as completely as he could. Not long afterwards, a friend, anxious to share a book that had shaken his own life to the roots, passed along a copy of *The Late Great Planet Earth*, a book of apocalyptic speculations by the Protestant fundamentalist writer Hal Lindsey.

Unable to put the book down, the young man, now working as a plastics engineer, read it from cover to cover. Without adequate religious training to challenge the book's premises, and trusting in his friend's sincerity, he accepted the book's teaching, hook, line, and "rapture."

In time, the book's emphasis on the notion of a "rapture"— an imminent "secret" coming of Christ—led the young man to question his vocation: "If Jesus were to return *tonight*, would He be pleased with what I'm doing with my life? Would I be content to tell Him that I'm dedicating my life to making better plastic cups, butter tubs, and coffee decanters?" Eventually this was one reason that the engineer decided to leave his secular career and enter the seminary instead.

In case you haven't guessed, I was that young man, and for several years I was caught up in the apocalyptic views expressed in books such as Hal Lindsey's little volume and the more recent *Left Behind* series. During my years of study at an evangelical seminary, I was confronted with every Protestant "end times" notion imaginable. Often during theology classes, or especially around the dinner table, seminarians would debate over the details, the timing, and the imminence of Christ's return.

Sometimes contradicting views would split us along denominational lines. (The majority of mainline Protestants actually do not believe in the secret rapture.) Too often these debates led to unchristian anger. I must even admit, shamefaced, that I once lost a close friendship because my friend and I could not see eye-to-eye about whether the timing of Christ's second coming was preordained or whether it was dependent upon man's free will in his efforts to reform the world.

I encountered again these same issues constantly during my years as a Protestant minister. In every congregation I served, some member or members would challenge the long-term planning of the church because the rapture of true believers, snatching them out of the world into heaven, was to occur any minute. "Forget tomorrow!" they insisted. "We must insure that all are ready to meet their Maker tonight!"

Unfortunately, I was not aware at the time of any books as thorough and helpful as *The Rapture Trap*. Dr. Paul Thigpen, a Catholic convert coming from an evangelical background himself, is well equipped to outline and critique the apocalyptic views so prevalent in Protestant thinking. This extremely well-researched and well-written book clearly explains the background and dangers of certain "end times" views in vogue today. But in this volume you will also find a hidden treasure: Dr. Thigpen addresses as well, in simple layman's terms, the larger doctrinal and apologetical issues that surround these renegade apocalyptic theories.

I wish that *The Rapture Trap* had come along years ago for other reasons as well. After nine years as a Protestant minister, by the grace of God and through the witness of faithful Catholics (and Catholic converts such as my co-seminarians

Scott and Kimberly Hahn), my family and I were led "home" to the Catholic faith. We rejoiced to discover the trustworthy guidance of the Catholic Magisterium in union with Peter.

Not long after our conversion to the Catholic Church, my wife and I encountered the stories of the apparitions of Our Lady of Guadalupe and Fatima. As Protestants, we had never heard of these events, nor the miracles and conversions that accompanied them. Since the Church has officially approved these particular private revelations, we were able to embrace their message, and we grew in holiness as a result.

Our interest in private revelations was piqued, however, and soon we discovered that Catholics have their own versions of "end times" fever. Through books and the witness of seemingly trustworthy and theologically astute Catholic friends, we learned about the many contemporary reports of Marian apparitions. We even met several visionaries and became close friends with well-known Marian authors and speakers.

In time, we thoroughly absorbed the dire implications of these more recent claims to private revelation, waiting for "the miracle," "the warning," "the three days of darkness," "the chastisement," "the apostasy," and eventually "the age of peace." Along with so many Catholics equally convinced of the validity of the messages predicting such events, we hunkered down for what we believed might prove to be difficult days ahead at the turn of the millennium. And though I was well aware that great spiritual writers such as St. John of the Cross and Fr. Benedict Groeschel had cautioned against becoming too focused on such external phenomena, the unbridled enthusiasm of our respected Marian friends drew us along with abandon.

I certainly wish that *The Rapture Trap* had been around at that time to guide our enthusiasm. In this diamond of a book, Dr. Thigpen not only addresses misguided apocalyptic thought among Protestants, he also presents the history of certain strands of popular apocalyptic thought among Catholics. As a bonus, he provides a tremendously helpful summary of how to discern the validity and trustworthiness of private revelations. On this topic and many others, you will learn much about your Catholic faith from this wonderful book.

As I look back at the times when I was drawn so sincerely into the dangers addressed by Dr. Thigpen, I recognize that these ideas were so palatable because they were communicated to me by otherwise trustworthy friends. And isn't this usually the case? Most Catholics are led out of the Church by seemingly trustworthy friends. And most Christians are led into heresy by people they think they can trust. This is why, as Dr. Thigpen emphasizes, we must trust the Church that Jesus Christ gave us to guide us into all truth. Amid the countless apocalyptic speculations of Protestants and Catholics alike, Dr. Thigpen offers a perspective on Christ's second coming based firmly on the teaching of the Magisterium.

Jesus warned us not to speculate about the day or the hour of His coming for an important reason. He wants us rather to "watch" and "be ready," because He can come at any moment, and "the Son of Man is coming at an hour [we] do not expect" (see Matthew 25:42–44). In the meantime, we are to "seek first His kingdom and His righteousness" (Matthew 6:33). We are to live lives of detachment, lives of love for God and our neighbor, lives in imitation of Jesus.

When, however, we become transfixed on some imminent date or period of time—whether it's for the "rapture" or for a "chastisement"—then our spiritual preparations come to be focused on that date or time as well. And when that period comes and goes without fulfilling such sharp expectations, as has happened so many times in Church history, the motivation for our spiritual preparation dwindles. Once-enthusiastic believers grow depressed and discouraged, and in some cases they turn away from God altogether.

This is why Dr. Thigpen's book is so crucial for contemporary Christians. We must put our faith in Jesus Christ and trust His Church, not the theories of men. My advice to you is this: Rather than being anxious about the "signs of the times" so you can determine the imminent "day and hour" (Matthew 24:36), read this wonderful book by Dr. Thigpen. In the end, in the midst of so many contradictory voices, you will be better equipped to follow Jesus' advice more assuredly: "Watch, therefore. . . . Be ready" (Matthew 25:42, 44).

Marcus C. Grodi
President, The Coming Home Network
Host, The Journey Home

"The Truth Will Set You Free"

An Introduction

What do the numbers 200, 380, 838, 1000, 1260, 1533, 1844, 1914, and 1988 all have in common?

No, these are not winning lottery ticket numbers. They are all dates when large groups of people thought the world would come to an end. And that is to name only a few.

One of those dates I remember well. Back in the summer of 1988, some years before I became a Catholic, excitement was sweeping through evangelical Protestant circles. All the talk in my congregation seemed to center on a new book by a man named Edgar Whisenant, who carefully laid out eighty-eight reasons why Jesus would be returning to earth in 1988. The little volume was selling fast nationwide, and people were breathless over the author's claim that Jesus was coming back to earth in September of that year.

The kids at church, who had to go back to school in late August, were praying that He would consider arriving a little *early*.

I must say honestly that I never gave the book's thesis any serious consideration. For starters, my Ph.D. is in church history, with a specialty in American religion. One of the university courses I have taught focuses exclusively on the many groups throughout history who have claimed that the end of the world was at hand, only to be disappointed. Many volumes could be filled with accounts of mistaken ideas about the "end times" and the sad consequences of such wrong notions.

In any case, I did read the book as background for a magazine article I was writing. When I did, it was immediately clear that Whisenant was not qualified to be writing Bible expositions, especially on so difficult a subject. He was a former NASA engineer who claimed no special revelations from God. (If he had, I might have had to pay a little more attention to what he said.) Instead, the author simply thought he had been able to make some important numerical calculations from Scripture and history. The results, he insisted, pointed conclusively to Rosh Hashana, the Jewish New Year, in September of 1988, as the time of Christ's return.

Somehow, I could not imagine how such an age-old puzzle as the date of Christ's return could be solved using a calculator. More importantly, I knew that Jesus had stated flatly to His disciples that "of that day and hour no one knows, not even the angels of heaven, nor the Son, but the Father only" (Matthew 24:36).

Needless to say, the world is still here. Whisenant's failed predictions proved once again that it doesn't take a NASA rocket scientist to figure out when Jesus is coming back.

It takes God the Father.

The second coming of our Lord is no doubt in many ways a mystery. We will never figure it out completely and certainly not before it happens. But there is still a great deal we can know about Christ's return, and no Christian should be ignorant of what God the Father has revealed to us.

Why does it matter? Because "the truth will set you free" (John 8:32, NAB) and a whole lot wiser and holier, too. Jesus Christ, who died and was raised from the dead, who ascended into heaven and is reigning there in glory with the Father, is coming back to earth! He is coming to raise the dead of every generation and then to judge the living and the dead, to set this messed-up world aright.

You may not think often about these impending events.

But they concern you deeply. You will be one of those whom Christ judges. How well you are able to prepare for that sobering occasion depends in part on your knowing the truth —the truth about the reasons He came to earth the first time, the reasons He is coming back, and the plans He has for you in the meantime.

The "Secret Rapture"

Sadly enough, a mistaken and rather novel idea about Christ's return, rooted in fundamentalist Protestant teaching, is making the rounds of our culture these days. It claims that Jesus is coming back, not once more, but twice. One of those times, this teaching asserts, He will come secretly to snatch away true believers from their troubles on earth. This event has been dubbed the "rapture" (or "secret rapture"), from a Latin verb that means "caught up" or "snatched."

If you are Catholic when Jesus comes, many of the preachers of this idea insist, you had better be careful. If you have failed to renounce some of the essential beliefs the Church has taught you, too bad. You are not a true Christian. You will be left behind.

That claim is simply not true. It is a dangerous error. And that is why this book was written. In recent days many unsuspecting Catholics have gotten caught in the "rapture trap." I want to help them get free of this unbiblical idea and the anti-Catholic theology to which it is typically shackled. I want to warn other Catholics who might be in danger of getting ensnared. And I hope to help equip Catholic pastors and teachers to dismantle the trap whenever they encounter it.

At this writing the runaway best-sellers in the *Left Behind* series of novels, and the other media products being promoted with them, have achieved remarkable popularity in America. These books push the misguided "secret rapture" agenda, and their teaching can be seductive because they are packaged as entertainment. Catholics are often urged by their non-Catholic friends to read the novels or view the movie version. My hope is that this book will help to expose the troublesome *Left Behind* agenda in particular.

Catholics With Common Sense

The Rapture Trap is written primarily, then, for everyday Catholics who accept the God-given teaching authority of the Church and who have a good dose of common sense. They will find here ample grounds for rejecting the rapture teaching as misguided and alien to both Sacred Scripture and Sacred Tradition. I trust they will also discover much more in these pages: an overview of Catholic teaching on the "close of the age" (Matthew 24:3; 28:20); some insights for responding to other questionable claims about the end times; and encouragement to grow spiritually strong in the rich soil of the Catholic faith.

Readers of all backgrounds who are curious about the history of Christian thought—especially with regard to ideas about the end of the world—will find plenty here to pique their interest.

Some readers taking up this little volume may deny or seriously doubt the Catholic Church's unique gift from God to interpret the Scripture according to the mind of the Holy Spirit. They will find the book less to their liking. This is the case because such readers have larger issues to settle before they can go very far toward understanding and appreciating Catholic teaching about the close of the age.

One of these larger issues should be immediately apparent. Intelligent, sincere Christians disagree sharply over the meaning of biblical texts about the end times and other subjects of equal importance. If God has left us without an objective, authoritative interpreter of the Bible, then how can anyone have confidence in any particular interpretation?

All the tedious and prickly debates over the true meaning of a biblical Greek term used by St. Paul, or over the true significance of a horned beast pictured in the book of Revelation, really count for very little until this larger issue of authority is resolved. And once the larger issue is resolved, some of these minor debates may count for nothing at all.

For this reason, readers who have not yet settled the issue of who has the God-given authority to interpret the Scripture should probably read, along with this text, some books grappling with that subject. I would recommend, as a good place to begin, a simple, brief, and insightful book entitled *By What Authority? An Evangelical Discovers Catholic Tradition* by Mark P. Shea (Our Sunday Visitor, 1996).

At the same time, Catholic apologists whose work leads them into complicated debates with rapture believers may be looking for a more detailed presentation of arguments over specific biblical texts. I would caution them that such arguments often prove to be of limited value: first, as I have noted, because they tend to ignore or obscure the larger, more definitive, issues; second, because such debates may yield too much ground to faulty fundamentalist presuppositions about biblical interpretation.

Nevertheless, Catholic apologists who are willing to brave these treacherous waters of contention may find useful historical points in this text, as well as more general comments about the flaws of "biblical" arguments made by rapture teachers. In addition, Catholic apologists should try reading the arguments presented by certain evangelical Protestants who also oppose the rapture teaching. This is not really, after all, merely a Catholic-Protestant debate; even among non-Catholic Christians throughout history, rapture believers are a decided minority, often viewed as somewhat eccentric by their fellows. So the Catholic apologist can actually challenge the idea largely on an opponent's own terms, if necessary, simply by quoting the arguments of a respectable evangelical Bible scholar such as Robert H. Gundry. I recommend in particular Gundry's books *The Church and the Tribulation: A Biblical Examination of Posttribulationism* (Zondervan, 1973) and *First the Antichrist: A Book for Lay Christians Approaching the Third Millennium and Inquiring Whether Jesus Will Come to Take the Church out of the World Before the Tribulation* (whew!) (Baker, 1997).[1]

Getting the Big Picture

The meaning of Christ's second coming cannot be adequately understood apart from the meaning of His first coming. Nor can it be understood apart from the meaning of the present age—the time between His two comings. The work of Christ on behalf of the human race is of one piece; it stretches from the first moment of the world's creation to the last moment of history and beyond. So chapters two, three, and four of this book provide in simple terms an outline of Catholic teaching on these subjects.

If you are interested solely in a discussion of the rapture teaching, you may want to skim those three chapters quickly or perhaps even skip to chapter five, "'As the Lightning Comes'—What Does the Bible Say About the Second Advent?" If you skip over this material, however, you should keep in mind that you might be missing some important aspects of the big picture. Though chapters two through four admittedly provide mostly background, such background is critical for understanding the rapture notion and how it differs from the teaching of the Catholic Church.

The Foundation of Our Hope

Above all, I want this book to help readers move beyond less important end-times issues so they can focus on the Lord Jesus Christ—the One who stands waiting at the end of history, who will bring the age to a close. His promise to return in triumph is the foundation of our hope that one day, God will be "all in all" (1 Corinthians 15:28, NAB).

To know Christ, who is Himself "the Truth" (John 14:6), we gladly turn to the teaching of "the Church of the living God, the pillar and bulwark of the truth" (1 Timothy 3:15). After all, it was the Holy Spirit's preaching through the Catholic Church that first told the world about the good news of Christ's coming. And it is the Holy Spirit's teaching through the Catholic Church that can keep us safely in the truth about His coming again.

Paul Thigpen
The Feast of the Ascension of Our Lord
in the year of our Lord 2001

1

Left Behind?

The Puzzling Popularity of an Odd Idea

Imagine the scene: High above the Atlantic, a 747 jetliner pierces the night on its way from Chicago to London. Inside, passengers are settling down to sleep—children clutching their teddy bears, young professionals shutting down their laptops, elderly couples holding hands while they doze off to the drone of the engines. With no more requests for blankets or pillows, the flight attendant relaxes and chats with the captain. The rest of the evening, she concludes, should be uneventful.

But just then, toward the rear of the cabin, an elderly woman stirs and finds that her husband is missing. Within moments other passengers have made similar discoveries. All the children and many of the adults have left their seats and are nowhere to be found. In a sealed aircraft at thirty-five thousand feet above the ocean, scores of people have simply vanished.

Stranger still, they seem to have disappeared naked. Their clothing, eyeglasses, and jewelry have been left behind neatly in their seats—shirts and blouses still buttoned up, neckties and scarves still knotted, belts still threaded through belt loops and buckled. Mothers call out for their little ones, first in puzzlement, then in desperation. Their panic spreads. Soon the cabin is in chaos, and the flight crew searches for some explanation of this frightening development.

As the captain turns the plane around to head back to Chicago, he learns by radio that the same mysterious phenomenon has occurred in other places. The passengers on his flight actually got off easy. On many planes pilots have disappeared, and in many airports air traffic controllers have vanished. Planes are colliding and falling from the sky, taking countless victims to a fiery death.

On the ground, things are even worse. Millions of vehicles seem to have suddenly lost their drivers while still in motion, leaving highways littered with wrecks while stunned, bloodied passengers scream for help. Everywhere, mothers wail hysterically, convinced that their babies have been snatched right from under their noses by some invisible kidnapper. Is America suffering from some kind of mass hysteria?

No—the event has taken place worldwide. Millions of people, from every nation, have dissolved without leaving a trace. And the billions of bewildered people left behind must face an unprecedented global nightmare of terror, death, and destruction.

Who or what is behind it all? Has some powerful international terrorist organization coordinated an attack? Has some bizarre plague swept the globe? Have malicious extraterrestrials invaded the planet?

No, say the authors of the best-selling novel whose plot emerges from this fantasy scenario. The mastermind behind all this horror is none other than Jesus Christ.[2]

Rapture Fever

Welcome to the world of *Left Behind*, religious fiction about the "end times" by evangelical Protestant writers Tim LaHaye and Jerry Jenkins. LaHaye, a graduate of Bob Jones University, has been a popular author, speaker, and pastor in American evangelical circles since the 1970s. Writing about biblical prophecy has been one of his specialties. Jenkins is a professional writer with more than a hundred books to his credit.

Breaking new ground in the religious publishing world, these authors' vision of the end of history has created a multimillion-dollar apocalyptic industry: at the time of this writing, nine best-selling books for adults in the *Left Behind* series, fourteen more for children, compact discs, video- and audiotapes, websites, chat rooms, and a full-length feature film. You can send friends electronic cards with scenes from the movie or download *Left Behind* images as wallpaper and screen savers.

What exactly has Jesus to do with this startling story line? Why in the world would He want to make people disappear and throw the human race into chaos? According to LaHaye and Jenkins, Jesus is coming back secretly in an event known as the "rapture"—a name that (as we noted in the Introduction) comes from the Latin verb that means literally "caught up" or "snatched." These two authors believe that Christ will invisibly snatch true believers and innocent children, both living and dead, up into heaven. Their divine abduction will cause massive, worldwide turmoil, and once they are gone, the Devil will be free to take control of the world through his puppet, the Antichrist.

Gross horrors will accompany this diabolical man's wicked reign. But the rapture will have taken place because, according to the authors, God has promised to spare true believers from the evil by snatching them off the planet before the "great tribulation" begins. Later, after the tribulation has reached its climax, Christ will come back yet once more, this time publicly in "a glorious appearing," to defeat the forces of evil and bring history to a close.

In this scenario, then, Christ comes to earth a total of three times: once at His birth in Bethlehem two thousand years ago; once at the secret rapture; and once in glory at the close of the

age. Not surprisingly, this notion sounds alien to Christians
who are familiar with the Church's ancient teaching about
the Second Coming but have never heard about a third one.

Such talk about an extra or "third" coming of Christ raises
a theological red flag, as it should, for the majority of Christians (Catholics, Eastern Orthodox, and many Protestants as
well), who adhere to the traditional belief in only two: the
First Advent (two thousand years ago) and the Second Advent (Christ's final appearance in glory). So rapture teachers
usually protest that they don't really believe in three comings.
Rather, they insist, Christ's second coming has two *phases*—
the secret rapture and the glorious appearing.[3]

Nevertheless, in their belief system Christ does indeed
come down from heaven and return there again twice before His final coming, making a total of three descents. As
one evangelical scholar comments: "Two separate movements
from heaven to earth cannot by any stretch of fancy be considered one coming."[4] For this reason, notwithstanding the
attempts to dodge the issue with references to two "phases"
of a single coming, in this discussion we will sometimes speak
of the rapture as the doctrine of a "third" or "extra" coming
of Christ.

However we may describe this proposed scenario of the future, millions of Christians, including most Catholics, would
find it mystifying. Some of its elements, of course, they would
recognize. The Catholic Church has taught since biblical
times about the Antichrist: A wicked and powerful figure
attempting to replace Christ, he will one day appear to trouble the world before the Lord returns in glory to raise the
dead and judge the human race. Most Christians also know
that Christ has come and Christ will come again; that He
has both a first and a second coming.

With this much, believers of every variety are acquainted.
But what about this notion of an invisible "third" coming

between the other two? Where does the idea of a "secret rapture" come from?

For countless Americans, even many who have neither read the *Left Behind* books nor seen the movie, the main outline of the plot is actually quite familiar. LaHaye and Jenkins are only providing speculative details for a story that numerous evangelical and fundamentalist Protestants believe is literally the gospel truth. Though the rapture doctrine was nearly unheard of before the nineteenth century, since that time it has spread like a fever throughout the United States and beyond, wherever a particular brand of Protestant fundamentalism has flourished.[5]

And no wonder. If you are convinced that the end of the world is coming soon (as Protestant fundamentalists tend to be), and that the Antichrist is thus right around the corner, you are probably terrified at the prospect of facing him or of suffering the catastrophes prophesied in the Bible for the last days of earth's history. The secret rapture doctrine relieves your fears because it promises you an escape from all the horror of brutal persecutions, wars, earthquakes, famines, plagues, and worse. No doubt the current popularity of such a comforting teaching accounts to a great extent for the phenomenal sales of the *Left Behind* media products.

It's in the Bible?

If you ask a fundamentalist Protestant why he believes in the rapture, he will quickly tell you that it is in the Bible. He will usually be able to cite several verses from Scripture that he offers as "proof" of his doctrine, some from St. Paul's epistles and some from our Lord's statements in the Gospels.

Once he begins to lay out his notions of the end times, he will soon reveal that the secret rapture is only one item in a much longer spreadsheet of ideas—ideas he claims can map out events soon to bring human history on earth to a close. You will likely hear vivid descriptions of the Antichrist and predictions of specific political events in the Middle East, tossed about with a number of mysterious terms mined from the last book of the Bible, the book of Revelation: "the four horsemen," "the mark of the beast," "the false prophet," "the whore of Babylon," and that most infamous of numbers, "666."

Nevertheless, that same Bible, when read or heard by more than a billion other Christians—other kinds of Protestants, as well as Catholics and Eastern Orthodox—tells no such story. Though the rapture teachers insist they are only interpreting "the plain sense" of Scripture, the truth is that they are reading it through a peculiar theological lens. In other words, they already have in place a certain set of assumptions about what they will find there. These assumptions have often been ingrained in them since childhood through repeated sermons, full of dramatic intensity, about the end of the world, a favorite theme of countless fundamentalist preachers.

As we shall see, though these apocalyptic Christians may be proud of calling themselves "Bible believers," their cherished doctrine simply does not appear anywhere in the Bible. But their assumptions keep them from seeing the obvious meaning of several scriptural texts that the Church has always interpreted in a straightforward way: namely, as prophecies of a single return of Christ to the earth, bodily and publicly, arrayed in a glory so magnificent that it could never be kept secret.

Catching the Fever

Sadly enough, even some Catholics are catching rapture fever these days. Their evangelical Protestant friends and relatives may have urged them to read the *Left Behind* books or listen to the tapes; they may even have received complimentary tickets for the movie. Perhaps they have attended a "revival meeting" with an evangelical acquaintance, where they heard fiery preaching on the end times.

When Catholics encounter these presentations, they may be able to recognize and affirm in them certain basic elements of biblical prophecies about the close of history: the coming of the Antichrist, the unprecedented suffering that awaits the world, the second advent of Christ, the resurrection of the dead, the Last Judgment. Yet they may not know the traditional Catholic interpretation of the relevant Scripture passages well enough to discern the errors, the speculative and often contradictory ideas, that have grown up in the tangled thicket of fundamentalist "Bible prophecy teaching." In fact, if they are like many Catholics in contemporary America, they have had minimal religious training about what the Church teaches even on the basics of this subject.

In that kind of spiritual vacuum, Catholics who hear the secret rapture teaching for the first time may find it seductive. Who would want to refuse a promise that God will provide a miraculous escape from horrifying diabolical attack? In this way, an increasing number of Catholics today have fallen into this dangerous theological trap.

Dangers of this Doctrine

At this point someone might object: Why should we consider this error "dangerous"? Does it really make much difference whether people believe in a rapture? If they are wrong about getting suddenly snatched out of the Antichrist's clutches, then history itself will prove them wrong. What does it · matter in the meantime?

Actually, it matters a great deal. If, as our Lord insisted, "the truth will set you free" (John 8:32, NAB), then false

doctrine can destroy your freedom. If you embrace error in
your thinking, it can lead you to significant errors in behavior
as well.

Anywhere the truth is denied or even obscured, danger
is lurking, especially when it is a question of truth about so
important a matter as the final outcome of human history.
Our convictions about how the world will end, and what
role we ourselves will play in that ending, can shape deeply
the ways in which we live in the world day to day. If you
doubt that such a powerful connection can operate between
our views of the future and our behavior in the present, you
need only recall the fate of several religious groups who met
a tragic end in recent years because they believed a lie. Both
the People's Temple followers of Jim Jones and the disciples
of the Heaven's Gate community, for example, committed
mass suicide as a way of acting out the role they believed
they had in an apocalyptic drama.

This is not to suggest, of course, that fundamentalist Protestants are likely to commit mass suicide because of their belief
in the secret rapture. Nevertheless, such a belief often affects
Christians' attitudes and behaviors in a way that is no less
real, if less dramatic. If you are convinced that one day soon
you will joyfully slip away to heaven and escape the worst
the world has to offer, you may dismiss most efforts to fight
against evil in that world. What good is a struggle against
the culture of death, against the propaganda of immorality's
champions, against the erosion of basic freedoms, if we are
soon to be snatched away? Why bother, if the social and
political fate of the world we will leave behind has already
been sealed?

Ironically, evangelical Protestants in America before the
Civil War were a dominant force in the social and political
arenas because of their optimism that they could improve

the world according to gospel mandates (see, for example, Matthew 25:31–40). Much like countless Catholic activists of every generation, they founded and energetically maintained a vast network of organizations to transform society. Evangelicals figured prominently in nationally organized efforts to abolish slavery, care for the sick and orphaned, educate children, oppose alcohol abuse, and support numerous other causes.

Sadly enough, the tragedy of the Civil War was followed by serious disruptions in American life caused by massive immigration and industrialization, among other factors. Feeling overwhelmed by the resulting changes, the American evangelical community as a whole lost confidence in its ability to influence society. The maintenance and control of older evangelical institutions for the most part passed over to their more "liberal" Protestant brethren, who tended to welcome the changes in society, believing that the Holy Spirit was somehow hidden within the spirit of the age.

As evangelicals were growing deeply pessimistic about their world, their views about the end times began to change accordingly. As we shall see in chapter six, during this period the rapture doctrine grew in popularity and became a central element in the framework of their religious beliefs. Did that doctrine cause evangelical social and political apathy, or did such apathy make evangelicals more likely to embrace the doctrine? Whichever the case, the notion of a secret rapture was certainly compatible with such attitudes, and it was capable of strengthening and entrenching them—just as it can strengthen and entrench them today.

Of course, not every believer in the rapture shuns social and political activism. For example, Tim LaHaye's wife, Beverly LaHaye, shares his theology yet has worked tirelessly on behalf of numerous social and political causes. At the same time, plenty of Catholics and other Christians who have never heard of the rapture certainly seem oblivious to the critical battle against evil being waged on so many fronts in our day.

Nevertheless, anyone who has sat through many fundamentalist sermons has likely found that frequent attention given to rapture doctrine rarely spurs preaching about why Christians should volunteer at soup kitchens or lobby elected officials for more just laws. The temptation to retreat is certainly sharpened by the conviction that God's own plans for His "troops" call for escape rather than engagement.

An Unbiblical View of Suffering

The secret rapture doctrine is dangerous in a second way: It can foster an unbiblical view of suffering for the Faith. It can be understood to imply that ultimately God wants to shield contemporary Christians completely from the injuries of those who oppose them for taking their stand with Him. Yet the life of Jesus Christ and the lives of His saints throughout history amply demonstrate otherwise.

The new official list of martyrs of the Catholic Church, recently published by the Vatican, includes more than seven thousand new names, many of whom died for Christ in our lifetime. These brave souls—only a few of perhaps millions of Christians put to death for their faith in the past century alone—faced the horrors of lesser antichrists who hated and devastated the Church, foreshadowing the great Antichrist and the great tribulation still to come (see 1 John 2:18, 22; 4:3; 2 John 7). Yet these believers certainly were not "raptured" away to heaven when the going got tough.[6]

The *Left Behind* series assumes a worldview that is seriously limited, displaying the cramped horizons of all too many comfortable, suburban, middle-class Americans. A broader range of vision would show that even now, Christians in places such as China and Sudan are being imprisoned, enslaved, tortured, murdered, some even brutally crucified, for their faith. Could we dare to look them in the eye and tell them that God has promised to spare true believers from such persecution? No. Instead, we would have to humble ourselves to learn from them, and from the martyrs before them, a powerful lesson, written in their own blood: "All who desire to live a godly life in Christ Jesus will be persecuted" (2 Timothy 3:12).

Ties to Anti-Catholic Teaching

The rapture doctrine is dangerous in yet a third way: It is often tied to a larger, complex body of religious teachings that are explicitly anti-Catholic. As we will see in chapter seven, when fundamentalist authors such as LaHaye and Jenkins write nonfiction books to explain the theology behind their novels, they make it clear that they believe the Catholic Church is a creation of the Devil and will be a tool of the Antichrist. They go so far as to associate the Vatican with the bloodthirsty "whore of Babylon" pictured in the book of Revelation, who drinks the blood of the Christian martyrs in the last days of the world (see Revelation 17:1—18:24).[7]

Of course, not every Christian who believes in the secret rapture also believes that the Catholic Church is demonic. Yet many of the preachers who promote this doctrine work hard to persuade Catholics to leave the Church and join their own congregations instead. They warn that those who remain Catholic could well be left behind at Christ's secret coming, become pawns of God's enemies, and be damned to hell for eternity.

Catholics who read the *Left Behind* books or see the movie are thus at risk of being deceived into thinking that the very Church Jesus Christ founded on St. Peter and through the other Apostles is actually a counterfeit church. Drawn into reading other books or attending religious meetings that use these spiritual scare tactics, they may not be prepared with an adequate defense against such high-pressure fundamentalist propaganda.

Once we become aware of the spiritual damage the rapture doctrine can do to Christians who embrace it, we realize why it is so important to establish a basic understanding of the Catholic Church's solidly biblical teaching about the end of the world. To do that, however, we have to take a few steps back to view the biblical picture of human history as a whole.

Getting the Big Picture

To repeat what we noted in the Introduction: The meaning of Christ's second coming cannot be adequately understood apart from the meaning of His first coming. Nor can it be understood apart from the meaning of the present age—the time between His two comings. So the next three chapters (two, three, and four) provide in simple terms an overview of Catholic teaching on these subjects.

If you are interested solely in a discussion of the rapture teaching, you may want to skim these next chapters quickly, or perhaps even skip to chapter five, "'As the Lightning Comes'—What Does the Bible Say About the Second Coming?" If you skip over this material, however, you should keep in mind that you might be missing some important aspects of the big picture. This background is critical for understanding the rapture notion and how it differs from the teaching of the Catholic Church. Consider, for example, these questions:

- Why exactly does Christ need to come back? What "unfinished business" will He take care of that He didn't complete the first time He came?

- What are some of the possible reasons why Jesus has not yet returned to earth, even after two thousand years?
- What important connection exists between the Eucharist and the second coming of Christ?
- Why will a mere profession of faith—which some non-Catholics view as a kind of eternal "fire insurance"—be insufficient to keep us out of hell when Christ comes back to bring Judgment Day?
- How do the answers to all these questions reveal errors in the larger system of theology that typically lies behind the rapture doctrine?

These and other significant issues will be addressed in the next three chapters.

In the book of Revelation (also known as the "Apocalypse," a word that means the same thing), our Lord identifies Himself as the One "who *is* and who *was* and who *is to come*" (Revelation 1:8, emphasis added). In the next three chapters, then, let's take a look at the scriptural texts dealing with the three historical segments of Christ's work as reflected in this statement: first, His initial coming to earth two thousand years ago; second, His ministry through the Church now; and, finally, His return to earth on a day still to come. What does the Bible *really* say about Jesus' mission—past, present, and future?

2

"The Word Became Flesh"

Why Did Christ Come the First Time?

It was a night unlike any other since the beginning of the world.

A newborn Baby cried out in hunger—and the voice that pierced the darkness was the voice of the One who had spoken light itself into being. The tiny hand His mother stroked was the hand of the One who had set the galaxies spinning, who had filled up the seas and shaped the first man from the dust.

That night, time gave birth to Eternity. Space gave a home to Infinity. The Potter climbed inside His clay.

God Himself had come to earth.

All Christians, whatever their views of the future, agree that the central event of human history occurred two thousand years in the past: God took on our human nature, joined it to His divine nature, and was born on earth as a Man. That Man was Jesus Christ. As St. John's Gospel puts it, the Son of God, who was Himself God, "became flesh and dwelt among us" (John 1:14). In Christ, St. Paul tells us, "all the fulness of God was pleased to dwell" (Colossians 1:19).

Jesus was born in the town of Bethlehem to the Blessed Virgin Mary: "And she gave birth to her firstborn son and wrapped Him in swaddling clothes, and laid Him in a manger" (Luke 2:7). This coming of Christ into the world is known as His first "advent" (the word literally means "coming"). From this term we get the name of the annual liturgical season leading up to our celebration of His birth.

"Jesus Christ is the same yesterday and today and for ever" (Hebrews 13:8). The same God-Man who was born in Bethlehem is the One who now gives Himself to the world through the Church and who will come again one day in glory. So only when we appreciate why the Son of God appeared on earth the first time, and what happened when He did, can we understand His present activity and make sense of biblical prophecies about His return.

The Need for a Savior

In this first coming, Jesus Christ came as a Savior. But why did the world need to be saved? After all, according to the Scripture, in the beginning the world was created good in every way. And our first human parents lived at the start in friendship with God (see Genesis chapter 1).

As their Creator, God knew what was best for these first human beings, and they owed Him their grateful obedience in love. But instead, they came to prefer their own will above His. So they sinned—that is, they disobeyed God, breaking their friendship with Him (see Genesis chapter 3).

The result? "Sin came into the world . . . and death through sin, and so death spread to all men because all men sinned" (Romans 5:12). To turn away from God, the very Source of life, was necessarily to choose death. And beginning with that tragic choice, our first parents and their descendants wrecked the world and brought on themselves all the terrible consequences of rebellion against Him: not only physical and spiritual death, but also moral depravity, disease, social disorder, decay, ignorance—and ultimately, the prospect of damnation, which is spending eternity totally cut off from God's friendship.

Meanwhile, an angel who had himself rebelled against

God, and had been cast out of heaven for doing so, took advantage of the situation to become what St. Paul called "the god of this world" (2 Corinthians 4:4). That is the Apostle's way of saying that this fallen angel, the Devil, was able to gain considerable power on earth and to manipulate people to further his own agenda: to mock God and take revenge against Him. In order to get back at God, and in envy of the human race created in His image, Satan used his considerable abilities (after all, he is an angel) to deceive and to tempt people in ways that would keep them separated from their Creator.

The Devil persuaded some people to deny God's existence. He tricked others into losing trust in God's goodness. Still others he simply seduced into loving themselves and other things more than they loved God. Whatever the strategy, he had a single goal: to pull down with him as many people as possible on the way to his final destination in hell—the place reserved for those who ultimately forsake God and are forsaken by God forever (see Matthew 25:41).

In time, then, "the whole world" came to be "in the power of the evil one" (1 John 5:19). The earth was utterly without hope unless God Himself acted to save it from the evil of its own making. We can be glad to know, then, that the same Lord who had created the world had never stopped loving it, despite its rebellion against Him. In fact, "God so loved the world that He gave His only Son, that whoever believes in Him should not perish but have eternal life. For God sent the Son into the world, not to condemn the world, but that the world might be saved through Him" (John 3:16–17).

What Did Christ's First Coming Accomplish?

How could the Son of God save the world by becoming a Man? What exactly did His *incarnation*—that is, His "becoming flesh"—accomplish? The full answer to that question remains a mystery to us until, God willing, we see Him face-to-face in heaven. Then we "shall understand fully" (1 Corinthians 13:12). But even now we are able to know a great deal about what Christ accomplished when He came to earth the first time.

Revelation

First, Christ revealed to us the truth about God and ourselves. As we have already noted, because of the Devil's lies and our own foolishness, much of the human race had been deceived about a number of critically important issues: who created us, how much He loves us, how we turned away from Him, and how desperately we need to turn back to Him. "All men," says St. Paul, "are under the power of sin. . . . 'None is righteous, no, not one; no one understands, no one seeks for God. All have turned aside, together they have gone wrong; no one does good, not even one'" (Romans 3:9–12).

We could not be reconciled to God and learn to obey His will unless we first knew who He truly is and what is His will for us. We needed to have God Himself tell us and show us how to live at peace with Him and with one another. Above all, we needed to see God Himself "up close."

"Whoever has seen me," Jesus said, "has seen the Father" in heaven (John 14:9, NAB). He was God in the flesh. To know the character of God, then, we need only look at the character of Christ. To know what God seeks to do for us, we need only look at what Jesus did for those around Him: teaching and correcting them, healing and forgiving them, comforting them and providing for their needs.

This part of Christ's mission we call *revelation*. As we will see in chapter four, His revelation will not be complete until after He has come again. Why? Certainly not because Christ was anything less than fully God. Rather, Christ has not yet revealed to the world all that He is. When He comes again, He will display aspects of the divine nature in ways we have never seen before.

Reconciliation

Though Christ came to reveal the truth, He came to do much more for us as well. If all we needed was to be given theological and moral instruction, then any one of the Old Testament prophets could have accomplished that task through the Holy Spirit's inspiration. God had already told us through them much of what He told us through Jesus. And if all we needed was to catch a glimpse of God, then perhaps He would have appeared to the world in glory, as He did to Moses, on a regular basis.

Such actions, however, would not have been enough to change the world as it cried out to be changed. The human race lacked more than enlightenment. St. Paul tells us what was needed: "God . . . through Christ reconciled us to Himself" (2 Corinthians 5:18). To reconcile literally means "to reunite, to bring back into harmony." Another essential aspect of Christ's mission to earth was thus the restoration of our harmony, our friendship, with God.

Why was reconciliation necessary? Because sin corrodes our relationships. To confirm that reality, we need only look at the countless ways that human selfishness destroys the peace and harmony of families, friendships, businesses, communities, and nations. When we do wrong to another person, we damage our relationship with that person. Trust and even goodwill may be lost. The one who was close to us becomes distant. The one who was a friend may become a stranger or even an adversary.

So it is in our relationship with God. In rebelling against Him, we separate ourselves so far from Him that He becomes a stranger. Worse yet, by opposing Him—by setting ourselves against Him to thwart His will—we actually make ourselves His enemies (see James 4:4).

Now it is no small thing to be an enemy of the Creator and Master of the universe. Just imagine: Through our sin, we have declared war on the One who gave us life and who holds our life moment by moment in His hand. What a terrifying place to be! "Woe to him," warns Isaiah, "who strives with his Maker" (Isaiah 45:9). Only by God's mercy are we sinners still in existence at all. We must be reconciled to God.

But a serious problem arises here. Wrongdoing has a cost. When we injure others, we steal something from them. We rob them of health, happiness, reputation, property—something that is rightly theirs. So in sinning against someone, we incur a debt, and the greater the sin, the greater the debt.

If we want to right the wrong, we have to restore what was lost. If we want to see justice done, we must pay the debt. Yet sadly enough, even in human relationships, it is not always possible to give back what we have taken. By our jealous slander, for example, a person's good name may be lost, never to be recovered. By our negligence in driving, someone's life may be lost.

In that situation, as we see clearly in a court of law, we may have to pay by forfeiting something else of value that belongs to us. We may lose our possessions through fines. We may lose our freedom through imprisonment. And in the most serious cases of wrongdoing, we may even forfeit our life.

If that is the case in our dealings with others, how much more so is it with God! But how can we steal from God, you might ask? Who has the power to take anything away from Him?

We need only consider what it is we owe to God just because He is God. He is our Creator; so we owe Him our very existence: "In Him we live and move and have our being" (Acts 17:28). He is all-wise, all-knowing, all-powerful, all-loving; so we owe Him our faith, our loyalty, our gratitude, our confidence, our obedience. In fact, He is perfectly good in every way, the greatest Good of all; so we owe Him our deepest love and our highest praise.

All these things rightly belong to God, and all these things we sinners have refused to give Him. We have robbed Him of what is His own. Justice demands—and God is perfectly just—that we pay the price for what we have done. And just for starters, that means losing the life we owe Him but have refused to yield to Him.

Redemption

Nevertheless, Jesus came to tell us and to show us that God is merciful as well as righteous. The justice within the divine Nature demands that the price be paid, but the mercy within that same Nature seeks a way to forgive us the debt, to spare us from eternal death. So how could this "divine dilemma," as it has been called, be resolved?

The solution was simple but startling: If the price was to be paid, yet the debtors spared, then God Himself would pay the debt. He would lay down His own life; God Himself would die.

But God's own divine nature cannot die. The One who is Life Himself is immortal. So He took on a nature that could die—our human nature—in order to pay the price in our stead. God became a Man.

"God shows His love for us," says St. Paul, "in that while we were yet sinners Christ died for us. Since, therefore, we are now justified [made just] by His blood, much more shall we be saved by Him from the wrath of God. For if while

we were enemies we were reconciled to God by the death of
His Son, much more, now that we are reconciled, shall we
be saved by His life" (Romans 5:8–10).

This aspect of Christ's mission is known as *redemption*.
To redeem means literally "to buy back, to pay off." "Jesus
Christ . . . gave Himself for us," St. Paul tells St. Titus, "to
redeem us from all iniquity" (Titus 2:13–14). And he reminds
the Corinthian Christians, "You are not your own; you were
bought with a price" (1 Corinthians 6:19–20).

When we recall just how great a debt we owe God, we begin to recognize how steep a price Christ had to pay. No crime
we commit against one another could ever be as heinous as
the crime we commit when we reject God Himself.

All the pains and losses the human race has merited by
the accumulated weight of its wickedness down through the
centuries, Christ took on Himself. We may never know completely all that Jesus had to endure, how high a price He had
to pay, how precious a sacrifice He had to make, in order to
make it possible for us to be restored to God's friendship. But
we know that His rescue mission to earth cost Him more
than any of us could ever have paid.

Think about it. First, Christ's coming required that He
lay aside for a while the universal reign, power, and glory
that had been His from all eternity in heaven. He was like
a billionaire who became a homeless man for a season, or
an emperor who became a slave. "Christ Jesus . . . though
He was in the form of God . . . emptied Himself," wrote St.
Paul, "taking the form of a servant, being born in the likeness of men. And being found in human form He humbled
Himself" (Philippians 2:5–8).

Second, Christ's coming entailed His taking on our weak
and limited human nature. Though He was still fully God,
He was also fully Man. He learned firsthand how it feels
to have a growling, empty stomach; a dry, parched throat;

a back with aching muscles; eyelids heavy with exhaustion. He even knew what it was like to fear and to grieve.

Third, when Jesus came to earth He experienced the emotional pain that comes from being rejected and even hated by others. In heaven He was perfectly loved by God the Father and God the Holy Spirit, and He was perfectly adored by the angels. But on earth, He was perpetually opposed by human beings; he endured heated hostility and cold indifference. He was mocked and scorned by His enemies. He was misunderstood, betrayed, and denied by His friends.

Fourth, Jesus suffered the unspeakable agonies of torture and execution through highly refined methods at the hands of the Romans, who were experts in the infliction of pain. As if it were not enough that He sweated blood in anticipation of the horrors before Him on the night He was arrested, He was tormented by cruel soldiers who considered him a grisly play toy. He was beaten with fists and clubs; scourged until metal-tipped lashes tore open His flesh; crowned with long thorns that ripped his scalp apart; forced to carry a heavy, splinter-filled wooden cross down rough stone streets; and finally nailed to the wood, naked and humiliated, with massive spikes piercing His hands and feet.

He hung from the cross for hours, gasping for air, able to breathe only when He could manage to lift up His broken body on bloody feet with gaping holes. And all the while, the crowds around him jeered at Him and spit on Him.

The price Jesus paid for our redemption in His first coming can never be fully calculated. And in a sense, His redemptive work remains costly to our Lord even today. His Sacred Heart still grieves because He is still misunderstood and slandered by many of those He came to save. In His second coming, however, all that will change. He will at last be vindicated in the eyes of all creation and recognized universally as Lord.

Re-Creation

Having been redeemed, we can walk again in friendship with God. But without His help, we are powerless to do His will fully and to become perfectly holy as He is holy. As St. Paul lamented: "I can will what is right, but I cannot do it. For I do not do the good I want, but the evil I do not want is what I do" (Romans 7:18–19).

The problem is that our rebellion against God has damaged our very nature. In breaking from Him, we have broken ourselves. Our will has become disordered—too weak to choose what is good and right, too twisted even to desire what is good and right. Our minds have been darkened. Our spiritual senses have been dulled. Our emotions have raged out of control to enslave us or grown thick and tangled to ensnare us (see Romans 1:18–32).

In short, sinful human nature needs to be healed. The fractures have to be fixed. The strength must be restored. Whatever is twisted must be straightened out. God's once-perfect creation cries out for a re-creation: "Lord, have mercy on me; / heal me; I have sinned against you" (Psalm 41:5, NAB).

This second part of Christ's mission—*re-creation*—was a job only God Himself could accomplish. He did it by taking that sinful, broken human nature of ours and joining it intimately and permanently to His own holy, perfect nature. In Christ, God brought the two together—humanity and divinity—and since then, humanity has never been the same.

"If anyone is in Christ," St. Paul tells us, "he is a new creation; the old has passed away, behold, the new has come. All this is from God, who through Christ reconciled us to Himself" (2 Corinthians 5:17–18). This new creation was first manifested to the world when Christ rose from the grave. "We were buried therefore with Him by baptism into death," the Apostle declares, "so that as Christ was raised from the dead by the glory of the Father, we too might walk in newness of life" (Romans 6:4).

When we are joined to Christ in the Sacrament of Baptism, we are joined to the same Power that set the galaxies spinning, that raised Jesus from the dead, that holds together every atom in the universe. This supernatural energy—we also call it *grace*—can heal our disordered nature so that Christ's perfect goodness becomes our own. In Christ, we receive a share in the life of God Himself.

St. Peter put it this way: "His divine power has granted to us all things that pertain to life and godliness, through the knowledge of Him who called us to His own glory and excellence." By this gift of God, we "become partakers of the divine nature" (2 Peter 1:3–4).

As with other aspects of Christ's mission, however, the process of our re-creation is not yet complete, nor will it be until He returns to earth. Then all the dead will be resurrected, and those who belong to Christ will find their bodies transformed in the divine glory. In the meantime, "the sufferings of this present time are not worth comparing with the glory that is to be revealed to us. For the creation waits with eager longing for the revealing of the sons of God" (Romans 8:18–19).

Victory Over the Devil

As the writer of the biblical book of Hebrews insists, our Lord died so that "through death He might destroy him who has the power of death, that is, the Devil" (Hebrews 2:14). The New Testament shouts with joy that through Christ's ministry, suffering, death, and—above all—His miraculous resurrection, this glorious aspect of His mission was accomplished. Christ won a decisive victory over the Devil and his power. "The reason the Son of God appeared," says St. John, "was to destroy the works of the Devil" (1 John 3:8).

How was this accomplished? In Christ, God arranged things so that Satan's malicious plans backfired. The Devil prompted Judas' betrayal of our Lord, which led to the crucifixion (see John 13:2). But Christ's death turned out to be the price paid to redeem us and reconcile us to God. Then, our Lord's resurrection—which could only have taken place after His death—opened the door for humanity to a new, supernatural life with God, far away from Satan's grasp. No wonder St. Paul remarks that "none of the rulers of this age" (that is, the demons) understood God's strategy—"for if they had," he concludes, "they would not have crucified the Lord of glory" (1 Corinthians 2:8).

This is wonderful news to a race that has been duped and enslaved for so long by such a supernaturally powerful tyrant! Despite all his long centuries of deception and seduction, temptation and oppression, Satan has been defeated; his rule over this world is broken. And in one of God's sweet ironies, the Devil has been bested this time not by a mighty archangel, but by a Man, a member of the lowly race he has worked so hard to destroy.

Even so, during the present age, God's diabolical enemy has been allowed to remain active in certain limited ways. In the next chapter we will consider some of God's reasons for this arrangement. But for now, we should simply note that Satan's defeat, accomplished on the cross in Christ's first advent, will not be fully manifested to the world until His second advent.

The First Coming: Just a Beginning

When our Lord was dying on the cross, He declared, "It is finished" (John 19:30). At that moment one stage of the divine plan was reaching its consummation. But we recognize that at the same time, a whole new stage was just beginning.

The word translated here as "finished" was also used in the ancient world to describe a debt that had been fully paid. Perhaps we should consider Jesus' declaration in that light. Our debt has indeed been paid by His suffering and death. But not long after those words were spoken, our Lord burst forth from the tomb. His resurrection opened up new possibilities for redeemed humanity to assume its destined role in God's plan.

As we have seen, several aspects of Christ's mission that found their initial fulfillment two thousand years ago will find their complete fulfillment only after He has returned. In the meantime, however, Jesus is not in some sort of celestial retirement. His ascension to heaven signaled that much of His work would now continue through those who loved Him and had followed Him. For that reason, the risen Lord entrusted them—and us as well—with a far-reaching mission to share the fruits of redemption with a world in desperate need of them.

Christ's first advent was coming to a close. His second advent lay far in the future. The time had come to begin the thrilling drama between the two advents: the present age, the exciting era of the birth and growth of the Church.

3

"I Am With You Always"

God's Plan for the Present Age

There were only a dozen of them. They smelled like fish and talked like country bumpkins. They had loud mouths and hot tempers; they annoyed strangers and bickered among themselves. They were often slow to catch on to what was happening around them.

And they turned the world upside down.

Meet the Apostles. A more improbable choice for continuing the mission of Christ on earth could hardly be imagined. Impetuous Peter, doubting Thomas, ambitious James and John, and all the rest—a handful of fishermen, a tax collector, a political revolutionary, and a few more whose occupations were so unremarkable that no one seems to remember what they had done for a living before they began following Jesus.

So how did these twelve and their small circle of friends come to change the course of history? What was the secret of their success?

The Continuing Presence of Christ

After the Crucifixion it looked to the world as if Jesus had come and gone and His followers had been left behind. Pontius Pilate, King Herod, Caiaphas the high priest, and countless others were saying good-bye and good riddance. Born as a pauper, executed as a criminal, another troublemaker was in the grave, and if His rabble-rousing friends knew what was good for them, they would shut up and go back to fishing.

But the truth, of course, is that the "troublemaker" soon came back from the dead and began a little fishing of His own. Once the stone door of His tomb had been tossed aside, He started showing up in the most unexpected of places to reel in His scattered followers, and there was no telling where He might show Himself next. Within a few weeks of His resurrection, Jesus had appeared at various times in a garden (see John 20:14–17), on a hilltop (Acts 1:6–12), in a room whose doors were locked (John 20:19–21), on a highway (Luke 24:13–43), on the beach (John 21:4–14).

In this way He left the Apostles little room to doubt that He had come back from the dead—the evidence for His resurrection went far beyond an empty tomb. "To them He presented Himself alive after His passion by many proofs," reports St. Luke, "appearing to them during forty days" (Acts 1:3). St. Paul gives even more details: "He was raised on the third day in accordance with the Scriptures, and . . . He appeared to Cephas [Peter], then to the Twelve. Then He appeared to more than five hundred brethren at one time. . . . Then He appeared to James, then to all the Apostles" (1 Corinthians 15:4–7).

Since dead men don't usually come back to life, the Apostles and other disciples of Jesus needed these multiple proofs. And just to make sure they wouldn't wonder later whether they had only been hallucinating, Jesus provided material evidence as well. He sat down at the dinner table with them, blessed and broke the bread, and gave it to them (see Luke 24:13–35). He took a fish from them and ate it as they watched (Luke 24:36–42). He cooked breakfast for them and fed them (John 21:4–14). He had them touch the wounds in His hands, feet, and side (Luke 24:36–40; John 20:19–29).

No doubt about it: Jesus had come back, bodily, from beyond the grave. He was really, truly present among them, physically as well as spiritually. He had not abandoned them. They had not been left behind. Death and the Devil had no power to rob them of their Master.

Christ's Ascension: The Next Step

All this took place, of course, before Christ's ascension into heaven. But once the faith of His Apostles had been firmly established—once they knew for sure not only that He was alive, but that He was God and He was with them (see John 20:28)—it was time for that next startling step in God's plan. With a mixture of awe and puzzlement, joy and grief, the Apostles watched as Jesus rose bodily to heaven from the top of Mount Olivet: "As they were looking on, He was lifted up, and a cloud took Him out of their sight" (see Acts 1:9–12).

Once again, it might have seemed to the Apostles that their Lord had abandoned them and they had been left behind. Even though Jesus had promised that He would be with them "always, to the close of the age" (Matthew 28:20), His words and His actions at that moment seemed to be in contradiction. Having just insisted that He would always stay with them, He disappeared into the clouds.

Nevertheless, Jesus wasn't breaking His word. He had given the Apostles the key to understanding His promise some weeks before, in the Upper Room on the night He was betrayed. Though they would be devastated by His death, He had told them, they should take courage: "I will not leave you desolate; I will come to you. Yet a little while, and the world will see me no more, but you will see me; because I live, you will live also. In that day you will know that I am in my Father, and you in me, and I in you" (John 14:18–20).

That prophecy had now come to pass. Having ascended

to heaven, Christ was nevertheless still with them; but His presence was of a different sort from before. Jesus' human form would no longer be visible on earth; His humanity had entered into divine glory. In this new arrangement, His followers would not see Him face-to-face again until they died and joined Him in heaven—or until "the close of the age" (Matthew 28:20), when He would return in the glory He now shared "at the right hand of God" (Mark 16:19).

On the other hand, Jesus would demonstrate His loving, powerful presence in astounding new ways. The Apostles and other disciples would no longer simply have the Lord *with* them; they would now have Him *within* them as well (see John 14:17). And because of their new, more intimate union with Him, the world would come to know Him through His presence in them.

"As the Father has sent me," Jesus said to the Apostles, "even so I send you" (John 20:21). This was their mission: to continue Christ's own mission. This was the secret of their success: He Himself was within them, continuing the work He had begun in His first advent.

Three Ways Christ Remains Present With Us

How could Christ live within the Apostles and His other followers? How could His presence manifest itself in this surprising new way?

Before His death and resurrection, Jesus announced on a number of occasions three gifts through which He would continue His presence within His followers: He would give them His *Word*; He would give them His *Sacraments*; and He would give them His *Spirit*. On the night before His crucifixion, when He presented the Apostles with some of His most important instruction, He referred to all three of these gifts. In examining them, we find that they are closely intertwined, because in each of them, Christ is actually making a gift of *Himself*.

Christ's Word

As we noted in the last chapter, revelation was one of the essential aspects of Christ's mission on earth. He came to reveal to us the truth about God, ourselves, and our world. That's one reason the Scripture speaks of Him as "the Word of God" (see John 1:1–14). Just as a word, when spoken or written, expresses what is in someone's mind and heart, Christ expresses what lies deep within the mind and heart of God.

For three years the Apostles and other disciples lived with Jesus and learned from Him. (The term "disciple," in fact, means "student.") They asked Him questions, watched Him work, listened to Him teach, witnessed His death and resurrection. Along with His Blessed Mother—who of course had known Him from the beginning as only a mother can—these men and women knew the Word of God and His message better than anyone else on earth.

On the night of His betrayal, Jesus prayed for these people He was entrusting with His mission. In that prayer to the Father, He referred specifically to this particular gift. The Word of God had given them His own words. "Father . . . the words you gave to me I have given to them, and they accepted them and truly understood that I came from you, and they have believed that you sent me. . . . As you sent me into the world, so I sent them into the world" (John 17:1, 8, 18, NAB).

To have Christ's word within ourselves is to have Christ Himself within. "I pray not only for them," Jesus continued, "but also for those who will believe in me through their word, so that they may all be one, as you, Father, are in me and I in you, that they also may be in us, that the world may believe that you sent me" (John 17:20–21, NAB). Through His word, Christ lives in us to shape our thoughts and our reasoning, our feelings and our attitudes, our memories and our imaginations, our desires and our choices. Through His word, Christ continues to re-create us in preparation for the close of the age and the life to come.

Christ's Sacraments

The same night Jesus prayed for those who would receive His word, He presented to the Apostles a second gift of Himself: the gift of the Eucharist. "Take, eat; this is my Body. . . . Drink, . . . all of you; for this is my Blood" (Matthew 26:26–28). In giving them His Body and Blood, He offered them an unparalleled way to receive Him intimately into themselves.

The Blessed Sacrament is a marvelous provision of God the Father for the present age that makes it possible for His Son to live within us and for us to live within Him: "He who eats my Flesh and drinks my Blood," Jesus said, "abides in me, and I in him" (John 6:56). It is a Presence unlike any other.

Through His first advent—His coming down from heaven to become a Man—Christ took on flesh and blood, which He could then offer to us once He ascended into heaven. In that life-giving Flesh and Blood, His previous presence in the world as a solitary Man, walking the dusty roads of ancient Palestine, is now superseded by an ongoing miracle: the Real Presence of Christ in the Eucharist, a Presence that appears, not just in one place, but all over the world.

What a brilliant strategy on God's part! During this middle phase of His great plan for the ages, in between the two times when His Son's human form is visible on earth (that is, between His two advents), Christ nevertheless remains here. And He abides in us, not just as a memory of His first coming, not just as a hope of His second coming, but as a powerful, immediate reality. Though He is hidden under the appearances of bread and wine, nevertheless His Body, Blood, Soul, and Divinity can be handled and even consumed.

The Eucharist is actually a foretaste of the new creation that will be fully manifested when Christ comes again in final triumph. Just as the bread and wine are transformed now in the consecration at Mass, so too will the faithful be transformed to share His glory when He returns. On that day, "we shall be changed. For this perishable nature must put on the imperishable, and this mortal nature must put on immortality" (1 Corinthians 15:52–53).

In an ancient liturgical prayer, the Church speaks of the Eucharist this way: "O sacred banquet in which Christ is received as food, the memory of His passion is renewed, the soul is filled with grace, and a pledge of the life to come is given to us." In the Mass we not only look back to Christ's sacrifice in the First Advent; we look forward to His triumph in the Second Advent.

Yet the connection between the Eucharist and the Second Coming is more intimate still. Receiving our Lord in Holy Communion transforms us even now. The grace conveyed to us in the Blessed Sacrament continues Christ's work of re-creation and reconciliation, bringing us closer to being fit for life in heaven with God. St. Ignatius, the bishop of Antioch in the generation just after the Apostles, put it this way: In the Mass we "break one loaf, which is the medicine of immortality, the antidote that wards off death, the food that makes us live forever in Jesus Christ."[8]

The other sacraments also fill us with the life of Christ, though in ways different from that of the Eucharist. Jesus' words and actions in His first advent formed the foundation of these gifts to the Church. Now that He has ascended to heaven, the saving power He displayed in healing, forgiv-

ing, ordaining the Apostles, and other sacred acts is the same
power now dispensed by the Church in the seven Sacraments.

Through Baptism, Christ cleanses us of sin and joins us to
Himself. Through Reconciliation (also known as Confession
or Penance), He restores our relationship with Him when it
becomes marred or broken. In Confirmation He strengthens
us to grow into His image. In the Anointing of the Sick,
His healing power flows through us and may prepare us for
our final journey to full union with Him. In Matrimony, His
grace is given for a couple to become a living image of His
love for the Church and to cooperate with Him in bringing
new life into the world.

Finally, in the Sacrament of Holy Orders, Christ gives us
men who bear His authority and power, generation after
generation, to govern the Church, to offer the Holy Sacrifice of the Mass, to absolve sins in His name, and to make
available to us the graces of the other sacraments. By giving
us bishops and priests, He makes it possible for the mission
He entrusted to the first Apostles to be continued until His
second coming.

Christ's Spirit

On the same night when Jesus spoke of giving the Apostles
His word and His sacraments, He prophesied as well that He
would give them a third gift: His Spirit. The Holy Spirit, of
course, is God Himself, the Third Person of the Most Holy
Trinity, who is sent to us by God the Father and God the Son
(see John 14:26; 15:26; 16:7). For this reason, the Holy Spirit
is also called in Scripture the Spirit of God (see Matthew
3:16), the Spirit of the Father (see Matthew 10:20), and the
Spirit of Jesus (see Acts 16:7).

The Apostles were grieved to hear that Jesus would have to
go away. But He encouraged them by telling them how His
departure fit into God's larger plan: "It is to your advantage

that I go away," He insisted, "for if I do not go away, the Counselor [that is, the Spirit] will not come to you; but if I go, I will send Him to you" (John 16:7). And once His Spirit was sent, the Spirit could live inside them.

We get our first glimpse of what it would mean for the Spirit to fill Jesus' followers on the Day of Pentecost, a few weeks after Jesus ascended into heaven. The Lord had told the Apostles to stay in the city of Jerusalem until the promised Spirit met them there, and at that time they would be "clothed with power from on high" (Luke 24:49). That is exactly what happened at Pentecost, when "suddenly a sound came from heaven like the rush of a mighty wind, and it filled all the house where they were sitting. And there appeared to them tongues as of fire, distributed and resting on each of them. And they were all filled with the Holy Spirit" (Acts 2:2–4).

The Spirit in the Present Age

What did the coming of the Holy Spirit on the Day of Pentecost have to do with the second coming of Christ? According to St. Peter, plenty! That same day, after being empowered by the Spirit to preach to the crowds who were present, he explained the event by quoting an ancient prophecy: "This is what was spoken through the prophet Joel: / 'It will come to pass in the last days,' God says, / 'that I will pour out a portion of my spirit upon all flesh . . . / before the coming of the great and splendid day of the Lord'" (Acts 2:16, 17, 20, NAB).

St. Peter announced that the "last days" had come. By this he didn't mean what some people refer to as the "end times," the season of final tribulation under the persecution of the Antichrist. He meant instead the last great era of human history—the present age. He is speaking of the era that began with Christ's ascension into heaven and leads up to His return from heaven on the "great and splendid day of the Lord." God "poured out" His Spirit precisely for the purpose of accomplishing His plan for these "last days" in which we now live.

From the Day of Pentecost on, the Apostles received the power to continue Christ's mission as their own. They preached His word with stunning success; on the Day of Pentecost alone, three thousand listeners believed the Gospel and were converted (see Acts 2:41). They administered His sacraments through the power of the Holy Spirit; the new converts were baptized and brought to His altar for "the breaking of bread and the prayers"—the Holy Sacrifice of the Mass in its early form (Acts 2:42). And they laid hands on others so that they too could receive the gift of His Spirit through Confirmation (see Acts 8:14–17).

The Spirit and the Word

The Holy Spirit sent by Christ gave power to Christ's word. His role was to recall to the Apostles' minds what Christ had said and to help them understand what He had meant: "These things I have spoken to you, while I am still with you," Jesus had said. "But the Counselor, the Holy Spirit, whom the Father will send in my name, He will teach you all things, and bring to your remembrance all that I have said to you" (John 14:25–26).

Through the Spirit the Scriptures were written; they are "inspired by God"—literally, "God-breathed" (see 2 Timothy 3:16. The "breath" of God is a way of speaking of His Spirit; the two words are the same in the biblical languages.) We are told, for example, that it was when St. John was "in the Spirit" that he was able to hear Christ tell him, "Write what you see" (Revelation 1:10–11). St. John obeyed, and what he wrote became the last book of the Bible.

Throughout the present age, these Spirit-inspired writings continue to reveal to us Christ, the Word of God made flesh.

Despite the attacks of those who reject the Bible, its truth remains a mighty fortress for believers who continue Christ's mission until He returns in glory. "Heaven and earth will pass away," Jesus assured us, "but my words will not pass away" (Matthew 24:35).

Through the Spirit, not only the Scripture but also the larger Tradition of the Church was born and passed down, much of it unwritten. Not everything Jesus did was recorded in the Scripture (see John 21:25), nor did early Christians write down every detail of the lives of His Mother, the Apostles, and other early Christians. In fact, it was a number of years after Pentecost before the New Testament Scriptures were completed; during those intervening years, the Church had to depend on the Holy Spirit's speaking with Christ's authority through the unwritten tradition of the Apostles.

That is why St. Paul told the church at Thessalonica, "So, then, brethren, stand firm and hold to the traditions which you were taught by us, either by word of mouth or by letter" (2 Thessalonians 2:15). In his preaching and writing to early Christians of every city, St. Paul claimed, "We impart this in words not taught by human wisdom but taught by the Spirit, interpreting spiritual truths to those who possess the Spirit" (1 Corinthians 2:13).

By giving the Spirit to the Church, Christ arranged for His living voice to be heard in the world even after He had ascended into heaven. He gave the Apostles, and through them the Magisterium—the teaching office of the Catholic Church—the authority to speak on His behalf. "He who hears you hears me," Jesus told them, "and he who rejects you rejects me, and he who rejects me rejects Him who sent me" (Luke 10:16).

Why did the Church need a living voice—a Magisterium —to speak for Christ? First, because He could not tell the Apostles everything they needed to know in the few brief years of ministry during His first advent. Second, because they needed help understanding, interpreting, and applying what He did tell them during that time. And third, because they did not yet have the necessary spiritual maturity to handle some of what He wanted to tell them later.

"I have yet many things to say to you," Jesus said to the Apostles the night before He died, "but you cannot bear them now. When the Spirit of truth comes, He will guide you into all the truth; for He will not speak on His own authority, but whatever He hears He will speak, and He will declare to you the things that are to come" (John 16:12–13).

At the first Church council, for example, the Apostles exercised this authority when they were called on to render a judgment about which Old Testament laws were to be maintained in the Church. The Scripture in itself—the New Testament had not been written—did not give sufficient guidance for settling the matter. So they turned to Christ's living voice, the gift of the Holy Spirit that had been given to them. When the Apostles issued their ruling, they prefaced their words in a way that reflected their conviction that God Himself was speaking through them: "It has seemed good to the Holy Spirit and to us . . ." (Acts 15:28).

The Second Vatican Council's *Dogmatic Constitution on Divine Revelation* summarizes the Church's teaching about this precious gift from God:

> Sacred tradition and sacred Scripture form one sacred deposit of the word of God, which is committed to the Church. . . . The task of authentically interpreting the word of God, whether written or handed on, has been entrusted exclusively to the living teaching office of the Church, whose authority is exercised in the name of Jesus Christ. This teaching office is not above the word of God, but serves it, teaching only what has been handed on, listening to it devoutly, guarding it scrupulously, and explaining it faith-

fully by divine commission and with the help of the Holy Spirit; it draws from this one deposit of faith everything which it presents for belief as divinely revealed.[9]

The Spirit and Christ's Character

The Holy Spirit is "the Spirit of holiness" (Romans 1:4), the One who helps us become like Jesus. Only as we become holy can we enter into fellowship, or communion, with Him and with all those who live in Him (see 1 Corinthians 1:9; 1 John 1:6–7). This process takes time, of course; it is a growth into maturity, just as fruit ripens on a tree. For this reason, the virtues the Spirit helps us cultivate, through which our character comes to resemble Christ's character, are called in Scripture "the fruit of the Spirit"—virtues such as "love, joy, peace, patience, kindness, goodness, faithfulness, gentleness, self-control" (Galatians 5:22–23).

Through Christ's Word and Sacraments, the Spirit labors with us, cooperating with our free wills, until Christ is formed within us (see Galatians 4:19). His character, like His mission, becomes our own. In fact, Christ's mission is an *expression* of His character. When He fed the hungry, healed the sick, taught the ignorant, comforted the downcast, and forgave the sinner, He was baring His soul, demonstrating clearly that He loved others with a pure, unselfish love. And He calls us to do the same in the power of the Spirit.

Only as we become like Jesus, then, are we able to obey His command: "Love one another as I have loved you" (John 15:12). Only then are we able to care for others unselfishly, to seek the best for others at all costs, just as Jesus did. And this transformation in character takes place "because God's love has been poured into our hearts through the Holy Spirit who has been given to us" (Romans 5:5).

As our Lord's character is formed in us, and we express His character through selfless charity, a remarkable exchange takes place: Christ the Giver becomes the Receiver, and we the receivers become the givers. We discover our Lord's presence still with us in a new way, because He is present in the people most in need of our loving care.

When Christ returns to judge the earth, we hope to hear these glorious words of gratitude: "Come, you who are blessed by my Father. Inherit the kingdom prepared for you from the foundation of the world. For I was hungry and you gave me food, I was thirsty and you gave me drink, a stranger and you welcomed me, naked and you clothed me, ill and you cared for me, in prison and you visited me. . . . Whatever you did for one of these least brothers of mine, you did for me" (Matthew 25:34–36, 40, NAB).

In all these ways, then, we can clearly see that when Jesus ascended into heaven, He did not abandon His followers. Nor did He leave them behind with little to do except wait for His return in the clouds. The mission of God's Son to save a lost world, a mission He received from the Father, was passed on to His Church through the Spirit. "All this is from God," noted St. Paul, "who through Christ reconciled us to Himself and gave us the ministry of reconciliation" (2 Corinthians 5:18).

Flaws in the Theology Behind the Rapture Doctrine

What has all this to do with the secret rapture doctrine? Actually, a great deal. As we shall see more clearly in chapter seven, the rapture idea is typically embedded in a larger system of theology with serious flaws. To a large extent, these flaws result from the failure of most fundamentalists to grasp fully God's plan for the present age.

On the whole, fundamentalists have a deep appreciation for the gift of Christ's Word. But their view of the Church's role between Christ's two advents typically lacks an understanding of three other important realities we have noted:

Christ's gift of the Sacraments; the transformation of our fallen nature as a necessary aspect of salvation; and the Holy Spirit's work through the Magisterium of the Church.

Fundamentalists deny altogether the reality of Sacraments —that is, unique signs of grace instituted by Christ that actually give us the grace they signify. The Catholic Church, for example, insists that Baptism, the Eucharist, Matrimony, and Holy Orders are all Sacraments. But even though fundamentalists baptize, have a "Lord's Supper," perform marriage ceremonies, and ordain their clergy, they don't view these actions as conveying a supernatural grace from God. Consequently, this rejection of Sacraments necessarily leads to a low view of the Church, whose role as the dispenser of sacramental grace seems to them unnecessary.

Lacking an understanding of Sacraments, fundamentalists tend to focus their attention on the Bible as God's great channel of grace in the present age. They affirm, as Catholics do, that the Bible presents God's revelation, and that we must respond to that revelation with faith—an assent to the truth of what God has said and a trust in His mercy. But unlike Catholics, they insist that once we have believed God's Word, putting our trust in Christ's redemptive work, then God declares us "righteous" and we are "saved" in such a way that no good works are necessary for our salvation. We can rest assured, they teach, that we will go to heaven.

The Catholic Church, on the other hand, points to the Bible's declaration that "a man is justified by works and not by faith alone" (James 2:24). When Christ comes again, His plan will not be to snatch us away, but rather to examine our works carefully to see whether we spent our lives in the present age caring for our neighbors. "When the Son of Man comes in His glory," Jesus said, He will ask whether we fed the hungry, clothed the naked, welcomed the stranger, and cared for the sick and the prisoner. His evaluation of such works will enter into His judgment of our destiny (see Matthew 25:31–46).

What an irony, then, that the secret rapture doctrine often seduces people to give up on social ministry. Our Lord's words clearly tell us that the best way to prepare for His second coming, and the Judgment Day it brings, is not to withdraw from the world or to hope for an escape from it. The best way to prepare is to serve the world, especially those most in need.

So how do fundamentalists who believe in the secret rapture, and who reject the notion that faith must be accompanied by good works for salvation, deal with this Gospel passage about judgment? Just as their faulty theology leads them to conclude that there will be two more returns of Christ, it leads some of them to conclude that there will be four judgments. And the judgment Jesus describes here, they insist, doesn't involve them, nor any of the Christians who will be snatched out of the world—a rather convenient arrangement, it seems. Instead, these fundamentalists usually teach, this judgment applies only to non-Christians living on earth at the time of Jesus' final return.[10]

Fundamentalist theology leads to considerable trouble in the present age in yet another regard: It denies the Church's teaching authority. Catholics can accept with confidence what the Church teaches about Christ's second coming because, as we have seen, Christ Himself gave the Church the authority to interpret the Scripture. But fundamentalists, rejecting the Magisterium, are at the mercy of every persuasive preacher who may come along (more about this in chapter seven).

With the rule of "every man for himself" in Bible interpretation, fundamentalists can all too easily fulfill St. Paul's prophecy: "For the time is coming when people will not endure sound teaching, but having itching ears they will accumulate for themselves teachers to suit their own likings, and will turn away from listening to the truth and wander into myths" (2 Timothy 4:3–4). The secret rapture doctrine is one such myth.

In all these ways, then, a faulty understanding of God's plan for the present age leads to misguided notions about how it will come to a close. And both kinds of error diminish a Christian's ability to obey God in this life and to prepare for His judgment in the next.

Why Has the Present Age Lasted So Long?

With this brief overview of God's plan for the world between Christ's two advents, we have examined the role of the Holy Spirit and the Church in continuing Christ's mission. One last, intriguing question about the present age remains to be considered. Why has it lasted so long?

Despite the exciting mission of Jesus' followers to launch the era of the Church, they understandably "longed for his appearance" (2 Timothy 4:8, NAB), and their longing nurtured their hope that He would come back again in glory during their own lifetimes. It was not an unreasonable hope. After all, hadn't the Lord Himself told St. John, "Surely, I am coming soon"? No wonder John had answered, "Amen! Come, Lord Jesus!" (Revelation 22:20, NAB).

Nevertheless, God's calendar runs differently from ours, and "with the Lord . . . a thousand years [is] as one day" (2 Peter 3:8). Even in St. Peter's lifetime, scoffers were already asking, "Where is the promise of His coming?" (2 Peter 3:4). They waited for years, till the years stretched into decades, and the decades into centuries, and now the centuries have stretched into two millennia.

Divine Delay Is an Act of Mercy

Why, indeed, hasn't Jesus' second advent taken place by now? Why does God seem to be taking His time? St. Peter an-

swered such questions with a sobering reminder. He stressed
that we must not be like those who "deliberately ignore this
fact that . . . the heavens and earth that now exist have been
stored up for fire, being kept until the day of judgment and
destruction of ungodly men" (2 Peter 3:5, 7).

Christ's second coming, after all, is the great Day of Judgment, the time of our final reckoning with God. Think for
a moment of your family and friends, your neighbors and
coworkers—even yourself. Are you all ready today to meet
your Maker and to give an account for how you have spent
your lives on earth? Are there some who have yet to turn
from their sins, believe the gospel of Christ, and give their
lives to God? And are there others who are Christians but
who need more time to reform their lives and grow in grace?

Honest answers to these questions will confirm St. Peter's
conclusion that the divine delay is an expression of the divine
mercy: "The Lord is not slow about His promise as some
count slowness, but is forbearing toward you, not wishing
that any should perish, but that all should reach repentance.
But the day of the Lord will come like a thief, and then the
heavens will pass away with a loud noise, and the elements
will be dissolved with fire, and the earth and the works that
are upon it will be burned up" (2 Peter 3:9–10).

In the meantime, then, we should thank God for His mercy
and seek to live a life worthy of the One who has redeemed
us. "Since all these things are thus to be dissolved," St. Peter
continues, "what sort of persons ought you to be in lives of
holiness and godliness, waiting for and hastening the coming
of the day of God!" (2 Peter 3:11–12).

Our Negligence: A Cause for Delay?

Those last few words of the Apostle suggest an intriguing
—in fact, a startling—possibility: By our response to God's

grace in our lives, cooperating with His Spirit to grow in godliness, we can in some sense "hasten" Christ's return. By the same token, we may well be contributing to the delay through our negligence to do God's will.

How can that be? It's no doubt a mystery. But St. Peter's words seem to suggest that Christ's coming is coordinated with the accomplishment by His Church of certain tasks on earth. In fact, earlier the Apostle had preached that Jesus had to remain in heaven "until the time for establishing all that God spoke by the mouth of His holy prophets of old" (Acts 3:21). Apparently our Lord has some things to achieve in the world before He comes back—and their achievement may well depend on our cooperation.

The book of Hebrews says that Jesus is waiting: "Christ, offered once to take away the sins of many, will appear a second time, not to take away sin but to bring salvation to those who eagerly await him. . . . [He] took his seat forever at the right hand of God; now he waits until his enemies are made his footstool" (Hebrews 9:28; 10:12–13, NAB). Perhaps He is waiting for us to do our part in subduing whatever opposes Him, whether within ourselves or in our surroundings.

Filling up Heaven

Several scriptural texts point to at least one specific reason God didn't allow Judgment Day to follow Christ's resurrection immediately. In the book of Revelation, for example, St. John refers more than once to "the book of life," in which were "written before the foundation of the world" the names of those who would live with God forever (Revelation 13:8). This reference suggests that God has had in mind from before all time a certain number of human beings to fill the ranks of heaven's citizens, ranks that are not yet complete. St. Paul also speaks of those God "foreknew" (knew ahead of time) who would be "glorified" (allowed to take part in the glory of heaven) "according to His purpose" (Romans 8:28–30).

St. John tells how he saw in heaven "the souls of those who had been slain for the word of God and for the witness they had borne" (Revelation 6:9)—that is, martyrs of the Church. As with most of us, these souls were disturbed to see how wickedness continues to corrupt the world. When they asked God how long He would delay the Day of Judgment, they were told to "rest a little longer, until the number of their fellow servants and their brethren should be complete, who were to be killed as they themselves had been" (Revelation 6:10–11). This text refers explicitly only to the martyrs, and yet it suggests that in general God is allowing human folly to play itself out until a predetermined number of the redeemed have been obtained.

St. Paul also writes as if God is waiting for a specific number of people to be reconciled to Him before He brings an end to history. In discussing the reasons why many of his Jewish contemporaries rejected Jesus while many of the Gentiles (that is, non-Jews) became Christians, St. Paul speaks of a delay in their coming into His kingdom "until the full number of the Gentiles come in." Once that happens, he says, "all Israel will be saved" (Romans 11:25–26). We will say more a bit later about this coming inclusion of the Jews in Christ's salvation, but in any case, the Apostle insists here that this event is scheduled to take place before the end of the world.

The Devil Is Still at Large

In His first coming to earth, Christ displayed His power over the Devil and the other demons in numerous encounters with these forces of darkness. He bested Satan in the wilderness by resisting the arch-demon's temptations (see Luke 4:1–13). He healed people the Devil had bound through illness (see

Luke 13:10–17). He delivered victims of demonic possession from their bondage and sent the diabolical spirits fleeing (see Matthew 8:16).

On one such occasion, the terrified demons who met up with Jesus cried out, "What have you to do with us, O Son of God? Have you come here to torment us before the time?" (Matthew 8:29). The latter question points to an important reality: Though Jesus definitively defeated Satan, who has no chance of finally winning his war against God, nevertheless the enemy of our souls is still at large. "The time" that the demons referred to is the final Day of Judgment at the end of history. At that time, all the fallen angels and their allies will at last be permanently confined in the horror St. John describes as "the lake of fire and brimstone, where . . . they will be tormented day and night for ever and ever" (Revelation 20:10).

The Devil's fate is thus sealed, and his resistance to God is utterly futile. But until the day of his permanent confinement, he continues to rage and to do his worst against the human race that God loves so dearly. "Your adversary the Devil prowls around like a roaring lion, seeking someone to devour" (1 Peter 5:8). He is a dangerous spiritual predator— wounded, no doubt, but like a beast mad with pain, all the more dangerous for the wound.

Satan is much like the captain of a sinking ship who is still firing salvos at those who have wrecked his vessel. He is like a condemned prisoner maliciously trying to trick others into following him into the gas chamber, deceiving them with false promises that they will find there, not death, but happiness. And he has shown himself capable of inflicting considerable damage on his way to destruction.

So why does God allow the enemy to remain at large? Why didn't He simply send His Son once, defeat the Devil by His death and resurrection, pull the curtain on history,

and begin the Judgment Day? We can't know the full answer
to that question in this life. But the Scripture does provide a
few hints about the matter.

A Time of Testing

The time between Christ's two comings—the present age—
is a time of probation, a testing of the souls for whom this
world is the preparation for eternity. Each generation, like
the ones before it, is born in the brokenness of original sin,
and each generation remains in need of Christ's redemption
and salvation. God waits for each person to make the great
choice: to love Him above all things, or to reject Him; to become suited for heaven, or fit only for hell. His challenge to
the ancient Israelites echoes still today: "I have set before you
life and death, blessing and curse; therefore choose life, . . .
loving the Lord your God, obeying His voice, and cleaving
to Him" (Deuteronomy 30:19–20).

If this world is our place of testing for eternity, we can
begin to see why Satan has been allowed to continue exerting
his power. Just as He did in the crucifixion of Christ, God
continues to bring good out of the Devil's work. In this case,
He allows Satan's opposition to prove us and refine us.

The Old Testament story of Job offers the classic example
of this kind of testing. Satan asks permission to put Job on
trial, and the Lord grants the request. The fallen angel then
buffets Job with adversity and tempts him, through the bad
advice of his wife and friends, to respond to his tragic personal losses with rage or despair. But Job ultimately resists
these temptations, and though he questions God, in the end
he remains faithful: "The Lord gave," he concludes, "and
the Lord has taken away; blessed be the name of the Lord"
(Job 1:21).

The New Testament tells us that our Lord allowed the
Devil to test the Apostles as well. On the night Jesus was

betrayed, St. Peter was sure he would stand by his Master to the death. But Jesus knew that the chief of the Apostles, and the others as well, would fail that test. So He said to him: "Satan has demanded to sift all of you like wheat, but I have prayed that your own faith may not fail; and once you have turned back, you must strengthen your brothers" (Luke 22:31–32, NAB).

Though the Apostles failed that night, all but Judas later repented and went on to pass many other tests, offering up their lives for their Lord. Through the enemy's sifting, God ultimately refined them.

Not only our character but our faith as well is tested in the present age. If it was difficult for the Apostles to believe that Christ was alive, even after seeing Him themselves, then how much more difficult can it be for those of us who have never had that kind of evidence? Yet if by God's grace we can nevertheless trust in Him confidently, He will reward us richly. Remember Jesus' words to St. Thomas: "Have you believed because you have seen me? Blessed are those who have not seen and yet believe" (John 20:29).

Vessels of Wrath and Mercy

In the end, some people will enjoy the everlasting glories of heaven, and some will suffer forever the horrors of hell. St. Paul calls the first "vessels" of divine mercy and patience, and the second "vessels" of divine wrath and justice. Both types of souls, he suggests, will play their part in bringing glory to God by offering to all creation clear demonstrations of the divine attributes: "What if God, desiring to show His wrath and to make known His power, has endured with much patience the vessels of wrath made for destruction, in order to make known the riches of His glory for the vessels of mercy, which He has prepared beforehand for glory?" (Romans 9:22–23).

This text forms part of a longer argument by the Apostle with which we are not concerned here: a debate about whether God is truly just in allowing some people to be damned. However we may interpret St. Paul's teaching on this larger issue (and the correct interpretation has been the subject of sharp controversy for centuries), the particular point to note for our purposes is this: One reason God "has endured with much patience" (verse 22) the Devil's work on earth is that it ultimately contributes to the divine glory. In God's hand, Satan is a scouring pad to polish the "vessels of mercy" (verse 23) and help make them beautiful. But the Devil is also a bucket of filth that fills up the "vessels of wrath" (verse 22) like chamber pots (a crude image, but it is the Apostle's own—that is the implication of the words translated "menial use" in verse 21).

The vessels of mercy show God's grace and His holiness. The vessels of wrath show His justice and His hatred of evil. Both types show His power: on the one hand, to save; on the other, to destroy. And both show His patience: the former, because He endured so much to save them; the latter, because He put up with them so long despite their hostility toward Him. In this era between the two advents of Christ, the Devil, however unwillingly, has become God's instrument.

For believers, then, Satan's opposition can serve as an occasion for spiritual growth and even joy. "In this you rejoice," St. Peter declares, "though now for a little while you may have to suffer various trials, so that the genuineness of your faith, more precious than gold which though perishable is tested by fire, may redound to praise and glory and honor at the revelation of Jesus Christ"—that is, at His second coming (1 Peter 1:6–7).

In the present age, God desires to make use of those who love Him. He takes pleasure in allowing us to be His "fellow workers" in the task of laying down our lives for the world and calling the world back to Himself (1 Corinthians 3:9). Being appointed to such a noble task is a high honor, and it will lead to a share in God's own glory (see 1 Peter 5:1). If the Lord has remained in heaven in part so that we might have the chance to enjoy such a reward, we should be all the more grateful for His delay.

Two Thousand Years of Grace

When we look at twenty centuries of Church history, we may see a great deal that disturbs or disappoints us. Nevertheless, if we focus on those people in which God has most clearly demonstrated His grace, we find ample reason to thank our Lord for His decision not to close history immediately after Christ's resurrection.

Just take a minute to think what would be lost if Judgment Day had come so soon. The Church would never have produced the gloriously devout intellects of St. Thomas Aquinas, St. Teresa of Avila, Pope John Paul II. The world would never have been touched by the burning charity of St. Francis of Assisi, St. Anthony of Padua, Mother Teresa of Calcutta.

St. John of the Cross would never have penned his mystical poetry, nor St. Augustine his passionate *Confessions*. Heaven's joy would not include the laughter of St. Thomas More, the thunder of St. Bridget of Sweden, the tenderness of St. Thérèse of Lisieux, the fire of St. Ignatius Loyola. How many other saints, unknown to us but known to God, would never have been born? (Not to mention the fact that we ourselves would never have been born.)

Who can bear the thought of the table at the "wedding feast of the Lamb" (Revelation 19:9, NAB) without all these members of our spiritual family seated there? As Christ prays for us at the Father's right hand, they stand before Him, joining Him in intercession for us. Surely God's delay is serving to fill His house with countless sons and daughters who make unique contributions to His pleasure and glory, and to our salvation.

Christ in Us, the Hope of Glory

In different ways, then, yet ways intimately connected, Christ's Word, Sacraments, and Spirit continue after two thousand years to make Him present to us on earth through the work of the Church. Though His human form is no longer visible, He has by no means abandoned us. In fact, He is with us in wonderfully new ways.

Nor is the present age simply an era in which Jesus' disciples stand waiting on the hilltop, watching the clouds where He was last seen and hoping that He will show up again soon, coming back in visible glory for all the world to see. He has promised that He will come back that way, of course, but He doesn't expect us just to hang around in a kind of time-out between His first advent and His second. Not at all! Instead, we are living in a critical stage in the plan of God for the world—a plan in which we are called to take part.

For that reason, the mission of Christ, carried out by the Church in the power of the Spirit, continues. Generation after generation passes through the world on the way to eternity, while His people lovingly reach out to offer Jesus' gift of Himself, to make Him truly present until the day He returns to bring history to an end. And to those who accept that Gift, the Church is able to say with St. Paul: "The gospel which has come to you . . . is bearing fruit and growing . . . Christ in you, the hope of glory" (Colossians 1:5–6, 27).

4

"Our Blessed Hope"

Why Is Christ Coming Again?

The news headlines confirm daily at least one fundamental teaching of the Church: the doctrine of original sin. On any given day, it seems, the human race demonstrates anew its fundamental brokenness, wounding the world with war and civil strife, oppression and injustice, lust and greed, hatred and cruelty.

Not long ago, a certain Catholic husband was reading the morning's news stories and nearly fell into despair. On a single day, reports told of crucifixions in Sudan, race riots and looting in the Midwest, terrorist bombings in Israel. There were child molestations in California, forced abortions in China, government corruption in Washington. Ethnic cleansing troubled Indonesia, and huge corporate profits in New York were reported from virtual slave labor in developing nations. The husband turned to his wife and summarized the information.

"If I were God," he concluded, "I just couldn't put up with it. I'd bring the curtain down on history right now. Today would be Judgment Day."

"And that," she replied wryly, "is one reason why you're not God."

She was right, of course. God's infinite wisdom has judged, for all the reasons the last chapter noted and more, that human history on earth must still continue—for now.

Nevertheless, the present age will not last forever. Just as the Father sent His Son once to offer the world salvation, He intends to send His Son once more to render judgment and to bring an end to the wickedness. Christ has died. Christ is risen. *Christ will come again.*

The Cry for Justice

From the very beginning, the Church has declared that Jesus, though still present invisibly with us, will one day appear on earth again in a glory so magnificent, with a power so irresistible, that all will know without doubt just who He is, and all will have to submit themselves to Him (see Revelation 19:11–16). Christ already reigns as Lord of all things at the Father's right hand, "far above all rule and authority and power and dominion" (Ephesians 1:21). But "He must reign until He has put all His enemies under His feet" (1 Corinthians 15:25). When the victory He won in His first advent finds its perfect manifestation on earth as it has in heaven, His kingdom will fully come on earth (see Matthew 6:10).

This expectation is not a matter of mere wishful thinking on the part of Christ's followers. On the contrary, it reflects an essential aspect of God's nature and of human nature. And it points to the necessary completion of the gospel—the good news of salvation.

Deep within the human heart lies a demand for justice —an insistence that each person should receive what he is rightfully due. We have all heard that call for justice, for example, in the familiar complaint of little children: "That's not fair!" And we have seen it in the courageous faces of men and women staring down the armored tanks of dictators in the streets of Manila and Beijing.

The same cry echoes throughout the Scriptures; we find it especially in the Psalms. As one psalmist sang thousands of years ago: "The needy will never be forgotten, / nor will the hope of the afflicted ever fade. / Arise, LORD, let no mortal prevail; / let the nations be judged in your presence" (Psalm 9:19–20, NAB).

Sometimes the cry startles us with its passion: "Rise up, O Judge of the earth; render to the proud their deserts! O Lord, how long shall the wicked, how long shall the wicked exult? They pour out their arrogant words, they boast, all the evildoers. They crush Thy people, O Lord, and afflict Thy heritage. They slay the widow and the sojourner, and murder the fatherless; and they say, 'The Lord does not see' " (Psalm 94:2–7).

Nor is this demand for judgment merely a relic, as some would insist, of an "Old Testament mentality" that focuses on law rather than grace, justice rather than mercy. In the New Testament as well, we hear the anguished cry of those who long to see God set the world aright. When St. John saw in his apocalyptic vision the souls of the martyrs beneath the altar in heaven, "they cried out with a loud voice, 'O Sovereign Lord, holy and true, how long before Thou wilt judge and avenge our blood on those who dwell upon the earth?' " (Revelation 6:10).

Does God respond to them by saying, "Now, now, it's unchristian to want to see the wicked punished; we should just love them and hope they get better"? By no means. Instead, the martyrs are given a white robe (a symbol of their heavenly reward) and told to rest a little longer. And by the time the vision concludes, Christ Himself (who could hardly be called "unchristian") has appeared, "and in righteousness He judges and makes war. . . . From His mouth issues a sharp sword with which to smite the nations." He comes to "rule them with a rod of iron" and to "tread the wine press of the fury of the wrath of God the Almighty" (Revelation 19:11, 15–16).

God Is Both Merciful and Just

Does this mean that God is not merciful? Of course not! Mercy is an essential quality of His divine nature. When the Lord appeared on Mount Sinai to Moses, He proclaimed Himself "the Lord, a God merciful and gracious, slow to anger, and abounding in steadfast love and faithfulness, keeping steadfast love for thousands, forgiving iniquity and transgression and sin" (Exodus 34:6–7).

The Lord's mercy has been expressed abundantly throughout human history, beginning with His gracious provisions for our first parents after they sinned (see Genesis 3:21) and on through countless generations down to the present. Nowhere, in fact, is His mercy more evident than in the first coming of Christ. There we see His mercy "made flesh." When we consider that "while we were yet helpless, at the right time Christ died for the ungodly" (Romans 5:6), we know without a doubt that God is merciful. And His mercy continues in the present age as He invites all people, even the worst of us sinners, to be reconciled to Him and to grow in grace through His Word, His Sacraments, and His Spirit.

Such mercy, however, is not opposed to justice. In God, the two qualities converge until they perfectly coincide. His words to Moses on Sinai confirm that reality. After proclaiming Himself to be "merciful and gracious, slow to anger," He went on to add, "but who will by no means clear the guilty" (Exodus 34:7).

"*Slow to anger*." That is not at all the same thing as "never angry." Just how forbearing, how slow to anger, God has been we can see when we look at the human race's long record of wickedness. But the day is coming when "the fury of the wrath of God the Almighty" will kindle the world at last (Revelation 19:15). In Christ's first advent, God has shown

Himself to be utterly merciful. And one day, in Christ's second advent, He will show Himself to be utterly just.

In the end, a mercy that never permits judgment is no mercy at all. It is merely indulgence. Sooner or later, the world must be made right if justice is to be fulfilled.

It's not as if we have never been warned. At the very beginning of history, just after the Fall, God promised our first parents that the head of the Serpent would be crushed —that the Devil and His works would at last be brought to an end (see Genesis 3:15). The Hebrew psalmists frequently predicted such an event: "The Lord . . . comes to judge the earth. He will judge the world with righteousness, and the peoples with equity" (Psalm 98:9). The prophet Daniel foresaw in a vision that the time would come when "the Ancient One took his throne. . . . The court was convened, and the books were opened." Then, "One like a son of man" would appear on the clouds of heaven, be presented before God, and receive "an everlasting dominion" (Daniel 7:9–11, 13–14, NAB).

Even in Christ's first coming, He warned that the mercy displayed in His suffering and death as the Savior would be inseparable from the justice of His return as the Judge. Speaking of Himself, He prophesied both that "the Son of Man will be delivered up to be crucified" (Matthew 26:2) and that "when the Son of Man comes in His glory, and all the angels with Him, then He will sit on His glorious throne" to judge the world (Matthew 25:31). His Apostles, too, warned of His coming judgment; as we have already noted, St. Peter promised a "day of judgment and destruction of ungodly men" (2 Peter 3:7). No one familiar with the Scriptures can deny that from the very beginning the Church has preached that Judgment Day will come. It is an essential part of the gospel.

Becoming Holy As God Is Holy

What exactly do we mean when we say that on Judgment Day, God will set the world aright? We find a clue in the passages from Revelation cited earlier. When the martyrs called for justice, they appealed to the God who is "*holy* and *true*" (Revelation 6:10, emphasis added).

Consider first that God is *holy*. He is utterly good, utterly righteous, always desiring and doing what is perfectly loving and morally right. "In Him is no darkness at all" (1 John 1:5).

The human race, as we have noted in chapter two, was created to share in this perfection. Having fallen morally, however, we find now that the possibility of our salvation—of being rescued from our own moral darkness, healed of our spiritual disorder, restored to friendship with God forever—depends on our cooperating with God's grace. That grace has been offered in Christ and is available to us in the present age through the Church. But God has given each of us a free will, and individually we can refuse His grace if we choose.

If we accept Heaven's offer, then God begins His work of "fixing" us. The Son of God has paid with His own blood to keep us from the eternal death we merit. But we still need correction.

What is bent in us must be straightened out. What is stained must be cleansed. What is weak must be strengthened. That process is part of what God's justice is all about: To be "justified," as the Scripture calls it (Titus 3:7), is to be made "just," to be made "right." We become holy in this life through a proper response to God's often painful correction, through the aid of His word, sacraments, and Spirit—and, if necessary, in the next life through the cleansing of purgatory.

This justification is necessary if we are to live with the Lord in the joy of perfect fellowship forever. Just consider: If salvation meant (as some evangelical Protestants teach) that we are merely forgiven while remaining disordered, heaven would cease to be heaven when we arrived there. All the mess we have created in this world would be re-created there— and it would last *forever*. Worst of all, we could never see God face-to-face because, as the Scripture tells us, this "Beatific Vision" only comes about when we become holy like Him (see 1 John 3:2).

Sooner or later, then, we must become holy if we are to be saved; we must "strive for . . . the holiness without which no one will see the Lord" (Hebrews 12:14). But God will not override our wills to make us love Him. If we were *forced* to love Him, our obedience would not be love. After all, to love is a choice that can only be made by someone with a free will. Instead of the sons and daughters God created us to be, we would become robots merely programmed to act a certain way. Robots cannot love.

So we have the option—the horrifying option—of telling God we want nothing to do with Him. And in the end, if we refuse to say freely to God, "Your will be done," He will say to us, "*Your* will be done." We will indeed have nothing to do with Him forever.

Having turned away from God's mercy in Christ, we will find that His justice demands we receive the penalty for our sins. We will be called to account for our lives, and when our debts are reckoned, we will be forced to pay what we owe. All the horrible consequences of our wrongdoing will come crashing down on our heads, and we will get what we deserve.

In that case, since what is bent in us refuses to be straightened, and what is stained refuses to be cleansed, then we will end up where we belong: hell, the garbage heap of the universe. (In fact, the Aramaic word Jesus used for hell, *Gehenna*, originally came from the name of the dump outside Jerusalem where refuse was continually burned.) Nowhere else will be fit to hold the wreckage we will have become. Since what is disordered in us refuses to be healed, our wickedness will be isolated and buried there, like toxic biological waste that must be kept from infecting the rest of God's creation.

The choice, then, is ours. One day each of us will be called to account for his life, with Christ as our Judge. For every individual, the time eventually arrives when the Judge who is "standing at the doors" (James 5:9) comes in to be seated in His court, and it is simply too late to seek mercy. In the present age, that time arrives at death.

For the world as a whole, the same is true. One day the time of reckoning will arrive at last, and the time to seek mercy will be over. That time will be the end of the present age, the Judgment Day when Christ returns in glory.

When He comes, He will cleanse the world of all the wickedness we read about in the daily news. When He is done, the human race will have been sorted into "wheat" and "chaff," those who have given themselves to God and those who have refused. "He will clear His threshing floor and gather His wheat into the granary," St. John the Baptist tells us, "but the chaff He will burn with unquenchable fire" (Matthew 3:12). It is a fire prepared, not only for wicked men and women who reject God, but also for the Devil and His demons, who will at last be rendered utterly powerless to harm those who love God (see Matthew 25:41).

Facing the Truth

We have noted that the martyrs in St. John's vision declared God to be holy. They also insisted that He is *true*. In doing so, they were echoing the words of the Son of God. Jesus said, "I am . . . the truth" (John 14:6), and He called the Holy Spirit "the Spirit of truth" (John 14:17).

Those who sincerely seek truth are thus ultimately seeking God and His holiness. And those who reject truth are rejecting God and His holiness. St. John tells us that Christ's first advent was a light from heaven invading a dark world, the light of Someone who was "full of grace and truth," who came into the world "to bear witness to the truth" (see John 1:5, 9–10, 14; 18:37). But Christ was rejected, because "men loved darkness rather than light, because their deeds were evil. For everyone who does evil hates the light, lest His deeds should be exposed" (John 3:19–20).

Many people in our day, as Pontius Pilate did in Jesus' day, try to justify their failure to seek the truth by asking, "What *is* truth?" (John 18:38), as if the question cannot be answered. But St. Thomas Aquinas, the great medieval theologian, gives us a simple and straightforward definition in response: "Truth is the identity of thought and thing." When what we think or say is true, it reflects, it matches up with, it corresponds to, things as they really are.

The statement that "God is true" can thus be understood in two senses, both of which are correct. First, to say that God is true means that He really exists—in fact, that He is more real than anything else that exists, because all other things only exist through Him: "In Him we live and move and have our being" (Acts 17:28). God is the Ultimate Reality.

Second, it means that "God . . . never lies" (Titus 1:2). What He reveals to us we can know to be true, however difficult we may find it to believe. As St. Paul put it, even if every human being should be found a liar, nevertheless, "God must be true" (Romans 3:4, NAB).

As we noted in chapter two, when Christ came to earth, an essential aspect of His mission was revelation—to show us the truth about God, ourselves, and our world. His mission is not complete, then, until the truth is fully revealed to every human being and fully acknowledged by every human being and every angel, fallen or unfallen, as well. Those who have rejected God and His truth may resist admitting their errors and deceit. But in the end, they will have no choice but to do so.

"We shall all stand before the judgment seat of God; for it is written," insisted St. Paul, quoting the prophet Isaiah: "'As I live, says the Lord, every knee shall bow to me, and every tongue shall give praise [or confess] to God.' So each of us shall give account of himself to God" (Romans 14:10–12).

To praise God is to speak the truth about who He is, to declare His wonderful attributes. To confess (an alternate translation) means literally to agree with, to "say the same thing as," God. Both translations point to the same reality: In the end, every one of us will have to recognize God as the Almighty Lord of all things; every one of us will have to concede the truth about God, ourselves, and our world—whether we like it or not.

This, too, will be a part of setting the world aright, because truth is a part of justice. We owe it to ourselves and others to think and say what corresponds to reality. Think, for example, of how in recent years a growing movement has denied that the twentieth-century Holocaust—the killing of millions of Jews by the Nazis and their allies—ever took place. Most of the criminals involved in this horror have by this time either died or been punished, so why, some may ask, does it really matter at this point if some people choose to deny what happened?

For an answer to that question, we need only look at the faded prison number tattooed on the arm of a now-elderly Jewish woman who survived the death camps as a little girl. The truth is etched indelibly in her flesh, just as it is in her memory. What does she think and feel when she hears a Holocaust denier stand before a gullible crowd to convince them that her torment in the camps never took place?

Something deep inside of us—that perennial demand for justice—cries out that to deny her suffering is to torment her all over again. To lie about what happened to her is an offense against justice. The truth must—it simply *must*—be told if the world is to be set aright.

Imagine further that a Nazi prison guard, who used to beat and sexually abuse this Jewish woman when she was only a schoolgirl, has finally been brought to trial for war crimes. The former guard denies every charge brought against him, just as he has for more than half a century. But she knows the truth. Wouldn't she be justified in demanding that, once convicted, the criminal had to confess his wickedness publicly, before the same people he had sought to deceive?

Now think of how many other sins and horrors lie hidden in the mists of history. Imagine how many people have been terribly wronged. They await Judgment Day because they want the truth to be told, to be shouted from one end of the cosmos to another. And so they should. Could God be truly just if, in the end, he allowed the terrible truth to remain hidden forever and permitted the world to maintain its malicious lies?

Those who have done wrong may go to hell adamantly refusing God's forgiveness. But before they go to their damnation, they will be required to admit to God and to all the world the truth about their wrongdoing. Judgment Day must happen because truth must triumph. Anything less would fail to set the world aright.

We must keep in mind, of course, that it is not just the hell-bound who will have to give a public account of how they lived their lives. Even those who accept God's grace in Christ and remain faithful to the end will have to face the truth and confess it, drinking the cup of their shame all the way to its dregs. That painful reckoning will serve as part of the purging process necessary to prepare them for heaven.

Yet even though it will be a day of "the wrath of God the Almighty," it will also be a day of joyous celebration—for those who love justice, who love truth, who love the Lord Jesus. "Let the heavens be glad, and let the earth rejoice . . . before the Lord, for He comes, for He comes to judge the earth. He will judge the world with righteousness, and the peoples with His truth" (Psalm 96:11, 13). The psalmist knew, as St. Paul did, that for the faithful, Judgment Day is "our blessed hope, the appearing of the glory of our great God and Savior" (Titus 2:13).

The Glory Due Jesus

In yet another way Christ's second coming will achieve God's justice: It is just and fitting for Jesus to be glorified and vindicated.

Worthy of Glory and Honor

When the American War for Independence broke out, a Polish nobleman named Count Casimir Pulaski crossed the ocean to fight heroically for the new nation. The corps of cavalrymen he organized and led performed valiantly throughout the American South. But Pulaski finally died from enemy fire in 1779 at the Siege of Savannah, Georgia, as he attempted to defend the city. His comrades reported that the last words of this devout Catholic soldier were a simple invocation: "Jesus, Mary, and Joseph!"

Ever since that day, Count Pulaski has been revered as a hero in Savannah. To honor his sacrifice, the city erected a fine monument in his memory. A federal fort, a grade school, and a town square all bear his name. And the U.S. Congress confirmed that the nation shared the town's admiration for the Count by declaring October 11 "Pulaski Day."

Few would deny that Count Pulaski has deserved the honors bestowed on his memory. Here was a man who laid aside a privileged lifestyle, left his country for a foreign land, took up the cause of oppressed people to whom he was a stranger, and sacrificed his life for their welfare.

If a man such as Pulaski rightly merits such acclaim, then how much more honor does our Lord deserve! Think about it. In His first advent, as we noted in chapter two, in order to live among us He laid aside the unutterable glory He had enjoyed as the Son of God from before all time in His heavenly home (see John 17:5). In place of that glory, He took on obscurity and poverty on earth. When He had reigned with the Father and the Spirit in heaven, He had needed nothing. But because of the love He had for us, He took pity on our terrible plight, limited Himself to live as we do, and lowered Himself to suffer with us through hunger, thirst, weariness, and finally even death.

When Jesus ascended to heaven, of course, He returned to His glory at the right hand of the Father (see Acts 7:55–56). But isn't it only right and just that He should be glorified on earth as well? Shouldn't those who despised and rejected Him here have to recognize Him one day as the true Lord and God that He is?

St. Paul reminded the Philippians of what our Lord has done for us. "Christ Jesus . . . though He was in the form of God," he observed, "did not count equality with God a thing to be grasped, but emptied Himself, taking the form of a servant, being born in the likeness of men. And being found in human form He humbled Himself and became obedient unto death, even death on a cross" (Philippians 2:5–8).

What was Jesus' reward for such unparalleled humility? "Therefore God has highly exalted Him," St. Paul wrote, "and bestowed on Him the name which is above every name" (verse 9). But that's not all. God has done this so that when Christ comes again, "at the name of Jesus every knee should bow, in heaven and on earth and under the earth, and every

tongue confess that Jesus Christ is Lord, to the glory of God
the Father" (verses 10–11).

Even if He had never descended to earth for our sakes, the
Son of God deserves to be honored on earth as our Maker.
He is "worthy . . . to receive glory" because He "created
all things" (Revelation 4:11, NAB). How much more, then,
should He receive the world's honor as our Savior as well!

Worthy of Vindication

The film and television series entitled *The Fugitive* tell the
story of a man falsely accused of murdering his wife. He
becomes a fugitive from the law and spends the rest of his
life evading the authorities while he tries to find evidence
that will clear his name. The continuing popularity of the
story attests to the compelling nature of its theme: If the
innocent are wrongly blamed and punished, justice calls for
their vindication.

When our Lord joined our human nature to His divine
nature, He became like us in every way except one: He was
without sin (see Hebrews 4:15; 1 John 3:5). He was "the Lamb
of God, who takes away the sin of the world" (John 1:29) by
His own perfect innocence. Yet He submitted Himself to be
cruelly tortured and slowly executed in place of those who
had sinned in order to save them from eternal damnation.

Jesus was falsely accused of blasphemy and other misdeeds;
mocked and abused while in the custody of a council that
pretended to judge Him in the name of God; and finally
sentenced as a criminal, enduring the most gruesome and
humiliating form of capital punishment the ancients could
invent. Even if He were not the Son of God, wouldn't justice demand that such an innocent man be publicly vindicated and His good name restored? Shouldn't the people
who falsely accused Him and treacherously murdered Him
be made to confess at last that He was blameless?

Of course! And that is exactly what will happen when Christ comes again in glory. "Behold, He is coming with the clouds, and every eye will see Him, every one who pierced Him; and all tribes of the earth will wail on account of Him" (Revelation 1:7). Jesus' appearance in glory will be His triumphant vindication—to the utter horror and dismay of those who put Him to death.

To a certain extent, of course, Jesus' resurrection was a vindication. His appearances after that first Easter morning were enough to convince the Apostles and all His followers that His claim to be Messiah, Lord, and God was genuine (see John 20:28). And for many of His contemporaries who were left confused by His trial and execution, the record was set straight by the dynamic preaching of the Apostles, with their insistence that He had indeed been raised from the dead.

"Let all the house of Israel therefore know assuredly," St. Peter proclaimed on the Day of Pentecost, "that God has made Him both Lord and Christ, this Jesus whom you crucified" (Acts 2:36). Many in his audience were "cut to the heart," converted, and baptized (see verses 37–41). In their eyes, then, Jesus had been vindicated.

Nevertheless, many others remained unconvinced. And in the two thousand years since their day, many more have denied the innocence of Christ. The scoffers, the "enemies of the cross of Christ" (Philippians 3:18), continue to hold Him up to ridicule, to brand Him a troublemaker or madman who brought on Himself a terrible and unnecessary end.

For that reason, justice still demands Christ's vindication. And the Scripture assures us that on the Day of Judgment, He will indeed be vindicated before all the universe as the innocent, spotless Lamb of God. In the vision recorded in the book of Revelation, St. John saw the scroll containing divine judgment, sealed with seven seals, in the right hand of God the Father on the throne. "I saw a Lamb standing, as though it had been slain," reported St. John (Revelation 5:6). The Lamb, who is the sinless Man Jesus Christ, took the scroll in order to open it and thus bring about the world's final reckoning.

Why was it fitting for Christ to bring about the judgment and to be exalted in glory? St. John hears a chant of the citizens of heaven that tells why: "Worthy is the Lamb who was slain, to receive power and wealth and wisdom and might and honor and glory and blessing!" (Revelation 5:12). By His supreme sacrifice, the Lamb has merited such recognition.

He is deserving of exaltation. The truth about Him must be told, and the universe must affirm that truth: Jesus Christ is innocent, and Jesus Christ is Lord.

The God-Man As Judge

Finally, it is fitting for Christ to be the Judge of the world because He alone is both God and Man. Only God is worthy to pronounce judgment on the world, because only He knows everything that must be taken into consideration for a righteous judgment: the multitude of deeds, good and evil; the dark, cavernous depths of the human heart; the countless details of circumstance that have shaped an individual's life. "For I know their works and their thoughts," the Lord said through Isaiah, "and I am coming to gather all nations and tongues; and they shall come and see my glory" (Isaiah 66:18; see also 1 Chronicles 28:9; Psalm 139:2). When the Lord Jesus comes, St. Paul announced, He "will bring to light the things now hidden in darkness and will disclose the purposes of the heart" (1 Corinthians 4:5).

Yet Christ's manhood makes Him fitting to be our Judge as well, because He is one of us. He is able, as the book of Hebrews tells us, "to sympathize with our weaknesses" (Hebrews 4:15). Just as our law deems it only fair that a jury be drawn from among a defendant's peers, so also God the Father has justly decreed that the human race be judged by one of its own. "The Father judges no one," Jesus tells us, "but has given all judgment to the Son, that all may honor the Son, even as they honor the Father" (John 5:22–23).

And honor Him they will indeed—even those who condemned Him. The very Blood they shed will overcome them (see Revelation 12:11), and the wounds they left on His precious Body will be adored.

The World Needs Both Savior and Judge

In all these ways, then, the Church's firm belief in the second coming of Christ is justified. To say that Jesus will return as Judge is no wishful thinking on the part of Christians. It reflects no immature desire for petty revenge. It represents no mythological embroidery to provide a satisfying ending to an otherwise messy historical event. Unbelieving critics have made such charges against the Church, but they are dangerously mistaken.

No, Christ "will come again in glory to judge the living and the dead," as the creed insists, because God's nature demands it. Human nature requires it. And the gospel, the good news, of Christ is incomplete without it.

Our world desperately needs, not only a Savior, but also a Judge.

5

"As the Lightning Comes"

What Does the Bible Say About the Second Coming?

The year was 1843. Tens of thousands of Americans—perhaps as many as a hundred thousand—waited excitedly for Jesus to return to the earth on clouds of glory. Convinced that He would be coming any day, and certainly no later than early spring of the following year, they tried to convince their families, friends, and neighbors that history was coming to a close within a few short months at most.

They belonged to a number of Protestant denominations: Baptist, Methodist, Presbyterian, others. The majority of people in their congregations thought they were misled; some even asked them to leave for disrupting the peace with their strange teaching. But most of those who were convinced of Christ's imminent arrival persisted in their belief. Some even abandoned all efforts toward "worldly" goals; they quit their jobs, stopped working their farms, and gave away their possessions. If the Lord was right at the door, why spend time on anything but spiritual concerns?

How had so many people come to think they could predict the timing of the Second Advent? William Miller, a largely self-educated Baptist lay preacher, had come to the conclusion from his personal Bible study that the event was sure to take place sometime between March 21, 1843, and March 21,

1844. Between those dates, he insisted, Christ would appear in glory to "cleanse the sanctuary"—that is, He would come with all His saints to judge the earth.

For more than a dozen years this charismatic speaker and his preacher friend Joshua Himes had been traveling the country. Everywhere they went they persuaded eager listeners that they had calculated the right dates through a new interpretation of obscure Old Testament passages.

Miller and Himes were first-class publicists and promoters. They published books, tracts, and newspapers promoting their peculiar ideas (though they apparently didn't think of publishing a series of novels). They organized lectures, citywide campaigns, and conferences. They wrote articles for secular newspapers that urged their viewpoints. And everywhere they went, they displayed elaborate charts "proving" that the Bible supported their claims.

Needless to say, March 21, 1844, came and went without Christ's return. So a new calculation was made and a new date predicted: Judgment Day would be October 22. But of course Jesus failed to show in October as well.

The "Great Disappointment"

Tens of thousands of the "Millerites," as people called them, were devastated. Some were financially ruined by their abandonment of worldly pursuits. Many returned to their former congregations in humiliation. Others, feeling spiritually betrayed, gave up their Christian faith altogether. Still others despaired of life itself.

Miller himself could only offer the vague explanation that there might have been some human error in Bible chronology. But the morning after October 22 and the "Great Disappointment," as they termed it, an ardent Millerite named Hiram Edson had a vision while walking in a cornfield. He claimed God showed him that there had in fact been no miscalculation.

On the expected day, Edson announced, Christ had indeed "cleansed the sanctuary"—but it was a sanctuary in *heaven*, not on *earth*. Jesus had moved from one "apartment" of the "heavenly sanctuary" to another, and He had begun performing a work that came to be called the "investigative judgment." So Christ's second advent to earth was still to come, and it would come quickly.[11]

Edson's reinterpretation of Miller's predictions was welcomed eagerly by many who could not bear to think that their trust had been misplaced. In time, the doctrine of a "judgment" by Christ that had occurred secretly and invisibly to people on earth established itself as dogma in several new groups that ultimately sprang up as a result of Miller's teachings. Rejected and largely isolated by the more mainstream Protestant denominations, some of these "Adventists" (such as the Seventh-Day Adventists) developed other peculiar teachings as well, such as the idea that Christians must follow the ancient Jewish laws by worshipping on Saturday and refusing to eat pork.

Lessons for Our Day

So many lessons can be learned from the Millerite fiasco. First, it teaches us how earnest but misguided students of the Scripture can twist biblical texts to produce unbiblical ideas. Second, it demonstrates how savvy promoters can use their media and organizational skills effectively to provide visibility and an air of plausibility to such ideas. Third, it shows how easily some Christians can be persuaded to adopt an eccentric teaching about the second coming of Christ if it promises them a quick escape from the troubles of the world. And finally, it illustrates the grave dangers of being misled on such an important matter, when religious excitement turns to disillusionment and ultimately to a loss of faith in God.

In light of all these lessons, we surely want to avoid a twenty-first-century replay of the Millerites' nineteenth-century mistake. The parallels between Miller/Hime and LaHaye/Jenkins should be obvious. To their credit, most (though not all) of the contemporary promoters of the secret rapture doctrine have avoided making precise predictions about the timing of Christ's return. As they themselves point out, the Bible assures us that no one but God Himself has access to that privileged information (see Matthew 24:36).

Nevertheless, the believers in a secret rapture tend to assume that it will take place during their lifetimes, and they assure themselves that because of it, Christians will be spared the coming "tribulation." So if the Lord delays His coming another generation or more, and if Western Christians should have to suffer for their faith in the meantime just as many African and Asian Christians suffer now, how many people could become casualties of another "Great Disappointment"? How many might feel, not left behind by Christ, but betrayed by Him instead?

Catholics need not be among those who are misled by such unbiblical ideas. All we need do is take a look at what Scripture has to say about the Second Advent. What is the main outline of events that it foretells?

What Jesus Said About His Return

The obvious place to start if we want to find out what the Bible says about Christ's second coming is to read what Jesus Himself had to say about it. Who on earth could know more, or more accurately, about the nature of His return?

St. Matthew presents in chapters 24 and 25 of his Gospel the longest account of an extended prophecy about the future that was spoken by our Lord. The Gospels of St. Mark and St. Luke have parallel passages—that is, accounts of the same events differing slightly, with each writer including some material the others leave out (see Mark chapter 13 and Luke chapter 21). Because Jesus stood on Mount Olivet as He spoke (the same place where He ascended into heaven), this teaching is known as the Mount Olivet discourse.

All three Gospel writers note that Jesus' prophecies about the end of the world are prompted by His disciples' remarks about the magnificent Jewish temple in Jerusalem. Christ responds to their admiration of the great edifice with the sobering prediction that it will be destroyed (see Matthew 24:2). Not surprisingly, His disciples are disturbed by His response and ask Him, "Tell us, when will this be, and what will be the sign of your coming and of the close of the age?" (Matthew 24:3).

We should first note that the disciples are asking for information about both the destruction of the temple and the second coming of Christ. They seem to think that the events will coincide, or at least occur close in time. As it turned out in history, however, the temple was destroyed in A.D. 70, while the Second Advent obviously has not yet occurred. So the disciples were mistaken if they thought that the temple's devastation would occur close to Christ's return. In fact, the two events are widely separated in time.

For this reason, we have to keep in mind that in response to the question posed to Him, Christ had to speak about both events. Part of His answer, then, applies to the first event, while part applies to the second. At what point does He turn from speaking about the destruction of the temple to speaking about the end of the world? The answer to that question has long been debated. But in any case, nearly all rapture believers would agree that the texts we will cite as references to the close of the age do indeed refer to that event rather than to events of the first century.[12]

A Time of Tribulation

Jesus' response to His disciples' query prepares them for trouble ahead. Some of the tribulation He describes, found in details added in St. Luke's Gospel, seems clearly connected to the temple's destruction, such as the siege of Jerusalem (see Luke 21:20). The city was in fact besieged by Roman armies in the lifetime of many of Christ's listeners, and on their victory came the devastation of the temple and of all the city as well.

Jesus adds other details of this tragic occasion. He says: "Great distress shall be upon the earth and wrath upon this people; they will fall by the edge of the sword, and be led captive among all nations; and Jerusalem will be trodden down by the Gentiles [that is, non-Jewish people], until the times of the Gentiles are fulfilled" (Luke 21:23–24). After the fall of Jerusalem to the Romans, all these prophecies sadly came to pass.

Other prophecies of adversity in the Olivet discourse have found their fulfillment repeatedly throughout two thousand years of Church history, beginning with the first generation of Christians: persecutions, martyrdoms, betrayals, false prophets, apostasies, wars, earthquakes, famines (see Matthew 24:9–14). But Christ follows these predictions with a particularly dire warning: "For then there will be great tribulation, such as has not been from the beginning of the world until now, no, and never will be. And if those days had not been shortened, no human being would be saved; but for the sake of the elect [that is, those God will save] those days will be shortened" (Matthew 24:21–22).

Do these last words refer to a final, unprecedented time of trial for Christians just before Christ's second coming? That is the view of many Christians, including most believers in the rapture. On the other hand, some Christians believe that the "great tribulation" was endured by the Jews during the siege of Jerusalem.

Either way, the principle, which Jesus states clearly here and elsewhere, remains the same: Not the one who is snatched out of tribulation but the one "who endures to the end will be saved" (Matthew 24:13; see also 10:22). The days of trial are not a time of escape, but rather a time of sifting, proving, and purging, a season of strengthening the faithful and sorting them out from the unfaithful, the wheat from the chaff.

A Gloriously Visible Return

One of our Lord's stated concerns in His warnings to His followers is that they might be tricked into thinking He has come when in fact He has not. Plenty of deceivers will claim that He has arrived; how will people know that He has truly returned to earth? The answer is simple: "For as the lightning comes from the east and shines as far as the west, so will be the coming of the Son of Man" (Matthew 24:27). The event will be universally recognized, visible, arresting, and unmistakable. There is nothing secret about lightning!

Our Lord says more about his arrival: "Then will appear the sign of the Son of Man in heaven, and then all the tribes of the earth will mourn, and they will see the Son of Man coming on the clouds of heaven with power and great glory; and He will send out His angels with a loud trumpet call, and they will gather His elect from the four winds, from one end of heaven to another" (Matthew 24:30–31).

What exactly is "the sign of the Son of Man in heaven"? Jesus does not say. But it is obviously a public event that prompts a worldwide reaction and is directly linked to history's climax, a climax that is clearly visible and recognizable to all: "the Son of Man coming on the clouds of heaven with power and great glory" (verse 30). Add to this earth-shaking visual display the sound of a "loud trumpet call" commanding the angels, and you have a reentry of Christ to the world's stage that is anything but secret or invisible. The Second Coming is one event that no one on earth will miss!

At other times as well, Jesus spoke of His second advent in these terms. Soon after the Olivet discourse, when on trial before the Jewish council of elders, He was asked by the high priest whether He was "the Christ, the Son of God" (Matthew 26:63). He replied: "Hereafter you will see the Son of Man seated at the right hand of Power [that is, God the Father], and coming on the clouds of heaven" (Matthew 26:64; see also Mark 14:62). Note especially the words that appear in both of Jesus' declarations: "the Son of Man . . . coming on the clouds of heaven."

Daniel's Prophecies

Jesus' Jewish listeners would have recognized immediately that He was connecting Himself to certain ancient prophecies uttered by the prophet Daniel. When Jesus called Himself the "Son of Man" on these occasions, He was identifying Himself as the heavenly figure who appears prominently in Daniel's apocalyptic visions as a judge and ruler. The prophet wrote that he saw thrones set up in heaven, and the "Ancient of Days" (a poetic name for God) took His place on one of them. Then "the court sat in judgment, and the books were opened"—that is, books holding the accounts of each person's life on earth (Daniel 7:9–10).

Then, said Daniel, "I saw in the night visions, and behold, *with the clouds of heaven* there came one like a *Son of Man*, and He came to the Ancient of Days and was presented before Him. And to Him was given dominion and glory and kingdom, that all peoples, nations, and languages should serve Him; His dominion is an everlasting dominion, which shall not pass away, and His kingdom one that shall not be destroyed" (Daniel 7:13–14, emphasis added).

As evidence that Jesus' contemporaries—even His enemies —understood that He was claiming to be the heavenly "Son of Man" Daniel spoke about, we need only refer again to the account of His trial. When Jesus, as we have already seen, spoke of Himself to His judges as "the Son of Man seated at the right hand of Power, and coming on the clouds of heaven," the high priest was scandalized. He "tore his robes" (a traditional gesture of pious outrage or grief) and said, "He has uttered blasphemy" (Matthew 26:64–65).

Whether we read the prophecy from Daniel or the one from Christ, we find that the Judge comes to render judgment "coming on the clouds of heaven." And when we examine passages about the Second Advent from other books of the Bible as well, we find similar language, echoing Jesus' references not only to a descent with the clouds for judgment, but also to glory and power, to the sound of a heavenly "trumpet," and to the angels who accompany His coming. All these point to an arrival that simply could not be kept a secret.

Passages from Other Biblical Books

After the Gospels, the next reference to Jesus' return to earth is found in Acts, a book written by St. Luke as a sequel to his Gospel account. St. Luke tells us that on the day of our Lord's ascension into heaven, the Apostles were still asking about His plans, and He reminded them that they could not "know times or seasons which the Father has fixed by His own authority" (Acts 1:7). He promised once more to send them the Holy Spirit, and then, as they watched, "He was lifted up, and a cloud took Him out of their sight" (Acts 1:9).

While they stood gazing at the sky, two angels appeared and offered one more reminder of what our Lord had told them before: "This Jesus, who was taken up from you into heaven, will come in the same way as you saw Him go into heaven" (Acts 1:11). How would He return to earth? *Coming with the clouds of heaven.*

We should note here that in biblical history, clouds were associated with the glory of God's presence. The term "glory," as it is used in Scripture, has more than one layer of meaning. On a physical level, it refers to "brightness" or "splendor." On a deeper level, it means "praise" or "renown"—the honor publicly given to someone of magnificent greatness. And it also describes the kind of greatness that attracts such attention and acclaim.

The Scripture tells us that God's grandeur sometimes takes the form of a luminous cloud so that people can encounter His glory in a compelling way. For example, when the Lord brought the Israelites out of slavery in Egypt and led them through the wilderness, He appeared as a towering cloud during the day (Exodus 13:21). When Moses met with the Lord on the mountaintop to receive the Ten Commandments, "the glory of the Lord settled on Mount Sinai, and the cloud covered it six days" (see Exodus 24:12–18).

When the Israelites, at God's command, built a great "tent of meeting" for worship (also called the tabernacle), "the cloud covered the tent of meeting, and the glory of the Lord filled the tabernacle" (Exodus 40:34). The same thing happened centuries later when the construction of the first Jewish temple, under King Solomon, was completed: "A cloud filled the house of the Lord. . . . The glory of the Lord filled the house of the Lord" (1 Kings 8:10–11). After that temple was destroyed, the prophet Ezekiel had a vision of it in which "a cloud filled the inner court" and "the court was full of the brightness of the glory of the Lord" (Ezekiel 10:3–4).

In the New Testament as well, God's majestic presence takes this form. Most notably, on the Mount of Transfiguration, "a bright cloud overshadowed" Jesus, Moses, and Elijah, and God's voice spoke from the cloud (Matthew 17:5).

Given this recurring form of the "Majestic Glory," as St. Peter calls it (2 Peter 1:17), we should not be surprised when Jesus says He will return to earth "coming on the clouds of heaven with power and great glory." In biblical terms, He is describing an event of immense grandeur, a brightness of such intensity and magnificence that it could never be hidden. The entire world will witness the splendor of Christ's second coming as the Lord and King of the cosmos.[13]

Advent, Resurrection, Judgment

Our primary concern at this point is to understand the nature of Christ's second advent rather than the nature of the resurrection of the dead or the Last Judgment. But these three events are so tightly intertwined that we need to note their necessary connections.

As we saw in chapter four, a primary reason for Christ's return to earth is the last judgment of the human race. "He is the One ordained by God," says St. Peter, "to be judge of the living and the dead" (Acts 10:42). Daniel says that the "one like a Son of Man" will come in the clouds to take part in the world's judgment by the court of heaven (Daniel 7:9–14). And Jesus Himself, after teaching about His second coming, proceeded to tell His disciples the parable of the sheep and the goats to warn about the judgment that would follow soon after (see Matthew 25:31–46).

For the judgment of the dead to take place, however, the dead must first be raised. That resurrection is also the work of Christ. "The Father . . . has given Him authority to execute judgment," says Jesus, speaking of Himself, "because He is the Son of Man. . . . The hour is coming when all who are in the tombs will hear His voice and come forth, those who have done good, to the resurrection of life, and those who have done evil, to the resurrection of judgment" (John 5:26–29).

With these three closely related actions of Christ in mind
—advent, resurrection, and judgment—we can now examine the New Testament epistles to see what they might add
to our picture of the Lord's coming.

"In the Twinkling of an Eye"

St. Paul, St. James, St. Peter, and St. John speak briefly of
the Second Advent a number of times in their letters. They
refer to it in various ways, such as "His coming" (1 John
2:28); "the coming of the Lord" (James 5:8); "the revelation
of Jesus Christ" (1 Peter 1:7); "the end of all things" (1 Peter
4:7); "the appearing of the glory of our great God and Savior
Jesus Christ" (Titus 2:13).

In the Old Testament, the expected time of divine judgment was often called "the day of the Lord" (see, for example,
Malachi 4:5, RSV; Malachi 3:23, NAB). In a similar way, the
New Testament writers sometimes speak of Christ's coming
in judgment as "the day of the Lord" (2 Peter 3:10), "the
day of the Lord Jesus" (1 Corinthians 5:5), "the day of Jesus
Christ" (Philippians 1:6), or even just "the Day" (1 Corinthians 3:13). Most of these references occur in the context of
exhortations to Christians to live a godly life in view of God's
judgment or to take courage in the hope of His triumph.

As we saw in chapter four, St. Peter pursues the subject a
little more in depth as he responds to scoffers. In his second
letter he reminds them that the seeming delay in Christ's
return demonstrates God's mercy, because the "day of the
Lord" will be terrifying (see 2 Peter 3:2–17). St. John's first
letter briefly warns of the Antichrist (in fact, of more than
one antichrist, and of "the spirit of antichrist"; 1 John 2:18–
22; 4:3—more on this later). Beyond these two short passages, only three more extended treatments of the subject are
found in the biblical epistles: one in St. Paul's first letter to

the Corinthians and one in each of his letters to the Thessalonians.

Apparently, the Apostle had spoken more on the subject
than he had written. (As we have noted, the unwritten tradition was critical for passing on the Faith in the early Church.)
When St. Paul attempted to settle a Thessalonian controversy
about the Lord's coming, he had no need to lay out a detailed
picture. Instead, he simply reminded them of a point he had
previously made in a homily: "Do you not remember," he
chided them, "that when I was still with you I told you this?"
(2 Thessalonians 2:5).

The Christians at Corinth seem to have had some questions and even doubts about the resurrection of the dead (see
1 Corinthians chapter 15). In explaining the nature of the
resurrected and glorified body, the Apostle described how
the change will take place: "Christ has been raised from the
dead, the first fruits of those who have fallen asleep [that is,
who have died]. For as by a man came death, by a man has
come also the resurrection of the dead. For as in Adam all
die, so also in Christ shall all be made alive. But each in his
own order: Christ the first fruits, then at His coming those
who belong to Christ. Then comes the end, when He delivers
the kingdom to God the Father after destroying every rule
and every authority and power" (1 Corinthians 15:20–24).
Here is the trio of closely connected events we have already
noted: Christ's coming, the resurrection of the dead, and the
judgment (in this context, described in terms of His triumph
over evil).

St. Paul then went on to argue for the feasibility of a bodily
resurrection. He described the nature of the change a body
undergoes in resurrection and then continued his description
of the close of the age: "Lo! I tell you a mystery. We shall
not all sleep [that is, die], but we shall all be changed, in a

moment, in the twinkling of an eye, *at the last trumpet. For the trumpet will sound*, and the dead will be raised imperishable, and we shall be changed" (1 Corinthians 15:51–52, emphasis added).

We have heard about that trumpet already. Recall the words of Jesus: "They will see the Son of Man coming on the clouds of heaven with power and great glory; and He will send out His angels *with a loud trumpet call*, and they will gather His elect from the four winds, from one end of heaven to the other" (Matthew 24:30–31). St. Paul is clearly describing the same event Jesus described. The Son appears in clouds of brilliant glory, the trumpet sounds, and the angels do His bidding to gather His people for resurrection and judgment.

Coming With His Saints

The Christians at Thessalonica, like those at Corinth, had some bothersome questions about the resurrection of the dead. Would those believers who had already died have to wait longer to meet Christ than those who were still alive at his return (see 1 Thessalonians 4:15)? And what about the people who were telling them that the Judgment Day had somehow already taken place (see 2 Thessalonians 2:1–2)?

In his response to these concerns, St. Paul offered a few insights that expand on his comments to the Corinthians. With regard to the first question, he insisted that the saints—those who had died in friendship with God and whose souls were in heaven at the time of the Second Coming—would actually accompany Christ on His return to earth. Christians should be growing in holiness, he said, in preparation for divine judgment "at the coming of our Lord Jesus with all His saints" (1 Thessalonians 3:13). This statement echoes Jesus' words about the angels gathering the elect from the four winds to be with Him when He returns (see Matthew 24:31).

After a few more exhortations to godliness and warnings about the judgment, the Apostle returned to the theme of the saints accompanying Christ:

> For since we believe that Jesus died and rose again, even so, through Jesus, God will bring with Him those who have fallen asleep. . . . We who are alive, who are left until the coming of the Lord, shall not precede those who have fallen asleep. For the Lord Himself will descend from heaven with a cry of command, with the archangel's call, and with the sound of the trumpet of God. And the dead in Christ will rise first; then we who are alive, who are left, shall be caught up together with them in the clouds to meet the Lord in the air; and so we shall always be with the Lord (1 Thessalonians 4:14–17).

St. Paul gives enough details here to make it clear that he is talking, not about a secret rapture, but about the same event we have already heard described by Jesus to His disciples and by the same Apostle when he wrote to the Corinthians. Once again, we find Christ's descent from heaven, clouds, angels, the trumpet, and resurrection. St. Paul's remarks on the subject in his second letter to the Thessalonians focus more on the activity of the Antichrist (see 2 Thessalonians 2:1–12; more on this later). But we read there also about our Lord's appearance from heaven in bright glory with the angels and saints to judge the wicked—"when the Lord Jesus is revealed from heaven with His mighty angels in flaming fire, inflicting vengeance upon those who do not know God, . . . when He comes on that day to be glorified in His saints, and to be marveled at in all who have believed" (2 Thessalonians 1:7–8, 10).

Three critical points should be noted here: First, these descriptions of Christ's coming share enough common elements to indicate that they all refer to the same sequence of events. This sequence includes our Lord's glorious advent, the resurrection of the dead, and the judgment of the world. Second, the references to the trumpet, the blazing light, the glory of the saints, the judgment or conquest of evil, and the fact that people will "marvel," all show that this is no secret or hidden event.

Third, the text in 2 Thessalonians shows that this sequence takes place after the horrors of the Antichrist's deceptions and attacks on the Church: "For that day will not come, unless the rebellion comes first, and the man of lawlessness is revealed, the son of perdition, who opposes and exalts himself against every so-called god or object of worship, proclaiming himself to be God. . . . The lawless one will be revealed, and the Lord Jesus will slay him with the breath of His mouth and destroy him by His appearing and His coming" (2 Thessalonians 2:3–4, 8).

"Caught up Together"

One detail included in St. Paul's comments may raise a question. When Jesus and the saints come down from heaven, he insists, the faithful Christians who are still alive on the earth "shall be caught up together with them in the clouds to meet the Lord in the air; and so we shall always be with the Lord" (1 Thessalonians 4:17). What is the significance of that meeting?

First, we should note that this statement parallels Jesus' words about sending out the angels to "gather His elect from the four winds, from the ends of the earth to the ends of heaven," so they can be with "the Son of Man coming in clouds with great power and glory" (Mark 13:26–27; see also Matthew 24:31). In addition, St. Paul's remarks on the same subject in 2 Thessalonians are prefaced with a slightly different description of this meeting: "Now concerning the coming of our Lord Jesus Christ and our assembling to meet Him"

—a day when "the Lord Jesus is revealed from heaven with His mighty angels in flaming fire" (2 Thessalonians 2:1; 1:7).

As we have seen, the context of the 1 Thessalonians passage, with its references to the angel, the trumpet, and the clouds, shows that St. Paul is writing about the glorious public return of the Lord. The question that arises is this: What is the purpose of the faithful on earth being "caught up" in the glory of their descending Lord to meet Him as He arrives in triumph?

The answer is simple when we recognize an ancient custom common in St. Paul's culture. State dignitaries and victorious military leaders of his time often made grand public visits to a city. Such an appearance was called a *parousia*, the same Greek term that St. Paul and other biblical writers often use to write about Christ's glorious arrival at the close of the age (see, for example, 1 Corinthians 15:23; 2 Thessalonians 2:8; 2 Peter 3:4; 1 John 2:28).

When the illustrious visitor approached a city with his entourage, he was often met by the citizens who wanted to go out to welcome him and then accompany him back into the city. It was a way for the people to honor such a person's arrival and to take part in the celebration of his coming. This, in fact, was the custom that led to Jesus' triumphal entry into Jerusalem on the day we remember as Passion (or Palm) Sunday (see Matthew 21:1–17).

When we find that the Greek word translated here as "meet" or "meeting" (*apantesis*) is the same term that was used for the gathering of citizens to meet the approaching celebrity, the passage makes perfect sense. Those who are still alive on earth when Jesus returns, gathered together from the ends of the earth by the angels, will have a great privilege: They will be caught up in His clouds of glory to meet the approaching "King of kings and Lord of lords" (1 Timothy

6:15) and to join the saints whose souls have already experienced the rewards of living with Him in heaven. Then they will accompany Him as He enters the world in triumph.

On that day, each faithful Christian will become "a partaker in the glory that is to be revealed" (1 Peter 5:1). Those who "suffer with Him" (that is, for His sake) through the terrors of the last days will at that time "also be glorified with Him" (Romans 8:17).

The Apocalypse

This theme—suffering for our Lord so that we can reign with Him—is nowhere more powerfully presented than in the last book of the Bible, the Revelation to St. John—also known by its Greek name, the Apocalypse. The book was recorded at a time when the Church suffered terrible persecution at the hands of the Roman imperial government. St. John's dazzling vision of cosmic cataclysm has become so thoroughly identified in Western culture with the end of the world that the word "apocalyptic" has come to mean "foreboding final doom."

As we shall discuss more thoroughly in chapter eight, not all Christians believe that Revelation prophesies the end of the world. Some conclude that it actually describes historical events that occurred near the time it was written (at the end of the first century). Others suggest that it refers to the two-thousand-year span of Church history as a whole. Still others believe it simply represents in vivid symbols the perpetual struggle of good and evil in the world.

If the Apocalypse does not in fact portray the future, then we have little reason to consider its text in a discussion of the close of the age. But the book does at times use language that is strikingly similar to the biblical passages we have already examined, raising the strong possibility that at least portions of the book point to Christ's second coming. And since most rapture believers would agree that this is indeed the case, a brief look at these portions may be helpful. (For now, we will resist the temptation to speculate about the intriguing details of the book.)

Which passages might be relevant? Several grab our attention because they use language already familiar to our discussion—echoes of Old Testament words quoted by Jesus that we have already examined. The first reference occurs in the Apostle's preface: "Behold, He is coming with the clouds, and every eye will see Him, every one who pierced Him; and all tribes of the earth will wail on account of Him" (Revelation 1:7). From the beginning, St. John seems to be affirming Christ's own declaration that His coming will be glorious, a universally visible event.

After this opening statement, we must for the most part pass over the messages directed specifically to the seven churches of Asia (see Revelation 1:11), the stirring scenes of splendor in heaven, and the turbulent accounts of wickedness and disaster on earth. Of most importance in these chapters for now are the glimpses they afford of the Lord who is to appear in glory to judge the earth. Having already examined Daniel's vision of the "one like a Son of Man," we find what seems to be a similar portrait painted here.

Chapters four and five of Revelation especially show clear parallels to the seventh chapter of the Hebrew prophet's account: Both visionaries behold God's magnificently brilliant throne in heaven, around which are arrayed a myriad of angels serving Him. In both visions a book (or scroll) must be opened before the heavenly court as it sits in judgment. And in both, Someone is presented before God's throne who has the power and authority to render that judgment—in Daniel's account, "a Son of Man" (Daniel 7:13); in St. John's, "a Lamb who was slain" (Revelation 5:12, referring, of course, to Christ's sacrificial death).

Daniel speaks of this glorious One as a mighty ruler whose "dominion is an everlasting dominion," and whose "kingdom . . . shall not be destroyed" (Daniel 7:14). In a later chapter St. John, with imagery shifting from the Lamb to a conquering Warrior on a white horse, calls Him "King of kings and Lord of lords" (Revelation 19:16). With the declaration of this triumphant title, St. John provides us with what seems to be his picture of Christ's descent to earth in glory.

> Then I saw heaven opened, and behold, a white horse! He who sat upon it is called Faithful and True, and in righteousness He judges and makes war. His eyes are like a flame of fire, and on His head are many diadems. . . . The armies of heaven, arrayed in fine linen, white and pure, followed Him on white horses. From His mouth issues a sharp sword with which to smite the nations; and He will rule them with a rod of iron; He will tread the wine press of the fury of the wrath of God the Almighty (Revelation 19:11–15).

What do we make of this startling portrait? No doubt we could argue, as many have, over which details are to be taken literally and which as symbol. But whichever way we interpret the imagery, its implication is clear: If this is the Second Advent, it is no secret matter. Christ descends from heaven in overwhelming glory accompanied by the brilliant hosts of heaven, and when He does, no one on earth can resist Him.

Martyrs of the Great Tribulation

We have noted that the suffering of the Church appears as a prominent theme in Revelation, so we should make one last observation about the message of this book. No one who reads it can reasonably claim that God keeps Christians from suffering the great tribulation of the last days. We may, if we wish, discount the exhortations to persecuted Christians of the seven churches of Asia as a message only for St. John's contemporaries, though even then, that message still illustrates the principle that God does not always spare believers from oppression. But we must listen as one of the elders in heaven tells the visionary about the martyrs he sees "from every nation, from all tribes and peoples and tongues, standing before the throne and before the Lamb, clothed in white robes, with palm branches in their hands" (Revelation 7:9).

St. John had seen them earlier in the vision. He knew they were "the souls of those who had been slain for the word of God and for the witness they had borne," who were "each given a white robe and told to rest a little longer, until the number of their fellow servants and their brethren should be complete, who were to be killed as they themselves had been" (Revelation 6:9–11). But there was more. In answer to the question, "Whence have they come?" the elder declared: "These are they *who have come out of the great tribulation*; they have washed their robes and made them white in the blood of the Lamb" (Revelation 7:13–14; emphasis added).

What could be clearer? God did not pluck these faithful believers out of the horrors of persecution; in fact, He told them that others would be joining their ranks as martyrs. We may, of course, interpret this passage as an account of St. John's own times, thus concluding that the "great tribulation" these martyrs endured took place in the first century A.D. But even if that is the case (and rapture believers tend to reject that view), then we are still left with the solid affirmation that the Church is called upon to offer a suffering witness to God's truth at the hands of His enemies—not a sudden escape from their grasp.

Jesus' passionate intercession for His followers in the Garden of Gethsemane reflects this reality poignantly: "I do not ask that you take them out of the world," he prayed to God the Father, "but that you keep them from the evil one" (John 17:15, NAB).

A Summary

Having surveyed what seem to be the most straightforward biblical passages about Christ's second coming, we can now summarize what we find there. First, Jesus' own instructions about the events to come are confirmed by the apostolic teaching of Sts. Peter, Paul, John, and James. In every scenario presented, the Second Advent is not a secret or invisible event. On the contrary, in various accounts it is described as unmistakably public, universally visible, glorious, full of splendor. The Lord returns on magnificent clouds of glory with brilliant angels and saints and a trumpet blast announcing their arrival; the faithful on earth are gathered to Him, while the rest of the world wails at the terrifying sight.

Second, Jesus and the Apostles warn that the Church will face severe tribulation before His second coming. The demonic forces that have resisted God from the beginning of history will launch ferocious attacks on His people. Christians will not be spared this adversity, but God will provide the grace to endure, and those who endure to the end through such cleansing and strengthening trials will be saved.

Details, Details

Given these scriptural basics of our Lord's second coming, how could so many Christians adhere to the secret rapture teaching? In general, rapture believers seem to start with the notion of an extra coming of Christ, and then go looking for biblical passages that might be forced somehow into fitting the doctrine. Consider the testimony of Robert Gundry, an evangelical Protestant scholar with a Ph.D. in New Testament who specializes in passages on the close of the age:

> I grew up as an evangelical who . . . didn't even know of a disagreement on the topic [of the rapture]. Later I heard dark rumors that some Christians don't believe in a coming of Jesus before the tribulation—but they must be straying dangerously from the Bible and standard Christian doctrine. Or so I was told, and so I thought.
>
> I enrolled in a college. It was Christian. . . . [B]ut somehow the suspicion grew on me that their teaching on this topic didn't sit so easily with biblical texts as their other teaching did. So I decided to erase from my mind as far as was humanly possible everything I'd heard and read about the second coming, to read through the entire New Testament afresh, pay special attention to passages dealing with the tribulation and Jesus' return, and see what first impressions might be. They were that He is *not* said to return before the tribulation, but only afterwards.

At this point Gundry tried reading once more "reams" of literature that taught the secret rapture doctrine. But he could no longer see such a teaching in the biblical text itself. Instead, he concluded that the Bible said nothing of a secret rapture and that "throughout history the vast majority of Christians have never thought" of such a notion.[14]

As Gundry discovered, the secret rapture really isn't there in the pages of Scripture. The best a rapture believer can do is read the idea into the text. The usual strategy is a kind of grasping at straws: Look for some detail in one biblical passage about the Second Coming that differs slightly from a detail in a very similar passage. Then declare that the two passages must refer to different events!

For example, some rapture teachers make a great deal of the minor variations in the various scriptural phrases that refer to the Second Coming. As we have already noted, sometimes the Bible speaks of it as "the day of Christ" (Philippians 1:10; 2:16). Sometimes it speaks of "the day of the Lord"

(2 Thessalonians 2:2). Obviously, rapture defenders claim, these phrases must refer to different events because one says "Lord" and one says "Christ"! The first term must refer to the secret rapture, while the other refers to the coming of our Lord in glory.

The problem, of course, is that St. Paul himself shows no such intention of making a distinction. What are we to make of the fact, for example, that he speaks of "the day of our Lord Jesus Christ" (1 Corinthians 1:8)? If the "day of Christ" and the "day of the Lord" really refer to two different events, why would the Apostle refer to the same day as the day of "our Lord" *and* of "Christ"?[15]

Examples of such forced distinctions by rapture teachers are numerous. Some teachers have tried, for example, to distinguish between biblical uses of the Greek words *apocalypsis* ("revelation"), *parousia* ("coming") and *epiphaneia* ("appearance") in speaking of Christ's return. They say that even though all these terms refer to His coming, *parousia* means the secret rapture and *apocalypsis* means His final advent in glory. The problem, of course, is that biblical writers actually use the terms indiscriminately in passages that rapture believers say refer to different comings.

Rapture teachers may also emphasize that some passages about Christ's return to earth omit details that others contain. One passage, for example, may say nothing about tribulation and judgment, while another may say nothing about meeting Christ and the resurrection. Rapture teachers argue that these omissions occur because the descriptions refer to two different events.

Such claims, however, cannot be supported merely on the basis of omitted details. A noted evangelical Protestant scholar of the Bible, Douglas J. Moo, has observed in his arguments against the rapture doctrine: "New Testament texts are almost universally directed to rather specific situations in the life of the Church. This means . . . that the author will generally include only what he wants in order to make his point and he will omit much that is unnecessary for his immediate purposes."[16]

Moo goes on to insist that for this reason, such omissions in detail have no significance for the rapture debate. In one situation (1 Thessalonians 4:13–18), St. Paul is emphasizing the resurrection in order to comfort bereaved Christians. In another (2 Thessalonians 1:3–10), he is focusing on tribulation and judgment to encourage Christians who are suffering persecution. In both passages, however, St. Paul is still referring to the same event: the single, glorious return of our Lord to the earth.

As Moo also points out, we should recall the varying Gospel descriptions of Christ's crucifixion. Each one omits certain details included by others. St. Luke and St. John, for example, don't record Jesus' cry, "My God, my God, why have you forsaken me?" (Matthew 27:46, NAB; Mark 15:34, NAB). Jesus' prayer committing His spirit into His Father's hands (see Luke 23:46) is omitted by Sts. Matthew, Mark, and John. The thrusting of the spear into Jesus' side is described only by St. John (see John 19:34). Using the reasoning of the rapture teachers, we would have to conclude that these four Gospel accounts must refer to four different crucifixions of our Lord!

Other arguments to "prove" from Scripture that Christ will return twice do similar violence to the biblical text. Secret rapture teachers may insist, for example, that the coming of "the Son of Man" (Matthew 24:27) is a different event from the coming of "the Lord Himself" (1 Thessalonians 4:16). The "trumpet of God" (1 Thessalonians 4:16) is not the same as the "trumpet" of the "angels" (Matthew 24:31). The "gospel of the Kingdom" (Matthew 24:14) is not the same as the "gospel of the grace of God" (Acts 20:24).

Sometimes rapture advocates will even go so far as to divide up a single, brief biblical reference to the Second Coming as a way of claiming that Christ will return twice. *Left Behind* author Tim LaHaye quotes approvingly one teacher's notion that St. Paul was distinguishing the secret rapture from Jesus' final coming when he spoke of "the blessed hope and glorious appearing" of Christ (Titus 2:13 in the King James Version, often used by fundamentalists). "Blessed hope," the teacher insists, refers to the secret rapture, while "glorious appearing" refers to Christ's final coming.[17] Using this same method of forcing a distinction, we could just as well conclude that "the God of our Lord Jesus Christ" and "the Father of our Lord Jesus Christ" are two different Persons—simply because St. Paul once wrote of "the God and Father of our Lord Jesus Christ" (Ephesians 1:3)!

Employing such questionable methods for interpreting Scripture can lead to all kinds of strange variations on the secret rapture notion. At least one fundamentalist defender of the doctrine, for example, uses this approach to conclude that there will actually be *two* secret raptures before the final return of our Lord (for a grand total of *four* advents of Christ), as well as *four* final judgments![18]

All these examples serve to illustrate the glaring problem in most attempts to find two future comings of Christ somewhere in the Bible. There are two clear ways in which Jesus and the New Testament writers could have distinguished between a secret rapture and a glorious advent if that had been their intention. First, they could have made a clear distinction in their terminology for the two events. But they did not. Second, they could have included details in the description of each event that were not merely different, but contradictory—incapable of being harmonized. But again, they did not. The similarity of language and the harmony of detail in the various accounts of the Second Coming point to an obvious conclusion: Christ's return will be a single, glorious, and public event.

Sometimes rapture teachers will charge that those Christians who believe in only one return of Christ are failing to distinguish His two descents from heaven in the same way that many Jews in New Testament times failed to distinguish the prophesied two advents of Christ. Many rejected Jesus, they say, because He fulfilled the prophecies in Isaiah about the Servant who suffers for His people (see Isaiah 42:1–4; 49:1–6; 50:4–11; 52:13—53:12) but not the prophecies in Daniel about the "Son of Man" who comes to judge (see Daniel 7:13–14). If the ancient Jews had rightly distinguished between the two advents, secret rapture teachers sometimes insist, they would have found that the Suffering Servant passages in Isaiah were fulfilled by Jesus' first coming as Savior, and the Son of Man passages will be fulfilled by His second coming as Judge (see 1 Peter 1:10–12).

This argument fails, however, when we recognize that most Jews, when they read the prophets Isaiah and Daniel, did not actually make the mistake of failing to distinguish there the two comings of the Messiah (the Hebrew word for "Christ"). In fact, the historical evidence suggests that most did not associate the Servant passages in Isaiah with an individual Messiah at all. Instead, they assumed that the Servant described by this prophet had to be someone else altogether —the prophet himself, a royal figure, or perhaps the nation of Israel as a whole—because they expected the Messiah to come as a conqueror, not as a lowly victim (see, for example, Acts 8:27–34).[19]

In short, the mistake in interpretation made by many Jewish believers in Jesus' time, the error that misled them about how prophecy would be fulfilled, was more like the mistake made by today's rapture believers. They thought that various prophecies pointing to a single figure actually referred to two figures instead—just as secret rapture advocates think that various prophecies pointing to a single advent of Christ refer to two advents instead.

Who Really *Gets Left Behind?*

The single scriptural detail that most excites rapture believers is found in the passage we have noted in St. Paul's first letter to the Thessalonians: "Then we who are alive, who are left, shall be *caught up* together with them in the clouds to meet the Lord in the air; and so we shall always be with the Lord" (1 Thessalonians 4:17, emphasis added). Our English word "rapture" comes from the verb used here in the Latin translation for "caught up."

As we have already seen, the idea of meeting the Lord at His coming has a simple, straightforward interpretation without any reference to a secret snatching of believers well before Judgment Day. Those who are alive will simply go up to meet Christ as His escort while He descends to earth in triumph. All the rest of the details in this account match or harmonize with the details in the other accounts of the Second Coming—including those passages that rapture believers claim apply to Christ's final advent in glory.

Another text commonly quoted by rapture believers as evidence of a secret snatching comes from the Olivet discourse. Jesus said: "As were the days of Noah, so will be the coming of the Son of man. For as in those days before the flood they were eating and drinking, marrying and giving in marriage, until the day when Noah entered the ark, and they did not know until the flood came and swept them all away, so will be the coming of the Son of man. Then two men will be in the field; one is taken and one is left. Two women will be grinding at the mill; one is taken and one is left" (Matthew 24:37–41).

These words have been cited in fundamentalist sermons

countless times; a popular evangelical song of the seventies even alluded to it, warning in a haunting chorus that spiritually unprepared listeners could be "left behind."[20] The assumption here is that the man taken from the field and the woman taken from the mill were true believers "caught up" at the secret rapture. The two people left behind, then, were not believers.

Many Christians believe that this text applies to the destruction of Jerusalem by Roman armies in the first century, not to the close of the age. But even if we grant that it refers to the "end times," we need only read again the words introducing this scenario to see the flaw in a rapture interpretation. "As were the days of Noah . . . the flood came and swept them all away" (Matthew 24:37, 39).

In the days of Noah, who was "taken" ("swept . . . away"), and who was "left"? The wicked were taken away in judgment by the flood waters, and the righteous (Noah and his family on the ark) were left behind in safety. If the rapture teachers are correct in thinking that this passage applies to the close of the age, then it would seem to prove the opposite of what they teach about who gets taken and who gets left behind.

Yet even if we should allow that Jesus is saying the righteous will be the ones taken and the wicked will be left, then the passage still fits the Second Advent scenario we have described: When Christ returns, publicly and in clouds of glory, the righteous will be caught up to meet Him as He descends to earth, while the wicked remain to await His imminent judgment. No secret, invisible, "extra" coming of Christ is depicted here.

Escape From God's Wrath?

Yet another way in which rapture believers attempt to argue their position from Scripture is to cite verses that say Chris-

tians will be spared God's wrath. St. Paul promises the Thessalonian Christians, for example, that "Jesus . . . delivers us
from the wrath to come" and "God has not destined us for
wrath" (1 Thessalonians 1:10; 5:9). But when we examine the
Apostle's references to divine wrath throughout His letters,
we find that he usually is referring to the sentence of everlasting punishment in the next life, not to temporary trials in
this life.

For example, the alternative the Apostle presents to being
"destined . . . for wrath" is not escape, but eternal salvation
(1 Thessalonians 5:9). The "vessels of wrath" are the damned
(Romans 9:22). "By your hard and impenitent heart," he told
the Romans, "you are storing up wrath for yourself on the day
of wrath when God's righteous judgment will be revealed"
(Romans 2:5). In a similar way, St. John the Baptist speaks of
"the wrath to come" in referring to the "unquenchable fire"
of hell (Matthew 3:7–12).

Rapture teachers may respond that the final tribulation under the Antichrist, along with various natural catastrophes,
is in fact the beginning of the divine wrath that culminates
in damnation for those who have rejected God. But even if
it were true that this is what St. Paul meant when he wrote
about "the wrath to come," then rapture advocates still have
a problem in their scriptural interpretation.

They insist that even though true believers will be snatched
away from harm in the secret rapture, many unbelievers on
earth will convert after that startling event. They admit, then,
that these last Christians will have to go through the final
tribulation. But if God has truly promised Christians that
they will escape this divine "wrath" of the last days, then
why wouldn't the "post-rapture" converts escape it as well?
They too would be Christians. Couldn't they claim the same
divine promise for themselves?

Perhaps, on the other hand, the rapture believers would admit that, in their way of thinking, Christians still living on earth (the "post-rapture" converts) could somehow be preserved from God's wrath in the last days. Maybe He would hide them out in places of refuge, or perhaps they would experience the adversity as purification rather than "wrath." (The latter position would actually be closer to Catholic thinking.) If so, then all the biblical passages that rapture teachers quote about divine wrath would no longer support a secret rapture doctrine. If God will somehow protect Christians still living on earth from the final divine wrath, then there is no need for Him to "rapture" them away as an escape. His biblical promises of protection imply nothing about Christians being taken away to heaven.

Pre, Mid, Post, Partial?

Perhaps we should make one last observation about attempts to find a secret rapture doctrine somewhere in the Scripture. Not all rapture believers agree on how or when the great "snatch" takes place. Most rapture advocates insist that the "great tribulation" at the end of time will last seven years, and that the rapture will occur in that same general period of time. But will believers be "caught up" to meet Christ *before* those seven years, at the *midpoint* of those seven years, or *after* those seven years? And will *all* Christians be taken out of the world, or only *some* of them?

Those rapture believers who insist that, according to Scripture, the rapture comes *before* the tribulation are called (not surprisingly) *pretribulationists*. Those who believe the Bible points instead to a rapture *during* the tribulation are called *midtribulationists*. Those who claim that the truly biblical position is the doctrine of a rapture *after* the tribulation are called *postribulationists*. And those who teach the *partial rapture* doctrine believe that only some Christians will be raptured before the tribulation, while others will be caught up sometime later.

Disagreement among rapture believers over these issues has often led to fierce theological battles. Advocates of one view have sometimes refused to associate with those of another view. Such disputes certainly seem to undermine the claim of rapture teachers that their doctrine is based on "the plain sense of Scripture." Apparently, the issue is not so "plain" after all—even to rapture believers. [21]

Where Did They Get the Idea?

Despite the current visibility and success of the *Left Behind* books, the rapture notion is held by only a minority of Christians worldwide. Not only Catholics, but also Eastern Orthodox believers, non-evangelical Protestants and even many evangelical Protestants find the rapture notion alien. If, as we have seen, the doctrine finds no substantial support in the Bible, where did the idea come from? How could such an idea take hold of people who sincerely profess to be "Bible believing"—and who often condemn those who disagree with them for denying the "plain sense" of Scripture?

The answer to these questions takes us back many years ago, long before millions of Americans ever began worrying about who might be left behind.

6

The Late Great
Secret Rapture Doctrine

Where Did It Come From?

When the police are tracking down a criminal, they often put together a profile on the outlaw. What is his background? Who are his usual associates? What are his habits? How long has he been operating?

The secret rapture doctrine is much like a criminal in that regard. We might, in fact, best think of it as a spiritual counterfeiter. If we want to keep people from becoming victims of its dangerous and costly deceptions, we need to assemble a file on this "bandit." What is the background of the teaching —where did it come from? With what other religious ideas is it usually associated? What spiritual habits does it lead to? How long has it been operating?

Let's create a profile for the rapture trap.

Not in the Creed

"He will come again in glory to judge the living and the dead, and His kingdom will have no end."

Since ancient times Catholics and countless other Christians have recited those stirring words in the profession of faith known popularly as the Nicene Creed, which had its beginnings in the First Ecumenical Council of Nicaea in the year A.D. 325. This creed sums up the most basic beliefs of the Church, affirmed week after week, year after year, century after century, throughout the world for countless generations. Not only Catholic popes and Eastern patriarchs have embraced it, but also Martin Luther, John Calvin, John Wesley, and other founders of the major Protestant traditions.

The Nicene Creed declares firmly that Christ will come again in glory to judge the world, but it says absolutely nothing about an extra, "third" coming to snatch believers from the world before the final tribulation. Admittedly, a number of important Christian doctrines do not appear in this brief statement of faith. Yet when we consider that the creed does address specifically the doctrine of the Second Advent, it is only reasonable to wonder why, if Christians through the ages had believed in a secret rapture associated with Christ's return, nothing was ever said about it here.

The reason that the creed is silent about a third coming is of course simple: This novel, eccentric teaching only appeared late in Church history and has never been embraced by the great majority of believers, Catholic or otherwise. Neither ancient Christians, nor medieval Christians, nor even the founders of the major Protestant movements ever heard of the secret rapture doctrine. They knew of no invisible coming by Christ to catch believers up to heaven prior to His return to earth in clouds of glory. And when they wrote about that single, universally visible, glorious coming of the Lord, they often referred to the very same biblical passages that today's secret rapture advocates claim must refer instead to an invisible snatching away.

So where did the "rapture trap" originate? Before we trace the relatively recent beginnings of this doctrine, we will take a brief look at the history of what Christians have believed, down through the centuries, about the nature of Christ's return.

The Early Church Fathers

The writings of Christian leaders in the first few centuries of Church history hold a special authority for Catholics and many other Christians. And so they should. The first generation of bishops and other leaders knew the Apostles personally and received from them directly the Sacred Tradition about Christ's life and teaching. The generations of leaders immediately following them remained close to that Tradition. They were instrumental in defining the essential Christian beliefs by formulating the creeds of the Church. They identified which books were truly inspired by the Holy Spirit as authentic Scripture, and they assembled the Bible as we know it today.

Not surprisingly, these men came to be known as the "fathers of the Church," because they were responsible for the doctrine and discipline of the early Christian community, just as a father is responsible for the discipline of his family. They were known for defending the Catholic faith by their preaching, writing, and personal holiness. Who, then, would be in a better position than these men to interpret correctly the words of Scripture according to the apostolic Tradition?

Sometimes the writings of the Fathers hold varying opinions on subjects not essential to the Faith or in matters that were not authoritatively clarified by the Holy Spirit's work through the Magisterium until after the time of their writing. But when we find the Fathers speaking on a particular doctrinal issue in consensus, or near consensus, Christians should pay close attention. The Fathers' teachings on the Second Advent are a case in point.

If we search the surviving Church literature of the Fathers, we find that they know nothing of an extra, "third" coming of Christ—a secret snatching away of believers to escape the final tribulation. Like the writers of Scripture itself, with one voice they speak of a single advent, glorious and terrifying, bringing history to a close. And they assume that Christ's earthshaking arrival comes after the Church has suffered severely at the hands of the Antichrist. A few citations should be enough to represent the whole.

St. Justin Martyr (c. 100–c. 165)

St. John was probably the last of the original twelve Apostles to die. Only a few years after his death, St. Justin Martyr was born in Samaria, where Jesus and the Apostles had traveled. A brilliant philosopher convert who gave his life for the Faith, St. Justin wrote: "[In] the words of the [Old Testament] prophecy . . . two advents of Christ have been announced: the one, in which He is set forth as suffering, inglorious, dishonored, and crucified; but the other, in which He shall come from heaven with glory, when the man of apostasy [that is, the Antichrist—see 2 Thessalonians 2:3], who speaks strange things against the Most High, shall venture to do unlawful deeds on the earth against us the Christians."[22]

Clearly, according to St. Justin, Christ has only two advents. And the second one is glorious and takes place after the Church has been ravaged by the Antichrist. No secret rapture to escape tribulation is envisioned here.

St. Irenaeus (c. 125–c. 203)

St. Irenaeus, bishop of Lyons, was a student of St. Polycarp, who had been discipled by St. John himself. If anyone knew how to interpret St. John's revelation, surely it was St. Irenaeus. "In a still clearer light," he wrote, "has John, in the Apocalypse, indicated to the Lord's disciples what will happen in the last times." Having cited the passage from Daniel quoted by Jesus in the Olivet discourse—a reference, he believed, to the final Antichrist—St. Irenaeus went on to talk about what the Church would suffer after this monstrous enemy of God came to power.

At that time, he said, the "ten kings" described by both Daniel and St. John (Daniel 7:24; Revelation 17:12) "shall give their kingdom to the beast [the Antichrist], and put the Church to flight." But the believers will at last meet their Lord at "the resurrection of the just, which takes place after the coming of Antichrist, and the destruction of all nations under his rule."[23] Here again, the picture is clear: The Church must endure the great tribulation under the Antichrist, and then Christ will come to gather His saints together in the resurrection of the dead.

St. Hippolytus (died c. 235)

In the next generation, St. Hippolytus, a priest who may have been a disciple of St. Irenaeus, noted in a commentary on Daniel 12:1 ("There shall be a time of trouble"):

> For at that time there shall be great trouble, such as has not been from the foundation of the world, when some in one way, and others in another, shall be sent through every city and country to destroy the faithful; and the saints [that is, Christians] shall travel from the west to the east, and shall be driven in persecution from the east to the south, while others shall conceal themselves in the mountains and caves; and the abomination shall war against them every-where. . . . For then they shall all be driven out from every place, and dragged from their own homes and haled into prison, and punished with all manner of punishment, and cast out from the whole world.[24]

In his *Treatise on Christ and Antichrist*, St. Hippolytus wrote in depth about what he expected to take place during and after the great tribulation. In an extended commentary on relevant Scripture texts, he cited the passages we have noted

from Jesus' instruction in the Gospels, St. Paul's letters to
the Thessalonians, and the prophet Daniel. His comments
make it clear that they all refer to the same occasion after the
Antichrist's devastation: a single "coming of our Lord and
Savior Jesus Christ from heaven, who shall bring the con-
flagration [that is, the fire] and just judgment upon all who
have refused to believe on Him."[25] In this passage, St. Hippolytus includes all the elements of the events that we have
noted: Christ's dazzling descent from heaven like brilliant
lightning in the clouds of glory, with the angels and saints
accompanying Him, the faithful caught up to meet him, the
resurrection of the dead, and the final judgment. Again, we
find here no extra, "third" coming, no secret rapture to rescue
the Church from the final trial.

These quotes from the earliest Fathers are only a few
among many. Their teaching is confirmed by other prominent early Christian texts as well: the *Epistle of Barnabas*, the
Shepherd of Hermas, the *Didache*, and the *Constitutions of the
Holy Apostles*, as well as the writings of Tertullian, Lactantius, Melito of Sardis, and Methodius.

The Later Fathers

St. Jerome (c. 342–420)

The later fathers of the Church consistently maintained the
position of their predecessors on the glorious second coming
of Christ. St. Jerome, for example, was the greatest biblical
scholar of the ancient Church; his translation of the Scripture
from Hebrew and Greek into Latin served as a standard until
modern times. In a letter to a priest friend he once insisted,
"You are mistaken if you suppose that there is ever a time
when the Christian does not suffer persecution" from the
Devil.

Then St. Jerome went on to remind him:

It shall come, it shall come, that day when this corruptible [nature] shall put on incorruption, and this mortal shall put on immortality. Then shall that servant be blessed whom the Lord shall find watching. Then at the sound of the trumpet the earth and its peoples shall tremble, but you shall rejoice. The world shall howl at the Lord who comes to judge it, and the tribes of the earth shall smite the breast. . . . But then you shall exult and laugh, and say: Behold my crucified Lord, behold my Judge.[26]

In this rousing exhortation, St. Jerome combined allusions from several of the scriptural texts we have examined. In doing so, he revealed his conviction that the Christians would suffer in the final tribulation as they do in every generation. And he made explicit his expectation that only one more advent of Christ is to come—a universally visible event with the angelic trumpet that will prompt the resurrection of the dead and the final judgment.

St. Augustine (354–430)

St. Jerome's brilliant younger contemporary, St. Augustine, was bishop of Hippo and by far the greatest, most influential theologian and philosopher of the ancient Church in the West. In his massive work entitled *The City of God*, he laid out in detail his vision of God's plan for human history. The twentieth book of that work discusses the close of the present age.

Christians should not think, St. Augustine warned, that during the Church's final tribulation "there shall be no Church upon earth, either because the Devil finds no Church, or destroys it by manifold persecutions." No—the Antichrist will do his worst. But God will bring good out of the Church's suffering, as He always brings good out of evil.

Even though the Devil "shall rage with the whole force of himself and his angels," yet "those with whom he makes

war shall have the power to withstand all his violence and
stratagems. . . . For the Almighty does not absolutely seclude
the saints from his temptation, but shelters only their inner
man, where faith resides, that by outward temptation they
may grow in grace." Nevertheless, "this persecution, occurring while the final judgment is imminent, shall be the last
which shall be endured by the Holy Church throughout the
world, the whole city of Christ being assailed by the whole
city of the Devil, as each exists on earth." Then, the writer
went on to explain, Christ will return to raise the dead and
to judge the world.[27]

Later in the same book, St. Augustine commented on
1 Thessalonians 4:13–17. As we saw in chapter five, for those
who believe in a secret coming, this biblical passage seems
to provide the clearest basis for claiming that Christians will
be snatched from the world. As we also saw in that chapter, however, St. Paul's words to the Thessalonians can be
easily understood without any reference to a hidden coming
of Christ to rescue the saints. On the contrary, the elements
common to this passage and others concerning Christ's return—such as the clouds of glory, the angels, and the trumpet call—point instead to the magnificent public arrival of a
victorious King.

St. Augustine's analysis reflected that age-old interpretation concerning those who will be "caught up in the air" at the
Lord's coming: They are in fact meeting Him in His clouds of
glory so they can accompany Him in His triumphant descent
to the earth. "For the words, 'And so shall we ever be with
the Lord,'" the bishop insisted, "are not to be understood as
if he meant that we shall always remain in the air with the
Lord; for He Himself shall not remain there, but shall only
pass through it as He comes. For we shall go to meet Him
as He comes, not as He remains."[28]

The great theologian of Hippo had much more to say

about the end of the world, and his thinking on the subject has profoundly influenced countless Christians ever since. But for now we simply observe that he affirmed and passed down the consistent testimony of the Fathers about Christ's return: It will be a single, glorious, public event at the conclusion of the Church's great tribulation.

St. John Chrysostom (c. 347–407)

St. John Chrysostom has often been acclaimed as the greatest preacher of the ancient Church. He was a contemporary of St. Augustine and St. Jerome, and he served as patriarch (archbishop) of Constantinople, the illustrious Eastern capital of the Roman Empire.

St. John's comments on 1 Thessalonians 4:17 demonstrate clearly that he too believed the "catching up" of believers will take place at Christ's return in glory at the end of history, when our Lord appears in order to raise the dead and judge the world. Portraying the dazzling grandeur of that event as few preachers have, St. John exhorted his congregation: "Remove your thoughts . . . to that awful day in which Christ is coming. For then you will [see] . . . things that are big with a mighty awe, and strike such amazement that the very incorporeal powers are astonished." He continued:

> For "the powers of the heavens," [Christ] says, "will be shaken" [Matthew 24:29]. Then is the whole heaven thrown open, and the gates of those concave spaces unfold themselves, and the only-begotten Son of God comes down, not with twenty, not with a hundred men for His bodyguard, but with thousands, ten thousands of angels and archangels, cherubim and seraphim, and other powers, and with fear and trembling shall everything be filled, while the earth is bursting itself up, and all the men who ever were born, from Adam's birth up to that day, are rising from the earth, and are all "caught up" [1 Thessalonians 4:17], when He

Himself appears with such great glory that the sun, and the moon, and any kind of light whatsoever, will be cast into shade, being outshone by that radiance. What language can portray for us that blessedness, that brightness, that glory?[29]

In a homily on 1 Thessalonians 4:15–17, St. John addressed a question raised by that passage that we have noted before: "If Christ is about to descend," he asks, "why will we be caught up?" The answer is simple, he replied: "For the sake of honor."

When a king drives into a city, those who are in honor go out to meet him; but those who are condemned await the judge inside the city. And at the coming of an affectionate father, his children and all those who are worthy to be his children are taken out to him in a chariot, so that they may see him and kiss him. But those of his servants who have offended him remain inside the house. We are carried upon the chariot of our Father. For He received Christ up in the clouds, and we shall be caught up in the clouds [see Acts 1:9]. Do you see how great is the honor? And as He descends, we go forth to meet Him—and what is most blessed of all, so shall we be with Him [see 1 Thessalonians 4:17].[30]

So for St. John Chrysostom, the "catching up" St. Paul described was clearly a parallel to the ancient custom of going out to meet a dignitary in order to escort him to his destination. In fact, St. John added the helpful insight that even households often have the same practice when a father arrives home. It is all part of the grand finale of history when Jesus returns as Lord of the cosmos. The notion of a secret rapture is simply alien to St. John's teaching.

Pseudo-Ephraem

Several years ago an obscure passage from an ancient text by an unknown author was first cited by proponents of the secret rapture doctrine as evidence that the belief was held by at least some early Christians. The true meaning of the passage, however, is problematic. The author is called "Pseudo-Ephraem" because the text was long attributed to the fourth-century Syrian writer St. Ephraem. But the actual writer is now commonly believed to have been a later, anonymous figure who drew extensively from St. Ephraem.

Pseudo-Ephraem stated: "Why therefore do we not reject every care of earthly actions and prepare ourselves for the meeting of the Lord Christ, so that He may draw us from the confusion which overwhelms all the world? . . . For the saints and elect of God are gathered, prior to the tribulation that is to come, and are taken to the Lord lest they ever see the confusion that is to overwhelm the world because of our sins." A later passage added: "The elect ones are gathered together before the tribulation in order that they might not see the confusion and the great tribulation which is coming upon the unrighteous world."[31]

These words, taken out of context, certainly could lend themselves to a secret rapture interpretation. But serious problems arise in the attempt to do so. First, neither of the passages mentioned any of the basic elements of the Second Coming that we find in the relevant biblical texts: Christ's descent from heaven, a resurrection of the dead, and a transformation of the faithful who are still alive. Perhaps more telling is the fact that within this same sermon are remarks about how Christians will suffer in the final tribulation under the Antichrist; these would point away from the secret rapture notion of an escape. Third, the sermon as a whole spoke of Christ's coming in glory with the angels and saints to raise the dead for Judgment Day—as opposed to the notion that the faithful dead are raised at a third and secret coming.

Finally, texts that are genuine writings of St. Ephraem—texts we might reasonably use to help us interpret Pseudo-

Ephraem correctly, since the latter was drawing from the tradition of the former—state explicitly that the Church will suffer through the great tribulation under the Antichrist. In addition, certain statements in these genuine works of Ephraem suggest that when he speaks of Christians being gathered and taken to the Lord, he refers to their being converted. This reading would certainly make sense in the Pseudo-Ephraem passages.

At best, then, the Pseudo-Ephraem text contains enigmatic statements. And even if we could somehow claim with any assurance that it teaches a secret rapture, it still would only represent an isolated statement from ancient times by an unknown author who was not an authoritative teacher of the Church. In either case, against the consistent teaching of the Fathers, it really holds little significance for the value of the secret rapture doctrine.

The Middle Ages

After the ancient period, we continue to find a consistent interpretation of biblical texts about the Second Advent that excludes the idea of a secret rapture. We find it, for example, in the writings of the great medieval theologians—men such as Sts. Gregory the Great, Albert the Great, Bernard of Clairvaux, and Thomas Aquinas. All these, like Sts. Jerome, Augustine, and John Chrysostom, have been designated "Doctors of the Church"; that is, the Church recognizes them as Catholic teachers of outstanding merit and acknowledged saintliness.

With particular reference to the "caught up" passage in 1 Thessalonians 4, for example, consider the remarks of St. Thomas Aquinas. He noted that some Christians think the "trumpet" at Christ's return "will be nothing else than the manifest appearance of the Son of God in the world, according to the words of Matthew 24:27: 'As lightning comes out of the east, and appears even into the west, so also shall be the coming of the Son of man.' These rely on the authority of St. Gregory [quoted by St. Albert], who says that 'the sound of the trumpet is nothing else but the Son appearing to the world as Judge.' "[32]

Whether or not we agree with the idea that the "trumpet" is a figurative name for the startling arrival of Christ (and St. Thomas offers this as only one possible interpretation), still the implication is clear. St. Thomas, like St. Augustine, St. Gregory, and St. Albert before him, assumed that the "caught up" passage refers to our Lord's glorious public advent to judge the world, not to a secret snatching away. And this event will come after the horrors of Antichrist, which the Church will suffer. That fearsome enemy will "appear in our midst to seduce those who still abide in Christ, who remain faithful to His truth," warns St. Bernard. ". . . He is even confident that he will devour the humble and the simple who are still in the Church. For he is the Antichrist . . . 'who exalts himself against every god or so-called object of worship' [2 Thessalonians 2:4]."[33]

The Protestant Reformers

Though the consistent teaching of the Catholic Tradition rules out an extra, hidden coming of Christ, and the notion appears almost exclusively among evangelical Protestants, we would be mistaken to conclude that this difference simply reflects just one more age-old dispute between Catholics and Protestants. The truth is that the novel idea of a secret rapture was apparently unknown even to the men who founded the major communions of the Protestant Reformation. And it remains alien to millions of Protestants even today.

Martin Luther and John Calvin, the two major architects of the Reformation, broke with the Catholic Church in a number of critical areas of faith and practice. In their hostility to the Church they left behind, they went so far as to identify the Antichrist with the papacy, just as some medieval writers had identified him with Mohammed. But both Luther and Calvin were deeply influenced by St. Augustine, and in their teaching about the issues we are discussing here, they affirmed with him two convictions that rule out a secret rapture: The Church is not spared tribulation at the hands of Antichrist, they insisted, and when that tribulation has run its course, Christ will gloriously return in triumph.

The book of Revelation, Luther claimed, was largely a description "of tribulations and disasters that were to come upon Christendom" throughout its history.[34] The Antichrist, Calvin observed, accomplishes "a public scattering of the Church." But in the end, Christ "slays Antichrist with the Spirit of his mouth, and destroys all ungodliness by the brightness of His coming [see 2 Thessalonians 2:8]."[35]

Convinced that St. Paul's remarks about the Second Advent in 1 Corinthians 15:20–28 and 1 Thessalonians 4:13–18 refer to the same event—not to two different comings of the Lord—Calvin comments on the "trumpet" in the first passage:

> "With the last trumpet." Though the repetition of the term might seem to place it beyond a doubt, that the word trumpet is here taken in its proper acceptation, yet I prefer to understand the expression as metaphorical. In 1 Thessalonians 4:16, he connects together the voice of the archangel and the trumpet of God. As therefore a commander, with the sound of a trumpet, summons his army to battle, so Christ, by his far-sounding proclamation, which will be heard throughout the whole world, will summon all the dead. . . . Not one people merely, but the whole world will be summoned to the tribunal of God.[36]

For Calvin, then, the believers' being "caught up" clearly takes place at our Lord's glorious appearance to raise the dead and judge the world—not in a separate, secret coming. Following Calvin, Luther, and other Reformation leaders, millions of Protestants today have avoided falling into the rapture trap.

The Emergence of the Rapture Doctrine

So when and how did the secret rapture notion first come about? The doctrine as it is currently taught in fundamentalist circles seems to have evolved in the nineteenth century. In the previous century, however, similar notions cropped up occasionally in colonial America.

In the early part of the eighteenth century, for example, Increase Mather (1639–1723), a Puritan minister in Boston, wrote of Christians being "caught up in the air" before the world was consumed by the fire of divine judgment. In 1788, a Baptist pastor and educator of Philadelphia, Morgan Edwards, published an essay promoting a similar idea, teaching that Christians would be taken to heaven three and a half years before Christ judged the world. Edwards admitted in his essay that his ideas were uncommon among his peers.[37]

The next hint of such a doctrine appears, surprisingly enough, in the writing of a Chilean Jesuit named Manuel Lacunza. His book *The Coming of Messiah in Glory and Majesty* was published in Spanish in 1812. In this massive volume, Lacunza concluded that toward the end of the world, Jesus would snatch up from earth the faithful believers who regularly received the Eucharist. Then the Lord would keep them safe for forty-five days while terrible judgments chastised the world. Finally, He would appear with them on earth to judge the human race. This scenario is similar to the *Left Behind* scenario, though the latter assumes that the subsequent great tribulation will last seven years instead.[38]

Lacunza's book was translated into English in 1827 by Edward Irving, a minister of the Protestant Church of Scotland who was later excommunicated from his denomination for teaching that Christ's human nature was sinful. After being removed from his local congregation, he helped to organize a new denomination called the "Catholic Apostolic Church" (which was of course neither Catholic nor Apostolic), which was in some ways a forerunner of the modern Pentecostal movement. Apparently under Lacunza's influence, Irving began preaching the secret rapture, though he, unlike Lacunza, thought it would happen three and a half years before Christ's final coming.[39]

About the same time, a secret coming of Christ was being preached by John Nelson Darby, a leader of the British sectarian group called the Plymouth Brethren. This group experienced numerous conflicts and schisms, some resulting from disagreements over the secret rapture teaching. Historians debate the extent to which Irving may have influenced Darby, but in any case, both "Irvingites" and "Darbyites" came to adopt the secret rapture teaching.

In time, Darby traveled extensively preaching his ideas about the end times, making seven trips to Canada and the United States alone between 1859 and 1874. His ideas began to gain acceptance at the influential "Bible prophecy" conferences of the time, which in turn shaped the beliefs of tens of thousands of American Protestants. As a result, several popular evangelical Protestant leaders in America came under his influence, including the famous revivalist Dwight L. Moody, the shoe-salesman-turned-preacher who captivated enormous crowds of listeners on both sides of the Atlantic.

Dispensationalism

Sharply disenchanted with all organized forms of religion, Darby was hostile toward the Catholic Church and Protestant denominations as well—a hostility that deeply shaped a new system of scriptural interpretation he developed. Dispensationalism, as his ideas came to be called, spread like wildfire throughout hundreds of British and American congregations of his day and became a standard feature in much of what was then emerging as Protestant fundamentalism. The popularity of the new system, which included the secret rapture idea, was aided significantly by the publication in 1909 of *The Scofield Reference Bible*, at that time the best-selling Bible in American history. That book sold nearly two million copies in the first thirty years after its publication.[40]

A King James Version of the Scripture, this volume included extensive notes on nearly every page of the scriptural text by C. I. Scofield, an enthusiastic convert to Darby's dispensational beliefs. Scofield was a Kansas City lawyer with no theological training. But his legal training compensated in persuasiveness for what his background lacked as a biblical scholar. In time, millions of Americans were studying Scofield's marginal notes as eagerly as if they were part of the divinely inspired biblical text.

Dispensationalism is so called because it divides all history into seven "dispensations," or progressive stages in God's unfolding revelation to humanity. In each of these time periods, God reveals some specific aspect of His will and commands obedience to it to test humanity's faithfulness. In each period, however, mankind utterly fails the test. So each period must end in God's judgment, and a new period must follow, in which God makes a new set of arrangements in dealing with the human race to put it once more on trial. For that reason, the promises and commands God issues under one dispensation may be different from those under other dispensations.

Darby's dispensational scheme sharply divides between two divine plans for history, one for an "earthly people" (the Jews) and one for a "heavenly people" (the Church). He makes such a radical distinction between the two that Israel and the Church become utterly isolated from each other, with Israel under "law" and the Church under "grace." All continuity between God's dealings with the Jews and His dealings with the Church disappears.[41]

According to the Dispensational view, for example, the Bible must be divided up between those passages intended for Israel and those for the Church. Some Dispensationalists insist that Old Testament prophecies apply exclusively to Israel—none to the Church. They may even go so far as to claim that Jesus did not preach the Sermon on the Mount for Christians; it is actually for Jews who will live in Christ's future earthly kingdom.

God's plan for the Jewish people, Dispensationalism teaches, was revealed through a series of covenants, or agreements, which pointed to the establishment of an earthly kingdom by the Messiah (the Christ, the "Anointed One"). But Israel rejected the Messiah—Jesus Christ—when He came. So God had to postpone the founding of the kingdom. He turned away from Israel and created a new people, the Church, out of the Gentile nations (non-Jewish peoples).

According to this "postponement" theory, Israel's "prophetic clock" stopped ticking when Christ died. But it will start ticking again when the Antichrist arrives on the scene and the secret rapture takes place. With the Christians out of the way, the great tribulation will proceed, with Israel at center stage once more in God's dealing with the world. Once Christ returns to earth a final time, He will reign for a thousand years as Ruler of an earthly kingdom of Israel, with its capital at Jerusalem. (This last notion of a future earthly kingdom ruled by Christ in the flesh is one version of the doctrine called *millenarianism*. We will examine that doctrine more closely in chapter eight.)

Later Popularizers of the Idea

With its anti-organizational bias, the Dispensational scheme appealed to isolated Protestant congregations in America that were unaffiliated with any denomination. It also made inroads into denominations that view local congregations as independent of larger structures, such as the various Baptist associations. But the best-selling Scofield Bible and America's perennial love affair with emotional revival meetings helped to spread the rapture idea even into some of the more highly structured Protestant denominations as well. Especially influenced were Methodists and their spiritual heirs, Christians in the Holiness and Pentecostal movements.

After Scofield died in 1921, other fundamentalist Protestant leaders continued to spread Dispensational teaching. Dallas Theological Seminary in Texas and Moody Bible Institute in Chicago embraced the new ideas enthusiastically and trained thousands of young men to promote their views in the congregations where they were called to preach. Meanwhile, two world wars made countless Christians world-weary and eager for divine relief.

After the reestablishment of Israel as an independent nation in 1948—an event many fundamentalists saw as a sign of the end times—interest in biblical prophecy intensified. The tensions of the Cold War and the political, social, and cultural disruptions of the 1960s further prepared many evangelical Protestants to focus on the "promise" of escape from a seemingly hell-bent world. By the 1970s, the time was ripe for an array of best-selling books on the end times written from a Dispensational, secret rapture view.

Most notable among these was the best-selling American book of the 1970s, *The Late Great Planet Earth* (1970), and its sequels, which together have sold more than thirty-five million copies. Author Hal Lindsey's sensationalist style presented a heady mix of highly selective Bible quotes; news clips of world events that he claimed were "fulfilling biblical prophecy"; frightening "scientific" predictions of natural and man-made catastrophes; and a print version of the old revivalist "altar call," an appeal to readers to get "saved" so they would not be left behind at the rapture. With tantalizing chapter titles such as "The Yellow Peril," "The Future Fuehrer," "World War III," and "Polishing the Crystal Ball," Lindsey found a ready audience, especially among young people, for the Dispensational doctrine he had learned so well as a student at Dallas Theological Seminary.

Lindsey has had countless imitators, not just in print, but also in radio, television, film, and video. Not all of them are Dispensationalists, but they have all gotten great mileage out of the "snatched out of tribulation" message. It's attention-grabbing, it's titillating, it's comforting, and it sells.

The *Left Behind* secret rapture story line is thus only the latest incarnation of an old—but not very old—unbiblical idea. We turn now to focus on the dangers of that deceptive doctrine for Christians who embrace it.

7

Tribulation Farce

The Dangers of the Rapture Trap

Not all the early fundamentalists who witnessed the rapid spread of the secret rapture notion in America were pleased by what they saw. At least a few recognized that the teaching was as dangerous as it was novel. "I am glad to know," said one evangelist of the early 1900s, "there are some who are opposing this *Secret Rapture fly-away-from-tribulation theory*. It seems to me to be only a trick of the Devil to fool God's people so that they will not be on the firing line for God. Wherever I am I smite that God-dishonoring doctrine."[42]

A "trick of the Devil." A "God-dishonoring doctrine." These are strong words, spoken by a man who was in a position to observe at close range the pitfalls of belief in an extra, "third" coming of Christ. What specific dangers might he have been warning against in his preaching? What problems arise from the larger system of doctrines to which the rapture notion is tied? We will examine now several aspects of the faulty theology surrounding the rapture trap and the kinds of trouble to which it can lead.

The "Plain Sense of Scripture"

Left Behind authors LaHaye and Jenkins have written a non-fiction book to explain the theology behind their novels, entitled *Are We Living in the End Times?* To help us "understand the major events of Bible prophecy" and set the stage for their claims to scriptural support for the rapture doctrine, in the first chapter they quote approvingly a certain Bible scholar's "golden rule of biblical interpretation." This rule, stated in one form or another, is commonly advocated by fundamentalists: "When the plain sense of Scripture makes common sense, seek no other sense, but take every word at its primary, literal meaning unless the facts of the immediate context clearly indicate otherwise."[43]

St. Augustine, John Calvin, and countless other biblical commentators down through the ages—both Catholic and Protestant—would be puzzled to hear such a statement coming from rapture theorists. Dispensationalists appeal repeatedly to the "plain sense of Scripture" and accuse their opponents of ignoring that sense. Yet, as we saw in chapter five, the "plain sense of Scripture" nowhere supports their eccentric doctrine.

Look carefully through any book of the Bible you may choose. In no passage will you find a straightforward statement such as these: "Immediately before the tribulation of those days, the Lord Himself will descend from heaven." "Christ will return to earth once in secret to take His people to heaven, and then once again later in glory to judge the world." "The Lord will take His people out of the world before the reign of the Antichrist, in order to spare them from the divine wrath." In neither the Gospels, nor the Acts, nor the Epistles, nor Revelation does such a declaration appear —nor anything even resembling such a declaration.

As we have seen, there are indeed scriptural passages that rapture theorists have tried to twist or take out of context so they can read into the passage a preconceived idea. But what they claim the passages say certainly does not represent "the plain sense of Scripture." If it *were* the plain sense of Scripture, wouldn't most Christians be in agreement about it, as they are about the fact that Christ is divine?

What about the early Church fathers? They received their Tradition directly from the Apostles or from those who had known the Apostles personally. They knew Christ's teaching well enough to be able to identify which books were truly inspired as Scripture and which were not. If the secret rapture doctrine appears in the plain sense of Scripture, why did they know nothing of it?

Or what about the later Fathers, who formulated the creeds of the Church, stating in clear terms the faith of the Church through the pronouncements of infallible ecumenical councils? Wouldn't they have taught a secret rapture if it were according to the apostolic understanding of the Scripture?

Why is it that the great medieval theologians, revered Doctors of the Church, knew nothing of a secret rapture if it is the plain sense of Scripture? Why did even the fathers of the Protestant Reformation fail to grasp such a clear meaning? Why did such a thought apparently cross almost no one's mind until the eighteenth century? Why do millions upon millions of Catholics, Eastern Orthodox, and even Protestants who read their Bibles today fail to see this teaching in its pages if it is so obvious?

Are the Church fathers both East and West, the Doctors of the Church, the founders of the Reformation, and the great majority of Christians for the last two thousand years just clueless? Have they simply refused through stubbornness to concede a "plain" truth of the Bible? Or is it more likely that the ones who truly miss the "plain" sense of Scripture are actually these more recent end times enthusiasts—perhaps disenchanted with the state of the world—who somehow manage to find in its pages a secret rapture doctrine?

The Church, Authoritative Interpreter

In a church nursery full of active infants and toddlers, on the wall over the diaper changing tables, hangs a sign with a brief quote from one of the passages we have examined, 1 Corinthians 15:51. No doubt some Sunday morning wit hung it there. It reads simply: "We shall not all sleep, but we shall all be changed."

That jest provokes a smile from the parents who bring their children to the nursery. But it also reminds us of an important principle of biblical interpretation: *Context is critical.* Out of context, a statement can appear to mean something quite different from what the author intended.

Sometimes the needed context for a passage is provided by a few surrounding verses, as with the sign in the nursery. At other times we need the context of related passages from other places in Scripture, as we demonstrated in chapter five by comparing the texts of Second Advent references from various biblical books. At still other times we need the context of the cultural customs familiar to the scriptural writer, as in the case we cited of the citizens of a city going out to meet a dignitary.

In every case, however, we should seek one indispensable context: *the context of the Church.* The Bible belongs to the Church, because God gave it *to* the Church, and He gave it to the world *through* the Church. Those outside the Church —atheists, Hindus, or Muslims, for example—lack the necessary context for a trustworthy interpretation of Christian Scripture. This is why, despite extensive training, so many "Bible scholars" in secular settings who admit to having no personal religious faith end up with bizarre conclusions about the text. They stray far from the Bible's meaning because they are unbelievers, living outside the context of the Church.

As far as we know, Jesus never wrote any books to publish His message. Instead, He commanded the Apostles to teach and preach what they had seen and heard (see Matthew 28:18–21; Luke 24:45–49; Acts 1:8). God used the Church to spread that unwritten teaching Tradition and to write the

New Testament. He also used the Church to designate authoritatively which books rightly belong to the canon (that is, to the body of texts held to be part of the inspired Scripture). The Bible is thus part of the wider Tradition of the Church, which preceded the writing of the Scripture and has functioned as its context from the beginning. Without that Tradition, interpretation of the Bible leads to guesswork and inevitably goes astray on some point or another.

We are like the Ethiopian eunuch who was reading the Scripture when he met up with St. Philip, one of the first seven deacons of the Church as described in the book of Acts (see Acts 6:1–6). St. Philip heard the Ethiopian reading aloud from the prophet Isaiah and asked, "Do you understand what you are reading?" The eunuch answered simply: "How can I, unless someone guides me?" (see Acts 8:26–40).

When we read Scripture, we need someone to guide us. For this reason, in addition to Sacred Scripture and Sacred Tradition, we have the Sacred Magisterium—the Church's teaching authority, instituted by Christ and guided by the Holy Spirit, which seeks to safeguard and explain the truths of the Bible and of the Faith as a whole. The "plain sense" of the Bible is not always so "plain"; that is why Christians have debated its meaning from the beginning. And that is, at least in part, why we now have more than twenty thousand Protestant denominations (not to mention many thousands of independent congregations) who argue among themselves about the meaning of Scripture.

Christ had to give the Church an authoritative interpreter of the Scripture, a final court of appeal, that we can trust to settle such disagreements according to the mind of the Holy Spirit. (After all, the Spirit wrote the book in the first place and knows exactly what it means.) Through the teaching of the pope and the bishops in union with him, then, we can receive a trustworthy interpretation of the biblical text.

To see the tragic results of trying to interpret the Bible without the Magisterium, we need only look at Church history. Martin Luther and other leaders of the Protestant Reformation rejected the Catholic Church's teaching authority, claiming instead that the sense of Scripture was plain enough for individuals to interpret it on their own with the Spirit's help. But once Luther had broken from the Magisterium, he soon discovered otherwise.

As new Protestant leaders emerged with more novel doctrines, many of them challenged Luther's "plain sense" interpretations and called him a heretic. The Reformation movement shattered into a number of warring sects because each sect's leader claimed to have the correct interpretation—and none of them had a higher, decisive authority to which they could appeal. They argued especially over what the Bible had to say about the end times.

The teachings of these various new Protestant groups could not have all been true, since many of their ideas stood in contradiction to one another. So at least some were obviously being deceived. Interestingly, even LaHaye and Jenkins have admitted that the proliferation of "denominations, sects, and cults in Protestantism" is an indicator of spiritual "deception."[44] Church history bears out that observation.

Apocalyptic Deceptions

Some rapture promoters—LaHaye and Jenkins among them —criticize the Catholic Church for keeping the Bible "locked up" and out of the hands of the people during the Middle Ages. Others insist that the Church refused to translate the Scripture into the common languages so all could read it for themselves and find out the "truth" about Bible prophecy. But these claims are terribly mistaken.[45]

First, we should note that, far from hiding the Bible, the

medieval Church presented biblical teaching to the common people in a number of ways—not just at Mass, but also through the preaching orders, such as the Dominicans and Franciscans. Even in praying the Rosary, the faithful learned to recall and meditate on important events of salvation history recorded in the Gospels.

Second, we must remember that until recent times, most people were illiterate and could not have read a Bible even if they had possessed one. Those who could read were trained to read Latin, and they could make use of St. Jerome's fine Latin translation of Scripture known as the *Vulgate*. Even among the literate, however, the price of a hand-copied volume of the Scriptures (the only kind available before the invention of the printing press) was usually prohibitive.

Nevertheless, even in these circumstances, the Church permitted a number of translations and partial translations of the Scripture in the common languages of Europe, long before Martin Luther and the Reformation ever came along. Some partial translations of the Bible into English, for example, appeared as early as the seventh century. Once literacy spread in later centuries, a number of new translations appeared in English, German, Spanish, French, Italian, and other common tongues as well.[46]

By no means, then, did Rome forbid Bible teaching and reading. But the Church did urge caution in the public interpretation and teaching of biblical texts about the close of the age. For example, in the pronouncements of the Fifth Lateran Council (1512–17) at the close of the medieval period, the Magisterium specifically forbade the preaching of unorthodox "end times" speculations from Catholic pulpits.[47]

Was this an act of arrogant censorship (as some modern observers might claim) carried out by power-hungry Church bureaucrats? Not at all. We must keep in mind that the

Church had not only the right but also the responsibility to set boundaries on the public preaching of those she had authorized to teach in her name and from her pulpits. Irresponsible rhetoric about an impending end of the world could and did provoke tragic results. A brief look at a few of the apocalyptic movements that had emerged in the centuries leading up to the Council—as well as similar movements that were to spring up soon afterward in the Protestant Reformation—suggests that Rome was justified in taking strong pastoral measures on this issue.[48]

Eon the Breton

Consider, for example, the case of Eon, an uneducated layman of twelfth-century Brittany. This medieval con man began preaching outdoors, winning large crowds through his magnetic personality and a seductive message that fanned the flames of resentment toward the wealthy. He eventually organized his own "church" with "archbishops" and "bishops," whom he named for the virtues and the Apostles.

Eon even went so far as to call himself Christ, the Son of God, who had arrived on the scene to fulfill the biblical prophecies about the end of the world. He had come, he claimed, to judge the living and the dead and to cleanse the world by fire.

The Breton "Messiah" found a following of multitudes among the poorer classes. Soon his little army of disciples was terrorizing the people of Brittany and living by plunder. This restless, violent mob raided and devastated churches, monasteries, and convents. Wherever they passed through, they scoured the land like locusts, putting many people to the sword and leaving countless others to starve to death. Eon's apocalyptic savagery ended only when a band of armed men captured him and dispersed his outlaw followers.

The Taborites

A radical sect arising in Bohemia in the early fifteenth century, the Taborites mixed apocalyptic views with revolutionary political views. When the rulers in Prague resisted their ideas, their rhetoric grew even more violent. They taught that once their opponents were eliminated, Christ would return to rule the world from a mountain they had occupied and renamed Mount Tabor. There would be no need for clergy, church, or even books, because everyone would be taught directly by the Spirit.

In 1419 several Taborite preachers announced that the great consummation was at hand, and all evil would be abolished in preparation for the millennial reign of Christ. Between February 10 and 14, 1420, they insisted, every town and village would be destroyed by fire, just as Sodom had been. The wrath of God would consume everyone who did not flee for refuge to the five Bohemian towns occupied by the Taborites.

Multitudes of the poor found the message convincing. They sold all their belongings, fled to the Taborite towns, and threw all their money at the feet of the preachers. Meanwhile, Taborite leaders were calling for the massacre of all who resisted them, and their followers eagerly took up the sword. "Accursed be the man who withholds his sword from shedding the blood of the enemies of Christ," said one Taborite tract. "Every believer must wash his hands in that blood."[49] But an army of Germans and Magyars finally defeated and scattered them in 1434.

Thomas Muentzer

Once Luther threw off the authority of the Catholic Church, theological, spiritual, and even political anarchy soon followed among those who joined him in rejecting the

Magisterium. In 1524, the savage "Peasants' War" began in Germany, a revolt of peasants, miners, and urban artisans against the German nobility. Some of the rebels appealed to Luther's writings as justification for their actions. After all, they reasoned, yesterday we threw off the authority of the pope; today, the authority of the nobles.

But Luther was appalled by their actions and desperate to distance himself from them. So he exhorted the nobles to massacre the peasants, denying vehemently that his spiritual revolt had encouraged them to political revolt.

Thomas Muentzer was a well-educated Lutheran pastor who turned against Luther at this time and became obsessed with apocalyptic speculation. He gladly provided theological support for the revolt, pressing the rebels to intensify their violence. Muentzer preached a sermon just before the battle of Frankenhausen in 1525, using end times imagery and promising that with heaven's help, he himself would catch the cannonballs in his shirtsleeves.

The attack began as the rebels sang hymns and looked for Christ to return to help them. But the peasants were slaughtered; an estimated five thousand died in the battle. Muentzer was beheaded, and the rebellion was crushed. Ultimately, as many as a hundred thousand rebels may have died in the uprising.

The Muensterites

Thomas Muentzer was not alone in the so-called "radical wing" of the Reformation. In 1534 the followers of a Dutch religious leader named Jan Matthys gained control of the Westphalian city of Muenster, proclaiming it the "New Jerusalem." When some of the townspeople resisted the spiritual and political "reforms" he began introducing, they were driven out and their property confiscated. Soon afterward, Matthys declared that all property would be held in common.

Having prophesied that the world would end on Easter Sunday, 1534, he led a small band of followers against a force besieging the city, and all were killed. One of his converts, Jan Bockelson, succeeded him as ruler of the city. Bockelson was an erratic young man, a twenty-five-year-old tailor given to receiving "divine instructions" while in a trance.

Claiming that he was acting at God's command, the new ruler imposed absolute authority on the city, instituted polygamy, and took several teenagers for wives, along with Matthys' widow. Women who objected were put to death, along with dozens of men who resisted. The people of the city lived in utter terror.

Soon a wandering prophet came through and hailed Bockelson as "Messiah," a title he gladly accepted. Bockelson claimed to be given power over all the nations of the earth and had coins minted with apocalyptic inscriptions. With a small group of his Dutch followers enforcing his every whim, he issued decrees prophesying Christ's imminent return and declaring that the town of Muenster was a forerunner of Christ's millennial kingdom.

In 1535 an army blockaded the city. Bockelson and his inner circle lived in luxury, taking what little food remained in the city for themselves. Meanwhile the populace starved, trying to survive by eating rats, grass, shoes, and human corpses. Finally the city was overthrown, and Bockelson and his followers were executed.

The Need for a Magisterium

These selected historical cases of apocalyptic fervor illustrate vividly why an ecumenical council of the Church would find it necessary to forbid end times speculation in Catholic pulpits. The tragedies we have described also show why God gave us the Sacred Magisterium as the authoritative interpreter of Scripture. These bloody episodes involving Eon, the Taborite leaders, and the rest could have been avoided if the followers they had sought to recruit had recognized the apocalyptic claims as contrary to Church teaching—and then rejected those claims firmly. The Church's teaching authority is a great gift that can provide us a safeguard against such error.

Of course, end times speculation does not always lead to the violence of a Thomas Muentzer or a Jan Bockelson. Nor would we suggest that contemporary believers in the rapture are likely to raise a revolutionary army. The point to be made is this: Even in its milder forms, eccentric apocalyptic doctrines can lead to harmful delusions. The Millerite movement, which we examined in chapter five, provides one example of the disturbing possibilities. So when we seek the truth about the end of the world, we must not ignore the guidance of the Church.

Shortcomings of Reformation Principles

In passing, we should note that Martin Luther's response to the political revolt associated with his teachings illustrates clearly the shortcomings of Reformation principles of biblical interpretation. Some rebel leaders in the Peasants' War claimed, quite reasonably, to be working out in political terms Luther's religious idea that each individual is his own final authority. After all, Thomas Muentzer could stake the same claim to the Holy Spirit's guidance in scriptural interpretation that Luther had made for himself. On Luther's terms, who was to say which man was right?

Luther translated the Bible into German so every man could read it and act on it according to his own private interpretation. Wasn't that exactly what these radical Reformers were doing? When Bockelson instituted polygamy in Muenster, couldn't he point to God's apparent approval of the practice in the Old Testament? After all, Abraham had been a polygamist. Hadn't Luther offered Abraham as a model of faith?

The peasant rebels called themselves a "Christian association" and insisted they were acting "according to divine law." They cited Scripture as justification for their political and social demands, and they said they could be convinced to give up their fight only if they were shown to be wrong by "clear, plain, undeniable passages of Scripture." (There is that "plain sense" appeal again.) And they appealed to Luther for justification of their deeds.

Nevertheless, Luther panicked when the radicals claimed spiritual kinship to him. He worried that if he became associated with them in the minds of the rulers, then the nobles who had come over to his side might withdraw their approval. Without such political support, Luther's new religious movement might be stymied. Luther's response to the peasants' appeal was a couple of harsh tracts repudiating them, with the second tract calling for their massacre by the nobility. He also accused the revolutionaries of blasphemously misreading the Scripture, even though they had only applied his own rule of private interpretation.

Worse yet, horrified by the peasants' use of apocalyptic language, Luther dismissed the biblical book of Revelation as "neither apostolic nor prophetic," relegating it to a mere appendix in his German translation of the New Testament. "I feel an aversion to it," he admitted, "and for me this is a sufficient reason for rejecting it." These statements come from the same man who claimed that the Bible was the only source of divinely revealed truth to which believers must submit themselves! Even within his own lifetime, then, Luther's rejection of the Catholic Magisterium had begun to bear the inevitable fruit of confusion and inconsistency.[50]

A Faulty View of the Church

The Protestant insistence on denying the existence of an authoritative Magisterium reflects a larger theological problem: a fundamental misunderstanding of the Church and its role in the present age. That problem becomes acute among the rapture advocates, who—as we have seen—tend toward a Dispensational view of God's people.

The sectarian Brethren to which Darby belonged saw the institutional Church as largely apostate and assumed that only a few true believers were left in the world. They rejected sacraments, creeds, ritual, and priests—in fact, clergy of any kind. They viewed all ecclesiastical organization and ordering with suspicion.

Consider these words from Hal Lindsey's *Late Great Planet Earth* in a section entitled "Where Is the Church?": "The organization which the Bible says will be a definite part of this [false] one-world religion . . . is the visible church which is characterized by increasing unbelief and apostasy. . . . The apostate church is, always has been, and will be, the visible, physical gathering of people who may call themselves Christians. . . . The true church, on the other hand, includes all believers in Christ."[51]

Lindsey offers the usual Dispensational view: The Church is not the one, holy, Catholic, and apostolic body of Christ, sharing in Christ's own holiness, power, authority, and glory. Dispensationalists (and other secret rapture theorists) know nothing of a supernaturally planted and cultivated Church that grows down through the centuries as a magnificent living organism, spreading its branches around the world (the Church *militant*), into purgatory (the Church *penitent*), and even into heaven itself (the Church *triumphant*), where the saints are joined in powerful communion with those of us who have yet to be perfected.

Instead, Dispensationalists see the Church more as a collection of individuals with a correct belief, a voluntary association of those who are already "saved," each waiting his turn to escape a corrupt world and enter the safety of heaven. Faith is, above all, a direct one-on-one relationship with God that, once established, guarantees salvation. Given that view of Christian life, it is no wonder, then, that Dispensationalism holds out the promise that God will snatch true believers out of a troubled world. That way, He can get down to the apparently more important business of building a true kingdom of God on earth—the nation of Israel.

Short and Naked

One nineteenth-century Catholic writer, speaking of the Protestant religion, lamented, "So short a creed, and so naked a worship!" The stripped-down, truncated nature of Protestant belief and practice is nowhere more evident than in Dispensational *ecclesiology* (that is, teaching about the Church). The secret rapture idea is simply a token of a falsely spiritualized notion of the Church. It fails to understand that the Church is sacramental in nature, a supernatural reality embodied in space and time, nature and history.

In Dispensationalism (and in some other forms of Protestantism as well), elements of the ancient Gnostic heresy— characterized chiefly by a disdain for the material world— seem to have reappeared. The Dispensational theology fails to appreciate the full implications of the reality that the Word of God took on *flesh*; He did not remain simply the Word (see John 1:14). Infinity Himself entered space; Eternity Himself entered time; and in the process, both space and time were transformed. The Incarnation thus set the stage for the whole

sacramental reality on which the Church is based: Once God's
own nature was permanently joined to our nature in Christ,
the world was never the same again.

As we saw in chapter three, Christ's life comes to us in
the present age through His Word, His Sacraments, and His
Spirit. Most Protestants give almost exclusive priority to the
role of His Word and His Spirit. In doing so, they tend
to forget that the Word became flesh, and that the Spirit
works through flesh and through other material realities as
well.

Water and oil, bread and wine, human hands and even
(in the sacrament of matrimony) human bodies as a whole
become the vehicles of God's grace and glory. The power
of these Sacraments is conveyed through physical, material
settings: the ritual and furnishings of the liturgy. And the
ripples of sacramental grace, flowing by way of the prayers
of the Church, touch the world through an array of physical,
material sacramentals: blessings and holy water, palms and
ashes, crucifixes and statues, relics and medals and all the
rest. Just as divine power flowed through material elements
in biblical times—the bones of Elisha (see 2 Kings 13:20–
21), the hem of Jesus' garment (Matthew 9:20–22), the mud
applied to the blind man's eyes (John 9:1–7), the handker-
chiefs and aprons touched to St. Paul's body (Acts 19:11–12)
—God's grace can touch us today in similar ways.

The rejection of the Church's Magisterium by Protestants
is in its own way a rejection of the Church's sacramental nature. If, because of the Incarnation, God's mighty power can
flow through such humble elements as water and oil, then
His infallible teaching authority can surely rest on a man or
group of men, even though they in themselves are fallible.
Otherwise, the Scripture could not have been written in the
first place. The book that Protestants hold in such high (and

deserved) regard, after all, is itself a sacramental reality. In the natural words of men, we hear the infallible, supernatural words of God.

In short, when Protestants hold only to the Sacred Scripture, while refusing the Sacred Tradition and Sacred Magisterium to which it is so intimately joined, they tear the Church apart and settle for only a fragment of it. The false rapture doctrine is simply one symptom of a more extensive spiritual disorder.

The Church in History

Christians of the early centuries often insisted, "The world was created for the sake of the Church," the redeemed people of God. This startling affirmation may sound like a proud boast, but it actually reflects a humbling truth: The Church, as St. Epiphanius put it, is "the goal of all things," because God's purpose in creating the world was to have sons and daughters in communion with Him—and this communion finds its ultimate fulfillment in the Church.[52]

When we examine Dispensational teachings, we find a strikingly contradictory view, a radical devaluing of the Church's purpose in the world, especially in the present age. Darby, for example, went so far as to insist that our age was actually unforeseen by the Old Testament prophets. In a sense, the Church appears in his scheme to be something of a distraction from God's real work. It is no more than a tangent in the story of human history.

The rapture, say the Dispensationalists, is necessary to take the Church out of the way so that God can complete His dealings with the Jews. In fact, the long interim period between the "stopping" and "starting" of Israel's prophetic "clock" is known to Dispensationalists as the "great parenthesis." That means the present age, the age of the Church, is only an interruption in the main "sentence," so to speak, which is the divine plan for Israel.

Not surprisingly, Darby and the Brethren taught that the "true" church is purely spiritual in character and should have no involvement in earthly affairs. "The church," he insisted, "is properly heavenly, in its calling and relationship with Christ, forming no part of the course of events of the earth, which makes the rapture so simple and clear. . . . Our calling is on high. Events are on earth."[53]

Once again, we see the danger of such a view of the Church. It warns Christians not to dirty their hands with attempts to improve the conditions of the world, to work for peace or justice. After all, as Billy Sunday, a professional-baseball-player-turned-revivalist, was fond of saying: "The world is going to hell so fast it's breaking the speed limit." So why bother?

Dwight L. Moody, another wildly popular revival preacher who helped spread Dispensational ideas in the U.S. and Britain, expressed the common Dispensational attitude with a memorable image. "I look upon the world as a wrecked vessel," Moody said. "God has given me a lifeboat and said to me, 'Moody, save all you can.' "[54]

That "lifeboat" was the work of evangelization, and to their credit, many rapture promoters have worked hard to call people to faith in Christ. But many times this seems to be the extent of the role they envision for the Church in the present age. LaHaye's nonfiction book *Revelation Unveiled*, for example, in a section entitled "The Present Work of Christ," devotes only a few paragraphs to this most important of topics for understanding the purpose of His second coming (which is what the book is primarily about). In that section, LaHaye seems to confine Christ's present work to the conversion of individuals by a simple prayer of confession, through which they are "saved." Meanwhile, he seems to say, the work of the Church is merely to help others come to the place of praying that sinner's prayer.[55]

Of course we must be calling unbelievers to repentance and faith. But the faith to which we call them must be more than eternal fire insurance—a promise from God that if they will once "accept Jesus Christ as their personal Lord and Savior," they will forever be guaranteed an escape from hell. No—conversion, as we saw in chapter three, is not just a single act of mental assent to an intellectual proposition, or even a one-time commitment of a person's entire self to the Lord. Instead, it is a repeated, lifelong giving of the self to God, so that He can remake the soul, gradually restoring in us His image, making us fit for the privilege of taking part in His own nature, sharing perfect fellowship with Him and all His saints and angels for all eternity. And the role of the Church is to nurture us in this process over a lifetime.

"Work out your own salvation with fear and trembling," St. Paul tells us, "for God is at work in you, both to will and to work for His good pleasure" (Philippians 2:12–13). St. James speaks rather bluntly about the matter: "What does it profit, my brethren, if a man says he has faith but has not works? Can his faith save him? . . . Do you want to be shown, you foolish fellow, that faith apart from works is barren? Was not Abraham our father justified by works, when he offered his son Isaac upon the altar? You see that faith was active along with his works, and faith was completed by works. . . . You see that a man is justified by works and not by faith alone. . . . For as the body apart from the spirit is dead, so faith apart from works is dead" (James 2:14, 20–22, 24, 26).

Meanwhile, the work of the Church in the world includes much more than evangelism. The Church is the " 'universal sacrament of salvation' in the world,"[56] the body of Christ, the vessel carrying His grace and presence into every page of human history, into every little corner of human life—

not just the spiritual realm, but the social, cultural, political, and economic realms as well. The Church, proclaimed the Fathers of the Second Vatican Council, "is to be a leaven and, as it were, the soul of human society in its renewal by Christ and transformation into the family of God."[57]

In short: Soldiers in the "Church militant" should seek to *change* history, not to *escape* it by being snatched away when the going gets tough. For that reason we pray, "Thy kingdom come, Thy will be done, on earth as it is in heaven."

In fairness, we must repeat our earlier observation that the secret rapture teaching and its Dispensationalist trappings don't *necessarily* lead to social and political apathy. Though early fundamentalists tended to spurn social and political activism, beginning in the 1970s, Dispensationalists such as Beverly LaHaye and the Baptist pastor Jerry Falwell attempted to lead their fellow believers back into social and political activism. Nevertheless, whatever success they may have had in motivating fundamentalists to action came only through diligent efforts to overcome the inertia resulting from nearly a century of Dispensationalist teaching (an inertia that still exists in many quarters).

To quote once more that fundamentalist evangelist of the early 1900s: The secret rapture doctrine can easily "fool God's people so that they will not be on the firing line for God."

No Escape From Suffering

A Puritan writer of the seventeenth century once wisely observed: "God has one Son without sin, but He has no sons without suffering." This world of ours is broken, and living in it is painful—even if you are the sinless Son of God (*especially* if you are the sinless Son of God).

"For the creation was subjected to futility" through our sin, St. Paul tells us, and it "has been groaning in travail," waiting to "be set free from its bondage to decay and obtain the glorious liberty of the children of God" (see Romans 8:19–23). We all, without exception, suffer because of "natural evil"—disease, accidents, natural disasters; and we suffer as well because of "moral evil"—the consequences of sin, both ours and that of others.

One more danger of the rapture teaching, then, is that it promises an escape from tribulation. Of course, promoters of the doctrine don't deny that Christians suffer. But behind the "third" coming notion lies the mistaken claim that when God chastises the world in the last days, the Christians living then will not be left around to endure it because they don't merit the chastisement—only unbelievers do.

"Why should a child of God's grace," asks one well-known defender of the rapture, "who is saved by grace, who is kept by grace, who has all the wonderful promises of God—be forced to go through a period which according to Scripture is expressly designed as a time of judgment upon a Christ-rejecting world?"[58]

Look closely at the apparent assumptions in that question. First, it seems to assume that our suffering is not a channel of God's grace to us and to those around us. Second, it seems to assume that Christians don't deserve divine chastisement. And third, it seems to assume that God would not allow Christians to suffer because of the sin of others. Let's examine each of these notions in turn.

Grace Through Suffering

The Scripture tells us repeatedly that Christians must endure adversity. The various forms of the New Testament Greek word for "tribulation" occur fifty-five times in the Bible. Some forty-seven of those refer to the tribulation of believers.

Jesus warned us, "In the world you have tribulation" (John 16:33). The Apostles Paul and Barnabas preached that "through many tribulations we must enter the kingdom of God" (Acts 14:22). And in the same letter where he wrote about the Second Coming, St. Paul told the Thessalonians: "We sent Timothy . . . to establish you in your faith and to exhort you, that no one be moved by these afflictions. You yourselves know that this is to be our lot" (1 Thessalonians 3:2–3).

As we saw in chapter five, the Scripture affirms that such tribulations include the great tribulation of the last days under the persecution of the Antichrist. Christians have long suffered at the hands of his precursors (see 1 John 2:18), and they will suffer at his hands as well. "But he who endures to the end will be saved" (Matthew 24:13).

Why does God allow us to suffer? He sometimes allows it as an act of cleansing grace. "Through [Christ]," St. Paul exults, "we have obtained access to this grace in which we stand, and we rejoice in our hope of sharing the glory of God. More than that, we rejoice in our sufferings, knowing that suffering produces endurance, and endurance produces character, and character produces hope, and hope does not disappoint us, because God's love has been poured into our hearts through the Holy Spirit who has been given to us" (Romans 5:2–5). All this is to say that suffering, if we endure it with an attitude of trust in God, can become a form of healing chastisement, of strengthening correction—of restoring God's image in us and drawing us into a closer union with Him.

Merited Suffering

We also suffer because we often bring it on ourselves. Sometimes God's justice allows us to pay the price of suffering —the consequences we ourselves have created. Who among us can always say when we suffer, "I don't deserve this"? Instead, we often find ourselves saying to God, along with the psalmist, "Against you alone have I sinned; / I have done such evil in your sight / that you are just in your sentence, / blameless when you condemn" (Psalm 51:6, NAB).

Read in the Scripture what kinds of things will bring God's judgment on the world when it comes: "Immorality or any impurity or greed must not even be mentioned among you, as is fitting among holy ones, no obscenity or silly or suggestive talk, which is out of place, but instead, thanksgiving. Be sure of this, that no immoral or impure or greedy person, that is, an idolater, has any inheritance in the kingdom of Christ and of God. Let no one deceive you with empty arguments, for because of these things the wrath of God is coming upon the disobedient" (Ephesians 5:3–6, NAB).

Have you ever engaged in any of those things St. Paul says will bring God's wrath on the world? Most of us have probably sinned in at least one of the ways he mentions here. So if we should suffer in the great tribulation of the world's last days, our suffering would represent no injustice on God's part. On the contrary—being given the grace to endure it and live with Him forever would be an act of His boundless mercy.

Innocent Suffering

Finally, we suffer sometimes even when we are innocent, simply because we share this broken world with people who are sinners like ourselves. To recall this truth, we need only look at the faces of children photographed in the midst of war, or at the quadriplegic victim of a drunk driver—or the Man on the crucifix, for that matter. But as with all suffering, this kind, too, can be redemptive if we join it to Christ's own suffering in prayer and reparation for the sins of the world.

By making that sacrifice, we "share His sufferings" (Philippians 3:10). As St. Paul observed when he suffered on behalf of those he served: "Now I rejoice in my sufferings for your sake, and in my flesh I complete what is lacking in Christ's afflictions for the sake of His body, that is, the Church" (Colossians 1:24). Though Christ's perfect sacrifice lacked nothing in itself to make our redemption possible, yet St. Paul tells us that we can join our afflictions to His in a way that benefits others.

"Is Something Wrong Here?"

In all these ways, then, a dangerous misunderstanding of suffering lies behind the rapture doctrine. Christians must reject any teaching that assumes tribulation cannot be redemptive, or that we don't ever deserve it, or that we cannot turn it to good even when we suffer innocently. Any of the Christians enduring severe persecution today in China, Sudan, or a dozen other nations around the world—where lesser Antichrists already ravage the Church—could tell us that much.

Even evangelical Protestant critics of the rapture idea recognize the misguided attitudes toward suffering that often accompany it. The evangelical New Testament scholar Robert Gundry notes that the doctrine appears to many as "the wishful thinking of some upwardly mobile Christians who want a crown without a cross and who, despite their confessing the Bible to be God's very Word, eagerly if not consciously accept a bending of its meaning to match the comfort of their lifestyle."[59]

Secret rapture teachers often make matters worse by using the fear of suffering through the "last days," and the hope of escaping it, as a tool of persuasion. Carl Olson, a former fundamentalist, a Catholic convert, and now an apologist, recalls from his youth the words of a junior high Bible camp leader who was eager to spur conversions around the campfire one night: " 'What if Jesus were to come back tonight?' he asked. 'If the rapture happened tonight, would you go to meet Jesus in the air?' Afterwards he prayed and invited us to stand up if we had made a decision for Jesus. 'You don't want to be left behind. This may be your only chance.' "[60]

Such tactics are not limited to Bible camp leaders. In his book *No Fear of the Storm*, Tim LaHaye himself makes what Gundry calls a "shamelessly maudlin appeal to escapism" when warning about what will happen to unbelievers left behind by the rapture: "Are you able to look at your children playing in the sunlight," LaHaye asks, "and believe firmly in your heart that they will not have to endure the monstrous horrors of the Tribulation?"[61]

The sense of relief that LaHaye's rapture-believing readers might feel is suggested by an anecdote also reported by Gundry. A well-known Bible prophecy teacher, having described the "tribulation" in gruesome detail, went on to exclaim, "But the church won't be here!" At that declaration, his rather large audience of listeners burst into applause. Gundry concludes the anecdote by asking pointedly: "Is something wrong here?"[62]

Yes, something *is* wrong here. The rapture is a conveniently comfortable doctrine that has led many Christians into a kind of smugness about their own immunity to divine judgment. The resulting glib dismissal of the world's future agonies is perhaps best reflected in a sticker that has often appeared on the auto dashboards of fundamentalist drivers: "Warning—in case of rapture, the driver of this car will vanish. Ride at your own risk."

The Anti-Catholic Agenda of Left Behind

In *Tribulation Force*, the second novel in the series by La-Haye and Jenkins, a journalist named Buck Williams who was left behind by the rapture has written an article on the phenomenon. "Most interesting to Buck," the novelists say, "was the interpretation of the event on the part of other churchmen. A lot of Catholics were confused, because while many remained, some had disappeared—including the new pope, who had been installed just a few months before the vanishings." Since all "true believers" in Christ have been raptured, it sounds as if the writers are at least allowing for the possibility that some Catholics, even a pope, could be "saved."

But if you read on, you find out why these staunch Protestants think such a thing could happen. That new pope "had stirred up a controversy in the church with a new doctrine that seemed to coincide more with the 'heresy' of Martin Luther than with the historic orthodoxy they were used to." The implication is clear: The pope had become a true believer, had been "saved," only by renouncing the historic orthodoxy of the Catholic Church and adopting Protestant theology instead. That implication was repeated in a later reference to two women who were raptured after having left the Catholic Church.[63]

In writing the article, Buck (who had been converted to fundamentalist religion after the rapture) interviewed a Catholic cardinal named Peter Mathews who was left behind. The journalist pressed him with a Bible verse about being saved through faith rather than works, and of course the cardinal resisted his fundamentalist interpretation of the verse. But the prelate is portrayed as fumbling through with lame statements rather than quoting, for example, the biblical passage we cited above clearly teaching that "a man is justified by works and not by faith alone" (James 2:24).

Lucky for Buck that the cardinal didn't know his Bible very well! He had "failed to explain away the doctrine of grace." In fact, the cardinal reflects the ignorance of the novelists themselves, who not only seem totally unaware of the biblical book of St. James but who—judging from an error in this passage—don't even know the difference between the "Apocrypha" (the Protestant term for the books in the Catholic Bible not included in the Protestant Bible) and the "Apocalypse" (the biblical book of Revelation).[64]

It gets worse. The not-so-subtle anti-Catholic bias of the novels eventually hardens into blatant anti-Catholic propaganda, which is focused in the character of Cardinal Mathews. "A beefy, jowly man" who customarily drinks champagne in the morning, the Cardinal becomes pope through a papal enclave apparently rigged by the Antichrist. The Antichrist, the Cardinal confides ominously to the journalist, "has much more in mind for my papacy than merely leadership of the Holy Roman Catholic Mother Church."[65]

These diabolical plans include the amalgamation of all the world's religions into "an entirely new religion, one that would incorporate the tenets of all." And of course, "there will be need for a new head of the new religion. . . . What better place to headquarter it than the Vatican? And who better to lead it than the new pope?" In this way, the bubbly-sipping pope hands over the vast global resources of the Catholic Church to the Antichrist and becomes his great false prophet who deceives the world.[66]

Real History Gets Left Behind

If you have read the LaHaye/Jenkins nonfiction exposition of the theology behind their end-time fiction, you will not be surprised by this story line. What they wrap up in foolish fantasy in their novels, they unwrap for clear viewing in the book *Are We Living in the End Times?* This particular volume serves as a "companion outline" of the end time events and characters that were fictionalized in the *Left Behind* series.[67]

In chapter thirteen their anti-Catholic agenda comes fully out of the closet. The authors predict that in the end times, a "corrupt one-world religion" will emerge: "Revelation 17 gives us a graphic picture of this global 'church.' John calls it

'MYSTERY, BABYLON THE GREAT, THE MOTHER OF HARLOTS AND OF THE ABOMINATIONS OF THE EARTH.' "[68]

Now many Catholics would agree that a one-world religion is currently being promoted by many organizations around the world influenced by New Age thinking. These mistaken New Agers assume that all religions teach basically the same thing and that the human race must be "enlightened" to move beyond all religious boundaries and differences. But LaHaye and Jenkins, influenced by the Dispensational suspicion of organized religion, go beyond this reasonable observation to make an utterly false prediction: They insist that the pope, and the Catholic Church as a whole, will attempt to lead the world into this global deception.

Why? Because, they assert, Catholicism is already joined to the false "Babylonian" religion that is prophesied to fill the world in the last days. But this argument is skewed from the start by faulty historical premises.

In a section entitled "Mystery Babylon's Long History," for example, LaHaye and Jenkins make the absurd historical claim that "every false religion in the world can be traced back to Babylon."[69] They would no doubt throw together indiscriminately into that category the human sacrifices of the Aztecs; the poetic myths of the Romans, Greeks, and Norsemen; the shamans and fetishes of the aboriginal Australians and Africans; the secret rites of the Druids; the mantras of Buddhists; the yoga of Hindus; the precepts of Confucius; the pilgrimages of Muslims, and on and on. Who can take them seriously when they claim that all these religions—so mutually contradictory in their beliefs and practices, so far-flung in their geographical origins—come from a single ancient Babylonian religion? Pseudo-historical claims of this sort would startle and amuse real historians, including evangelical Protestant scholars who have traced the quite unrelated origins of various non-Christian religions of the world.[70]

The Catholic Church as the Daughter of Babylon

For those who are familiar with typical fundamentalist rhetoric against the Catholic Church, the next step in the La-Haye/Jenkins argument is predictable. "Rome is the mother of an unholy mixture" of these false religions and the true faith. "The pagan practices and teachings of Babylon began to worm their way into Christianity. These included prayers for the dead, making the sign of the cross, worship of saints and angels, instituting the mass, and worship of Mary."[71]

Catholics who know even the basics of their faith will recognize the silliness of such claims. The practice of praying for the dead was inherited by the Church from ancient Jewish tradition, is affirmed in the Scripture (see 2 Maccabees 12:39–45), and was practiced by Christians from earliest times. The sign of the cross obviously recalls for us the instrument of Christ's sacrificial death. Mary, the other saints, and the angels are not "worshipped" by Catholics in the modern sense of that term; rather, we honor (or "venerate") them as members of our spiritual family and ask for their prayers. And the Holy Sacrifice of the Mass was instituted by our Lord Himself on the night He was betrayed. Neither these nor any other distinctively Catholic religious beliefs and practices have even a remote connection to ancient Babylonian religion.[72]

Are there parallels between Catholic practice and the practice of non-Christian religions? Of course—just as there are parallels between fundamentalism and non-Christian religions. Hindus pray and read from sacred books, for example, just as Catholics and fundamentalists do. But that doesn't mean that the Christian practices of prayer and Scripture reading came from Hinduism.

Are there parallels between Christian beliefs and non-Christian beliefs? Of course. The ancient Babylonians taught a creation story with similarities to the first part of the biblical book of Genesis. They also believed in the existence of demons. Must both Catholics and fundamentalists, then, reject the opening chapters of the Bible and the doctrine that demons exist simply because their beliefs resemble certain ancient beliefs in ancient Babylon? Of course not!

Are there Catholic practices with actual historical roots in other religions? Of course—and fundamentalists share in some of those practices. The wearing of wedding rings, the coloring of Easter eggs, the decorating of homes at Christmas with evergreen boughs and trees, and even the very dating of the Christmas holiday on December 25 all have pagan beginnings. Are fundamentalists willing to give up these "pagan" traditions?

Is every custom with a pagan religious origin, even if it no longer carries pagan religious meanings, to be shunned? If so, then fundamentalists had better come up with new names for the days of the week and months of the year; the ones we now use in English come from the names of pagan gods and goddesses. Fundamentalists had also better give up the system of dividing time into hours, minutes, and seconds; that practice, after all, is itself rooted in the dreaded ancient Babylonian religion! Using fundamentalist "logic" of this sort, anyone wearing a wristwatch could be accused of having connections to "Mystery Babylon."

LaHaye and Jenkins's spurious claims lack not only logic, but historical documentation as well. Where exactly they encountered these strange ideas is not clear. But if they or their sources drew the notions from the book *Babylon Mystery Religion* by the Protestant evangelist Ralph Woodrow, or the oft-quoted and reprinted *Two Babylons* by Alexander Hislop (1858), they may want to reconsider their accusations against the Catholic Church. Woodrow, to his credit, has pulled his book from publication because he discovered serious flaws in Hislop's material, from which he himself had drawn. In its place, Woodrow has now published a new book called *The Babylon Connection?* (1997), which debunks and repudiates the notion that the Catholic faith has Babylonian roots.[73]

Woodrow seems to have learned what reputable historians have known all along: The Catholic faith is not an idolatrous blend of Christianity and "Babylonian mystery religion." The "whore of Babylon" in the book of Revelation is not the Church of Rome. And the claim that the Catholic Church is the offspring of ancient Babylonian mysticism is the religious equivalent of a supermarket tabloid headline screaming that Elvis' real mother came from the planet Venus.

Blame It All on St. Augustine?

LaHaye and Jenkins continue their attack on the Catholic Church with charges against St. Augustine, the great theologian of the ancient Church whose writings we cited earlier. They accuse him of adulterating "God's wisdom" by mixing it with "Greek humanism," or "man's wisdom," thus "further paving the way for more pagan thought and practice."[74]

Again, the claims of the *Left Behind* authors lack historical foundation. Though St. Augustine certainly made use of Greek learning to examine many theological issues, he was by no means the first Christian teacher to do so. A number of the Church fathers before him and in his day had employed Greek learning as well, especially great defenders of the faith against paganism such as St. Justin Martyr (c. 100–c. 165) and brilliant theologians who helped the Church understand the mystery of the Most Holy Trinity, such as St. Basil (329–79), St. Gregory Nazianzen (329–89), and St. Gregory of Nyssa (330–95).

In fact, even the Apostles St. Paul and St. John had made

use of Greek learning in their teaching. In the book of Acts, we find St. Paul quoting from a pagan Greek poet when he addressed the Greek intellectuals in Athens—and the words he quoted actually referred, in their original context, to the pagan god Zeus (see Acts 17:16–28). In his Gospel, St. John appropriated from the Greek Stoic philosophers the philosophical term *Logos* (Greek for "word" or "reason") and applied it to Christ as the Son of God (see John 1:1). In "mixing" Greek learning with Christian revelation, St. Augustine was apparently in good company.

LaHaye and Jenkins insist, as we have seen, on interpreting the Bible "literally" rather than "spiritually" or "symbolically," and they believe that "spiritual" interpretation has led the Church into error. They claim that St. Augustine was guilty of "spiritualizing" Scripture in this way, taking the Church away from the literal interpretation. He was thus responsible for having the Bible "removed . . . as the sole source of authority for correct doctrine."[75]

Yet the "spiritual" reading of Scripture did not originate with St. Augustine any more than did the use of Greek learning. Several influential Church fathers before him had insisted that Scripture displayed more than one level of meaning. In fact, St. Paul himself had interpreted Scripture "spiritually" rather than literally when he told the Galatians that the Old Testament story of Isaac and Ishmael could be read as an "allegory," with their mothers, Sarah and Hagar, seen as symbols of "two covenants" (Galatians 4:22–26).

We should note here as well that fundamentalists themselves interpret Scripture "symbolically" rather than literally when it suits their purposes. They believe, for example, that the "beast" of the book of Revelation (described in chapter thirteen and later passages) does not refer literally to an animal, but rather symbolizes a man. More importantly, they refuse to interpret literally Jesus' words about the Eucharist:

"This is my Body. . . . This is my Blood" (Matthew 26:26, 28); "Unless you eat the Flesh of the Son of Man and drink His blood, you have no life in you" (John 6:53). The Lord speaks here in "symbols," they claim. So much for the "literal" or "plain" sense of Scripture!

When the *Left Behind* authors go on to assert that St. Augustine was responsible for having the Bible "removed . . . as the sole source of authority for correct doctrine," they continue to reveal their ignorance of early Church history. At no time in the ancient period, before or after St. Augustine, did the Church teach that Scripture stood alone in this way. As we saw in chapter three, from before the time when the New Testament was completed, the Church has always recognized the doctrinal authority of Sacred Tradition and the Sacred Magisterium.

Finally, we should note that if LaHaye and Jenkins were looking for an ancient theologian to make a whipping boy for Catholic doctrinal "error," St. Augustine was the wrong choice. Ironically, the major architects of the Protestant Reformation deeply admired this brilliant saint. Martin Luther and John Calvin in particular quoted him repeatedly and approvingly—probably more often than they quoted any other ancient writer outside the biblical authors themselves. In attacking St. Augustine, then, LaHaye and Jenkins are pitting themselves against the most influential teachers of their own Protestant tradition.[76]

More "History"

The *Left Behind* authors go on to trot out even more false claims parading as history. "At the same time" as St. Augustine taught, they assert, "the Scriptures were kept locked up in monasteries and museums, leaving Christians defenseless against the invasion of pagan and humanistic thought and practice. Consequently, the Dark Ages prevailed, and

the Church of Rome became more pagan than Christian."
Christianity, they conclude, was thus almost destroyed by
"Satan's Babylonian mysticism."[77]

These assertions are wrong on several counts. First, as we
have already noted, the Church did not at all "lock up" the
Scriptures in this period. In fact, it was only through the
arduous labors of the Catholic residents of those monasteries
—who lovingly copied the Scriptures by hand through the
"Dark Ages"—that the text of the Bible survived at all.

Second, these so-called "Dark Ages," which lasted for
roughly five centuries after St. Augustine's lifetime, were
hardly an era of "invasion" of the Church by "pagan and
humanistic thought and practice," as LaHaye and Jenkins
insist. On the contrary, this period earned the name "dark"
from historians precisely because of the *collapse* in Western
Europe of the classical Greco-Roman learning and civilization that these authors have labeled "pagan and humanistic."
Few of the *real* invaders of that era—the barbarian peoples
from the North and the East—would have been quoting
Greek philosophers as they plundered!

Finally, we should note that "museums" as we know them
today were not even established in Europe until the eighteenth century. The Church could hardly have "locked up"
the Scripture in museums a thousand years before such institutions existed.

Perhaps the most outrageous anti-Catholic claim of the
Left Behind authors is that the Catholic Church murdered
up to forty million people—"true believers"—during the
Middle Ages.[78] Not surprisingly, LaHaye and Jenkins fail
to provide documentation for such a shocking statement,
because no such documentation (of a reputable sort) exists.
They are only parroting the wildly irresponsible assertions of
earlier anti-Catholic tracts, which have published "estimates"
of the Church's carnage ranging from twenty million to a

breath-taking ninety-five million. (This last figure is equal to the estimated total of people living in Europe in 1650, long after the population had grown well beyond medieval levels. In order to rack up those kinds of statistics, the Pope probably would have had to resort to importing victims from other continents just to kill them.)[79]

In many ways, then, the Church "history" presented by the *Left Behind* authors seems to have as many fictitious elements as their novels. Worse yet, their distorted views of the past lead to equally distorted visions of the future. They warn darkly that Pope John Paul's "infatuation" with Fatima and his "reverence" for Mary "concerns some who fear he could be setting up his church and the religions of the world" to create the one-world religion of "Mystery Babylon, the Mother of Harlots."[80] Pope John Paul II, they fear, could become the tool of the Antichrist.

Is it any wonder that secret rapture advocates with such misconceptions about the Catholic Church are eager to draw Catholics away from their faith?

The Antidote: True Catholic Teaching

Catholics should recognize all these explicit attacks on the Church as mistaken. Even the deceptions hidden behind the mask of the *Left Behind* fantasy can be discerned by Catholics who are forewarned. But unsuspecting Catholics may read the books or watch the video on the recommendation of a fundamentalist friend without knowing that the authors seek to undermine their beliefs. Their faith could be at risk; they need to know the truth.

Meanwhile, Catholics should realize that when the Antichrist comes, many Christians who *reject* the Church's Magisterium may actually be more likely to be taken in by him. After all, the Bible portrays him as a master spiritual deceiver. Perhaps, in the eyes of many, he will be able to "prove" his teachings from "the plain sense of Scripture." If such an utterly subjective standard is all some believers have to go by, then history teaches us that they could be in big trouble.

The rapture doctrine in particular will actually set up believers for the Antichrist's deception if they should be alive on earth at the close of the age. Imagine your situation if the Antichrist should actually come to power, but you were convinced that you would be snatched out of the world before God would allow such a thing to happen. In that case, you would refuse to recognize the Antichrist for what he was. Your misguided doctrine would blind you to his identity.

So once more we pose the question: Is the rapture teaching, and the system of theology that surrounds it, actually dangerous? In all the ways we have noted, most certainly *yes*. Deception is always dangerous. As an antidote to this spiritual poison, then, we must take a look at what the Catholic Church teaches about the end times.

8

"He Will Come Again in Glory"

What the Catholic Church Teaches (And Doesn't Teach) About the End of the World

Open the last book of the Bible, and you enter a strange and dazzling world. In quick succession you encounter there a baffling array of angels and beasts, saints and sinners, worshippers and warriors, celebrations and catastrophes.

There you find a great beast whose number is 666. Two prophets who are murdered and then raised from the dead. A scroll with seven seals. Seven angels, seven trumpets, seven thunders, seven golden bowls, seven plagues. Four men riding horses, each horse a different color. Hail and fire, mixed with blood. A battle named Armageddon. A star named Wormwood falling to earth. Crowned locusts with human faces, women's hair, lions' teeth, scales, and stinging scorpion tails. Invading nations named Gog and Magog. A red dragon with seven heads, ten horns, seven crowns. A bejeweled harlot drinking blood and riding a scarlet beast.

So what does the Catholic Church officially teach about the true meaning of all these puzzling symbols, figures, and events?

The short answer: Not much.

The Church has never claimed to know with certainty, for example, the true meaning of the locust with human faces.

But the Church does witness to a number of important truths about Christ's second coming and the close of the age.

A Humbling Perplexity

The Church teaches, of course, that the book of Revelation and the book of Daniel, with its similar imagery, belong among the Scriptures inspired by God. Both books extend to us God's invitations, promises, and warnings. Both contain useful exhortations to maintain a steadfast hope and faith.

Nevertheless, much of what is contained in these books is exceedingly difficult to understand. The rule of interpreting a biblical text as far as possible in its "plain sense" does not help much in many passages we find here. The "plain sense" of a red dragon with seven heads and ten horns is just not very plain at all.

"All Scripture," St. Paul tells us, "is inspired by God and profitable for teaching, for reproof, for correction, and for training in righteousness" (2 Timothy 3:16). If so, then why are these texts in some places so difficult to penetrate? What can we possibly learn from words that leave us squinting and scratching our heads in bewilderment?

We can learn *humility*, said St. Augustine. God includes these deep, murky waters of mystery in the Bible, he concluded, to teach us not to dive in over our heads. To remind us that we don't know it all and can't figure it all out. To send us to the Church for help in understanding divine revelation.

Those are rather valuable lessons for anyone to learn, whether Bible scholar or Bible beginner.

This is not to say that Catholics have never tried to make sense of these books. As we noted in chapter six, a Chilean Jesuit named Manuel Lacunza even published a book outlining something like a secret rapture thesis in the early nineteenth century. His work, not surprisingly, encountered little enthusiasm in Catholic circles. Ironically, through Lacunza's influence on Edward Irving, his ideas actually ended up having their most serious consequences among Protestants who thought his Church was the "Whore of Babylon." But he was largely forgotten among Catholics because his speculations were ruled out by the clear teaching of the Church.

We should note here that the teaching of an individual Catholic who is not speaking for the Magisterium, even if he is a trained theologian or biblical scholar, by no means has the same authoritative status as the official teaching of the Catholic Church. That distinction should be clear to most Catholics. But many Protestants, having no concept of a Magisterium, fail to understand it.

For that reason, we sometimes encounter an ironic and rather amusing claim made by certain evangelical Protestants who both reject the secret rapture and abhor Catholicism. Having heard about Lacunza's influence on Irving, they announce confidently that the Catholic Church teaches the rapture doctrine and that Protestants have thus been deceived by "Jesuit-spawned propaganda." "Roman leaven," claims one fundamentalist opponent of the doctrine, has "corrupted the prophetic teaching of almost all the fundamentalist world. Well might we say of the *'secret rapture,'* can any good thing come out of Rome?"[81]

In any case, after twenty centuries, you can well imagine that by now, even among Catholics, nearly every possible biblical interpretation and speculation on the end times has been proposed by someone. But on many issues emerging from these inspired texts, God simply has not chosen to speak clearly and definitively through Scripture, Tradition, or the Magisterium. On these particular issues, then, whatever ideas individual Catholics may have come up with on their own, the Church remains silent.

On the other hand, what the Catholic Church, by Christ's authority, *has* definitively declared about the end of the world

—and what is clearly implied by what it has so declared—Catholics are obliged to believe. In fact, what the Church has definitively declared, Catholics should be *overjoyed* to believe. After all, it's good news! Christ's second coming and the events surrounding it are just as much a part of the gospel as His first coming.

Essentials of Catholic Teaching on the Last Days

The Church has not yet attempted to define the precise significance of the four horsemen, the human-faced locusts, and the like. Why not? For this reason: Though the Church's understanding of divine revelation continues to unfold as the Holy Spirit guides the Magisterium, at this point the Spirit has not yet chosen to clarify these and other matters.

Nevertheless, this does not mean the Church has not spoken quite clearly about the basic revealed truths of *eschatology*—that is, the doctrine of the "last things."[82] We have noted a few of the phrases from the Nicene Creed that sum up the Church's teaching in this regard. Now we will expand a little on that understanding, drawing a few specific points from what Pope John Paul II has called a "sure guide" to faith: the *Catechism of the Catholic Church*.[83]

Jesus will return to the earth in glorious triumph. "Though already present in His Church," says the *Catechism*, "Christ's reign is nevertheless yet to be fulfilled 'with power and great glory' by the King's return to earth"[84] (671). Our Lord's return "could be accomplished at any moment"[85] (673) and will be universally visible and undeniable. No secret rapture here. This foundational truth has been affirmed many times over by the scriptural texts we have examined in earlier chapters.

First, however, the Antichrist will appear to deceive the world and persecute the Church. "The persecution that accompanies her pilgrimage on earth will unveil the 'mystery of iniquity' in the form of a religious deception offering men an apparent solution to their problems at the price of apostasy from the truth. The supreme religious deception is that of the Antichrist, a pseudo-messianism by which man glorifies himself in place of God and of His Messiah come in the flesh"[86] (675). The spirit of Antichrist has manifested itself many times already in history, most notably in recent times under the guise of atheistic Communism (676). Christians will be terribly persecuted at the hands of the final Antichrist, just as they have been at the hands of his forerunners.

The Church will suffer the great tribulation prophesied by her Lord. "Before Christ's second coming the Church must pass through a trial that will shake the faith of many believers"[87] (675). "The Church will enter the glory of the kingdom only through this final Passover, when she will follow her Lord in His death and resurrection"[88] (677). Again, we have examined a number of scriptural passages that confirm this teaching. Contrary to the rapture doctrine, Christians will not be spared the great tribulation.

The final victory of Christ on earth will not come through a gradual improvement in the world's spiritual condition. "The kingdom will be fulfilled, then, not by a historic triumph of the Church through a progressive ascendancy, but only by God's victory over the final unleashing of evil, which will cause His Bride to come down from heaven"[89] (677). This declaration rules out the end time expectations of certain Reformation traditions (see "postmillennialism" below). Calvinists in particular often teach that the Church will achieve in history, through the Holy Spirit, a gradual betterment of the world's spiritual condition that will climax in Christ's return to earth. But this mistaken notion offers only a false hope.

The final victory of Christ will not come within *history, but* beyond *it.* "The Antichrist's deception already begins to take shape in the world every time the claim is made to realize within history that messianic hope which can only be realized beyond history through the eschatological judgment. The Church has rejected even modified forms of the falsification of the kingdom to come under the name of millenarianism"[90] (676).

As we saw in chapter seven, down through the ages, some Christians have mistakenly claimed that Christ's "millennial reign" (more about this below) was already taking place within history and was coming to pass through a particular group of religious enthusiasts in a particular geographic locale. Typically, such *millenarians,* as they are called, have claimed a special status because of their connection to that realized "kingdom," leading to eccentric, questionable, or even immoral practices: strict vegetarianism, the condemnation of marriage and procreation, claims to bizarre private revelation, polygamy, sexual promiscuity, military conquests, the murder of their opponents, and the like. The Church condemns these false claims and the tragic consequences to which they typically lead.

The Jewish people will come to recognize Jesus Christ as their Messiah before He returns. We have only hints of this remarkable development in Scripture, in the Gospels and St. Paul's epistle to the Romans. "The glorious Messiah's coming is suspended at every moment of history until His recognition by 'all Israel,' for 'a hardening has come upon part of Israel' in their unbelief toward Jesus"[91] (674). "The 'full inclusion' of the Jews in the Messiah's salvation, in the wake of 'the full number of the Gentiles,'[92] will enable the People of God to achieve 'the measure of the stature of the fullness of Christ,' in which 'God may be all in all' "[93] (674).

The dead will be raised. "The Christian creed—the profession of our faith in God, the Father, the Son, and the Holy Spirit, and in God's creative, saving, and sanctifying action —culminates in the proclamation of the resurrection of the dead on the last day and in life everlasting" (988). What does it mean to be resurrected? In death, body and soul are separated, and the body decays. In the resurrection, the body will be granted "incorruptible life" by being reunited with the soul (997).

When Jesus was raised from the dead with His own body —He still had the scars of His crucifixion, which the disciples could physically touch—His body no longer experienced a merely "earthly life" (999). It was a "glorified body" (997), transformed in such a way that it could exercise new abilities such as passing through physical barriers. But it retained its former capabilities, such as the ability to eat.

When we are raised, "Christ 'will change our lowly body to be like His glorious body,' into a 'spiritual body' "[94] (999). Exactly how this happens "exceeds our imagination and understanding; it is accessible only to faith" (1000). But it will surely take place "definitively 'at the last day,' 'at the end of the world,' "[95] in close association with Christ's appearing (1001).

Christ will judge the living and the dead, and the Evil One and his allies will at last be utterly overthrown. "God's triumph over evil will take the form of the Last Judgment after the final cosmic upheaval of this passing world"[96] (677; see also 1038–1041). Again, we have reviewed in earlier chapters a number of scriptural passages that attest to this truth. As the God-Man who conquered death and the Devil, Jesus alone is worthy to judge the earth and bring a definitive end to its wickedness. "Jesus solemnly proclaims that He 'will send His angels, and they will gather . . . all evil doers, and throw them into the furnace of fire,'[97] and that He will pronounce the condemnation: 'Depart from me, you cursed, into the eternal fire!' "[98] (1034).

At the end of time, God's kingdom will come in its fullness, and all things will be renewed. "Sacred Scripture calls this mysterious renewal, which will transform humanity and the world, 'new heavens and a new earth.'[99] It will be the definitive realization of God's plan to bring under a single head 'all things in [Christ], things in heaven and things on earth' "[100] (1043). Not only humanity, but the entire universe as well will be perfected. In this consummation of all things, there will be no more sadness or sin, pain or sickness, death or decay. The saints will reign with Christ, glorified in body and soul, and will enjoy perfect fellowship face to face with God for eternity (1044–45). But we do not know exactly when or how this transformation will take place (1048).

The hope of God's coming kingdom should not tempt us to withdraw from earthly affairs. "Far from diminishing our concern to develop this earth, the expectancy of a new earth should spur us on, for it is here that the body of a new human family grows, foreshadowing in some way the age which is to come." We must never confuse earthly progress with the increase of God's kingdom (as some forms of liberation theology, for example, have done). But "such progress is of vital concern to the kingdom of God, insofar as it can contribute to the better ordering of human society"[101] (1049). Darby's notion of a Church that forms "no part of the course of events of the earth" is thus a spiritual fantasy.

In the meantime, Christ's presence with us through His Word, His Sacraments, and His Spirit draw us closer to the fulfillment of His promise. "The Holy Spirit's transforming power in the liturgy hastens the coming of the kingdom and the consummation of the mystery of salvation. While we wait in hope He causes us really to anticipate the fullness of communion with the Holy Trinity"[102] (1107; see also 1100–1106). "There is no surer pledge or clearer sign of this great hope in the new heavens and new earth 'in which righteousness dwells,' than the Eucharist"[103] (1405).

This, in summary, is the faith of the Church with regard to the close of the age. Admittedly, it is a short outline compared to the endless volumes of speculation that have been published by end times enthusiasts. But that is because God has not yet clearly revealed to the Church details such as the precise nature of "Wormwood," the identity of the two prophets, or the specific geographic locations, if any, of the nations Gog and Magog.

Fruitless Speculations vs. Fruitful Debates

Unlike the *Left Behind* authors and many other fundamentalist "prophecy scholars," the Catholic Magisterium does not spend much time speculating about who will be the Antichrist or whether he is now living on earth. It does not try to match up the vivid scenarios in Revelation and Daniel with the evening news and the mutually contradictory, ever-changing predictions of politicians, scientists, and economists. It does not seek to provide a definitive explanation of the millennium, or "thousand years," referred to in Revelation 20.

Perhaps as events unfold, God will make known His plan to the Church more clearly, in more detail. But unless and until He does, where the Holy Spirit has left a particular matter as a mystery, the Magisterium faithfully remains silent. In the meantime, imitating the Blessed Virgin Mary, the Church keeps within herself as a treasure all that God has said and ponders it in her heart (see Luke 2:19, 51).

If the rapture promoters (and some overly imaginative Catholics as well) would imitate such wise and modest reticence, they could spare themselves considerable embarrassment. After all, the plug-the-headline-into-the-Bible-verse game has always been a losing proposition.

In past generations, for example, Christians have mistakenly identified numerous historical figures of their own day as the final Antichrist: the Muslim Sultan, the Emperor Frederick, the Pope, Napoleon, Bismark, Hitler, Mussolini, Stalin, Gorbachev, Yeltsin, even former U.S. Secretary of State Henry Kissinger! Usually the candidate proposed for this dubious "honor" was the political leader who seemed to be the most sinister enemy at the moment. Consequently, some Americans have thought, for example, that the Antichrist was King George III of England in the Revolutionary War, the German Kaiser in the First World War, and Saddam Hussein in the Gulf War.

The same is true of Gog and Magog. Mentioned in Revelation 20:8 and a few Old Testament passages, these "nations at the four corners of the earth" are gathered for battle against God's people, but God sends fire from heaven to consume them. Christians given to apocalyptic speculation throughout history have tended to identify these hostile nations with whichever foreign people seems most to threaten them at the time: the Norsemen, the Huns, the Mongols, the Turks, the Russians. Perhaps a few contemporary Christians in Iraq think "Gog and Magog" refers to the United States!

This is not to say, of course, that all speculation and debate about the future of the Church and the world should be avoided. Sometimes we can gain from a careful, reasonable discussion of what Sacred Scripture and Sacred Tradition seem to suggest about the end times, even if we lack certainty about the issues under discussion. Meditation on the world's end can also put our everyday lives in a proper perspective, keeping us from too strong an attachment to fleeting pleasures and possessions.

Fretting over the nature of the human-faced locusts in Revelation will probably be of little spiritual benefit to us. On the other hand, wrestling with some of the more important, though unsettled, issues can press us to examine our theological biases and assumptions. It can acquaint us with elements of Scripture and Tradition that were not familiar to us before. And if it shows us the limits of our knowledge and understanding, it can humble us as well.

Several significant debates over the Church's future have been running literally for ages, ever since the earliest generations after Christ. Unless God settles these debates by giving more light to the Magisterium, they may well continue until Jesus returns—and answers our questions once and for all. Nevertheless, these subjects merit a closer look, even if only to make us aware that certain questions still have several possible solutions rather than a definitive answer.

The Book of Revelation

The last book of the Bible had a hard road on the way to getting approved by the Church as Scripture. For reasons obvious to anyone who has ever struggled to make sense of St. John's visions, a few early Christian leaders questioned its inclusion in the Bible. Nevertheless, the Church did finally affirm that God had inspired the book and that it was worthy of a place in the New Testament alongside the Gospels, the Acts of the Apostles, and the Epistles.

What the Church did not say, however, was just exactly how we are to read this particular book. Over the centuries, several schools of thought have developed, with quite different interpretations resulting. The differences stem primarily from disagreements over which segments of history the book is describing.

Most, though not all, Christians have agreed that the first three chapters of Revelation—the messages to the seven churches of Asia—describe the situation of St. John's contemporaries, though the messages are meaningful to later generations as well. Most also agree that the last half of chapter 20 (verses 11–15) and all of chapters 21 and 22 apply to the last things: Judgment Day, the consummation of all things, the eternal life of the saints with God. However, the time frame of the middle chapters (4:1—20:10) is disputed.

Futurist

The *futurist* school of thought holds that these middle chapters, along with the concluding passages, apply strictly to the future—the last brief segment of the present age, its conclusion when Jesus returns, and the events to follow His return. A number of early Church fathers apparently interpreted Revelation this way, but the approach fell into disfavor for many centuries. A Spanish Jesuit doctor of theology, Francisco Ribera (1537–91), revived this school of thought after the Protestant Reformation. St. Robert Bellarmine (1542–1621), a Doctor of the Church, was also a proponent of the futurist position.

Futurists typically conclude that the Antichrist will be an individual man who will reign for a few short years just before Christ's return in glory. The references to wars, plagues, and other disasters are usually taken literally as real historical events yet to come. Many elements of St. John's vision, however, are interpreted symbolically by futurists—for example, few would claim that the "Beast" is literally an animal rather than a man. Today, most evangelical Protestants (including the rapture theorists) and many Catholics hold to a futurist interpretation.

Preterist

The *preterist* school of thought, which also includes many contemporary Catholics, teaches that nearly all the events described in the book of Revelation took place in St. John's time or within a few centuries afterward. Some who hold this view, for example, believe that the book primarily describes the fall of pagan Rome, which is symbolized by the "beast" (19:20), and the growth of the Church, referred to as the "new Jerusalem" (21:2), while "Babylon the great, mother of harlots" (17:5) represents the Jewish religious system. Some preterists think that the only events described in the book that are still to take place are the Second Advent, the last judgment, and the consummation, leading to the new creation.

A few preterists go so far as to say that *all* New Testament prophecies—even those about the Second Coming—have been fulfilled. This position is obviously in error, as it contradicts the Church's clear teaching that Jesus will come again to the earth in glory.

One of the best-known champions of the preterist view was the Spanish Jesuit Luis de Alcanzar (1554–1613). Interestingly enough, he and Ribera formulated their opposing positions at about the same time. But even though they disagreed on which approach was correct, they agreed on which approach they opposed: the *historicist* school of thought.

Historicist

The *historicists* teach that the events described in the middle chapters of Revelation have found their fulfillment throughout the two thousand years of the Church's history. This particular view was popular among a few medieval dissenters in the Catholic Church and became widespread in the Protestant Reformation because it could be used as a tool of anti-papal propaganda. According to such historicists, the Antichrist is not an individual; it is a system—usually they say it is the papacy.

In this view, Antichrist's domination and persecution of

true believers began with the fall of Rome and lasted until the Reformation (or in some schemes, until the eighteenth century). Not surprisingly, this view was enthusiastically propagated by Martin Luther, John Calvin, Ulrich Zwingli, and many other vehemently anti-Catholic Reformation leaders. Historicists may also identify other historical figures or events with images in Revelation. For example, some say that the seven trumpets equal seven historic invasions of Christendom by enemy armies (the Goths, Vandals, Huns, Saracens, and so on.)

Spiritual/Idealist

The *spiritual* (or *idealist*) approach to interpretation says that particular historical events and characters have no one-on-one correspondence to the scenarios and figures in Revelation. St. John's imagery simply symbolizes spiritual realities: the fight between good and evil, God and the Devil, which Christians witness in every generation. Celestial bodies such as the sun, moon, and stars, for example, refer to political rulers; bodies of water refer to nations and peoples.

Progressive Parallels

Yet one more view takes its cue from a simple literary analysis of Revelation. This school of thought teaches that the book is structured in seven sections that run parallel to each other. Each of these sections portrays the Church and the world from the time of Christ's first advent to the time of His second advent.

For that reason, according to this view, though there is some overall progression through time within the book as a whole, we should not expect the order of the scenarios to correspond to a strict historical chronology. In effect, the story starts all over again with each new section, told from a slightly different perspective.[104]

Bible commentators, of course, do not always hold one of these positions in its "pure" form. They may teach, for example, that one scenario in the middle chapters of Revelation is a symbol of the present age, while teaching that another scenario is actually a prophecy of a future event. St. Augustine held that the "first resurrection" (Revelation 20:5–6) refers to the present regeneration of the soul through baptism, and that the thousand-year reign of Christ (Revelation 20:4–10) represents the era of the Church between the two advents. But he also insisted that the Antichrist is a specific individual who will appear toward the end of history to persecute the Church for a literal three and a half years.[105]

Some Bible scholars maintain that it is possible to embrace all these schools of thought at once. The Church has always taught that Scripture can have several levels of meaning. One of the "beasts" of Revelation, for example, might actually refer simultaneously to the ancient Roman emperor Nero, twentieth-century German Nazism, the final Antichrist still to come, and the perennial evils against which every Christian must struggle.[106]

Whichever school of thought we find most convincing, this much should be clear: Within the firm boundaries of the Magisterium's teaching, Catholics have considerable room to speculate and debate about how best to approach the last book of the Bible.

The Nature of the Millennium

Not only for Catholics but for Protestants as well, perhaps the most hotly debated issue connected to the end times is the nature of the thousand-year reign of Christ with His saints described in Revelation 20:1–10. At first glance this *millennium* (from the Latin for "a thousand years") seems to occupy only a minor role in the book's message. Nevertheless, the passage has shown itself capable of stirring up considerable enthusiasm and controversy in generation after generation of Christians.

To summarize the scenario: The Devil was seized by an angel and "bound . . . for a thousand years," thrown into a bottomless pit, and sealed inside where he could "deceive the nations no more, till the thousand years were ended. After that he must be loosed for a little while" (20:1–3).

Next, the saints martyred for their faith occupied thrones to reign with Christ a thousand years. "The rest of the dead did not come to life until the thousand years were ended. This is the first resurrection" (20:4–6).

When the thousand years were ended, Satan was loosed. He then deceived the nations and gathered them for war so he could attack "the beloved city." But fire fell from heaven to consume them, and the Devil was "thrown into the lake of fire and brimstone where the beast and the false prophet were, and they will be tormented day and night for ever and ever" (20:7–10).

Questions abound. Is "thousand" to be taken literally, or does it just refer symbolically to "a long time"? What does it mean for the Devil to be "bound" and "loosed"? Who exactly are the martyrs, and are their thrones on earth or in heaven, literal or symbolic? What is the nature of Christ's reign and their reign? Who are "Gog and Magog"? And most importantly, does this happen before or after Christ's final coming in glory?

In general, three schools of thought have developed among Christians in an attempt to answer such questions. We will briefly examine each of them in turn.

The Premillennial View

The *premillennial* position holds that after Christ returns to the earth in glory, He will reign for a thousand years before the final consummation of God's plan in the age to come.

Premillennialists take their name from their insistence that Christ's coming takes place *before* ("pre-") the millennium. (They are often affectionately dubbed "premills" for short.) Some premillennialists think that this reign of Christ takes place with the saints in heaven. But historically, this position has tended to view the reign as a literal earthly kingdom, with its capital city at Jerusalem. This latter position, as we have noted, is a form of *millenarianism*—a doctrine the Catholic Church has explicitly rejected.

Millenarians (also called "chiliasts," from the Greek word for "thousand") have debated whether the millennium lasts literally a thousand years or simply a long time. Either way, since Christ is immediately present on earth in human form during this reign and the Devil is bound, the assumption is that this era represents a golden age of civilization in which natural, social, moral, economic, and political conditions are optimal.

Millenarians tend to apply Old Testament prophecies of the Messianic kingdom to this time and to interpret these prophecies literally. "The wolf and the lamb shall feed together, the lion shall eat straw like the ox" (Isaiah 65:25); this means, they say, that the very nature of animals will change. There will be a healing of all physical ills: "No inhabitant will say, 'I am sick'" (Isaiah 33:24). Long life will be restored: "No more shall there be in it an infant that lives but a few days, or an old man who does not fill out his days, for the child shall die a hundred years old" (Isaiah 65:20). The soil will have increased fertility: "The wilderness and the dry land shall be glad, the desert shall rejoice and blossom" (Isaiah 35:1). Social and political relations will be perfected: "Neither shall they learn war any more" (Isaiah 2:4).

References to the millennial kingdom in a few of the early Church fathers show that some of them seem to have held to this view. The early Christian apologist Lactantius

(c. 240–c. 320), for example, alluding to Revelation 20:1–10, wrote this of the earthly kingdom ruled by Christ between His second coming and the loosing of the Devil:

> Throughout that time the stars shall be more brilliant, and the brightness of the sun shall be increased, and the moon shall not be subject to decrease. Then the rain of blessing shall descend from God at morning and evening, and the earth shall bring forth all her fruit without the labor of men. Honey shall drop from rocks, fountains of milk and wine shall abound. The beasts shall lay aside their ferocity and become mild, the wolf shall roam among the flocks without doing harm, the calf shall feed with the lion, the dove shall be united with the hawk, the serpent shall have no poison; no animal shall live by bloodshed. For God shall supply to all abundant and harmless food.[107]

Other early writers who seem to have held millenarian notions include St. Justin Martyr (who noted that many Christians of his time disagreed with his position); the second-century bishop Papias; St. Irenaeus; and Tertullian, the great third-century African apologist and theologian. Some Catholics insist, however, that not all these writers were truly millenarian. Even though they expected a millennial "golden age" to come, not all of them explicitly affirmed that Christ would be ruling the world visibly during that time.[108]

In any case, at least one of them—Tertullian—eventually joined the schismatic and undeniably millenarian movement known as Montanism. This sect taught that the kingdom of God was about to descend physically from heaven to the region of Phrygia in Asia Minor. Ecstatic prophets and prophetesses led the Montanists to severe rules of religious practice, such as strict forms of fasting, banning second marriages for widows, and forbidding Christians to flee when persecuted. They considered Christians who did not follow their rules of discipline to be mere "soulish men," while they referred to themselves as "spiritual" people.

Montanism was ultimately condemned by the Magisterium. After enduring the troubles caused by the Montanists and by later millenarian movements (we noted several such movements from the medieval and Reformation periods in chapter seven), the Church finally rejected millenarianism. A 1944 pronouncement of the Congregation for the Doctrine of the Faith in Rome clarifies the Church's position in the matter:

> In recent times on several occasions this Supreme Sacred Congregation of the Holy Office has been asked what must be thought of the system of mitigated Millenarianism, which teaches, for example, that Christ the Lord before the final judgment, whether or not preceded by the resurrection of the many just, will come visibly to rule over this world. The answer is: The system of mitigated Millenarianism cannot be taught safely.[109]

The language here is difficult, but in simpler terms it means this: We must reject the doctrine that before the final judgment day, Christ will come again in the flesh and in human history to rule visibly in an earthly kingdom.

Under the influence, perhaps, of fundamentalist friends or television preachers (most fundamentalists are millenarians), some Catholics have adopted a millenarian position without realizing that it contradicts Church teaching. Others tend in this direction through following the spurious messages of Catholics who claim a private revelation about it. This development (like the seduction of Catholics by the secret rapture doctrine) stems at least in part from a significant void in contemporary Catholic teaching: Catechesis about the "last things" is largely absent from Catholic pulpits and classrooms.

In recent days, an increasing number of Catholics have adopted what might well be called "spiritual millenarianism"—a belief that is not explicitly millenarian but resembles millenarian teaching in many ways. With the Church, these Catholics reject the claim that Christ will reign on the earth visibly and in the flesh for a period before Judgment Day. But they insist that Christ will nonetheless have an *invisible spiritual reign on earth* before history comes to a close.

This earthly "reign" or "temporal kingdom," they say, will be mediated—either through Mary and the other saints in heaven, who will influence humankind by their intercession, or through Christ's Eucharistic presence on earth (or both). Correlating this notion with certain alleged private revelations, Catholics who expect this "kingdom" sometimes speak of it as "the era of peace," "the Eucharistic reign," "the reign of Mary," "the Second Pentecost," or "the new era." They anticipate, before the final Judgment Day, the coming of a terrestrial paradise, an era resembling the golden age that was anticipated by the ancient writers we have noted.

Since this end time scenario does not include a visible earthly reign of Christ before Judgment Day, it does not appear to be fully millenarian in the sense that was explicitly rejected by the Magisterium in 1944. Nevertheless, Catholics who hope for any kind of future golden age should keep in mind, to repeat the declaration of the *Catechism*, that we must not expect even a spiritual reign of Christ on earth "to realize within history that messianic hope which can only be realized beyond history through the eschatological judgment"[110] (676). Perhaps in time the Church will offer a formal evaluation of the teaching that Christ will have an invisible spiritual reign on earth before Judgment Day.[111]

The Postmillennial View

Historically, the premillennial view has tended toward pessimism about the destiny of human society as a whole. It usually assumes that conditions on earth are certain to deteriorate, with the human race growing so wicked that Christ has to pull the curtain down on history before it is too late to save anyone. In John Calvin's wing of the Protestant Reformation, however, there emerged a position called *postmillennialism*, which exhibited a much more optimistic attitude toward human history.

Contemporary "postmills," who still tend to be Calvinists, teach that the kingdom of God is now being extended through the world by the preaching of the gospel, social activism, and the work of the Holy Spirit in conversion. Through this process, the world is eventually to be Christianized, and the return of Christ to the earth will take place only at the close of a long period of righteousness and peace—that is, at the *end* of the millennium. (The "thousand years" in this view means simply "a long time.")

John Calvin himself had insisted that Christians should aggressively shape society according to their vision of righteousness. He drew heavily from Old Testament sources to provide the theological justification for his own iron-fisted rule in the Swiss city of Geneva. There he held the populace under a tight religious, social, and political control more ambitious than any pope had ever attempted at Rome. Eventually, Calvin's program for a Reformed theocracy was exported to America with the Puritans.

These stern and sturdy men and women arrived with a deep conviction that America could become "a city set on a hill" (Matthew 5:14), a beacon of righteousness to the world. Their most brilliant theologian, Jonathan Edwards, once mused that the dawn of the millennium just might be breaking in the New World. Largely due to such influences, through the first century of our nation's history the post-millennial view was dominant among American evangelical Protestants, even those who were not Calvinist. Indomitably optimistic and tirelessly activist, they sought by their efforts to enlighten and transform society through movements for the prohibition of alcohol, the abolition of slavery, the banning of commerce and public recreation on Sundays, and similar religious causes.

Though the Civil War won success for the abolitionist cause, that agonized and protracted conflict nonetheless put a damper on national optimism. Soon after, the great social dislocations that took place toward the end of the nineteenth century drained such enthusiasm even more. An emerging "liberal" movement within the Protestant denominations held up the banner of Christian social activism to transform society, but the emerging fundamentalist movement reacted with a fervent premillennial (and Dispensational) pessimism.

After enduring two world wars, even many of the liberals lost confidence in the postmillennial dream. In the twentieth century, evidence for a gradual spiritual transformation of the world was hard to come by. Still, in recent years postmillennialists have increased in number among American Protestants. They exhibit a renewed, if yet unsupported, confidence that the United States could become a righteous theocracy.

As for Catholics, the issue is already settled. We noted before how the *Catechism* states clearly the teaching of the Church in this regard: "The kingdom will be fulfilled, then, not by a historic triumph of the Church through a progressive ascendancy, but only by God's victory over the final unleashing of evil, which will cause His Bride to come down from heaven"[112] (677). Even those Catholics who anticipate a coming "era of peace" usually expect it to end before Christ returns visibly, because they believe that Antichrist must appear before the close of the age to dominate the world.

If Catholics are optimistic, it is not because we look for a gradual emergence on earth of lasting peace, justice, and prosperity. It is solely because we know that in the end, after the Devil has done his worst, *God will triumph*.

Amillennialism

Since the time of St. Augustine (nearly sixteen centuries ago), most Catholics have tended toward the so-called *amillennial* position. "Amillennial" means literally "no millennium," which is something of a misnomer. In fact, amillennialists, who might more accurately be termed "present millennialists," *do* believe in the millennium of Revelation chapter 20. They simply insist that it refers symbolically to the present age between Christ's two advents rather than to a future, literal thousand years.

St. Augustine's powerfully moving *City of God* has influenced, directly or indirectly, millions of Christians to adopt this position. In that book he lays out the doctrine this way: When Christ defeated the Devil through the cross in His first advent, that "ancient serpent" was bound. Satan was not totally disarmed, of course, but he was "bridled and restrained" from "the exercise of his whole power to seduce men" and from seducing those who belong to God. Since that time, Christ has been reigning on earth through His saints because He is reigning in the hearts of those on earth who love Him.

Just before the close of the present age, however, God will loose the Enemy once more for a brief time. Then the Devil "will rage with the whole force of himself and his fallen angels for three and a half years." (Some "amills" do not insist on the three and a half years as St. Augustine does.) This is the period of the great tribulation under Antichrist's oppression.

At the end of the tribulation, Satan will be conquered and judged by Christ at His coming in glory. So why did God loose him in the first place? "So that the City of God might see how mighty an adversary it has vanquished, to the great glory of its Redeemer, Helper, and Deliverer."[113]

We should note that St. Augustine's views on the symbolic nature of the millennium, though they have dominated Catholic thinking for many centuries, have not been officially adopted by the Church. The Magisterium has never defined the "millennium" as the present age of the Church (in fact, it has never defined the "millennium" at all). Nevertheless, the Church does teach that Christ reigns even now, and the Church is the sacrament of that reign in the world.

So there you have it—all the parties involved in the centuries-long debate over the meaning of St. John's "thousand years." A fine assortment of "premills," "postmills," "amills," and "windmills" (long-winded authors filled with hot air).

The Antichrist

No book on the end times would be complete without saying at least a few words about that mysterious, most sinister of characters, the Antichrist. But keep in mind that the Magisterium has had little to say about this matter, other than the fact that Antichrist will surely come and will ravage the Church before being defeated by Christ at the Second Advent. Nearly all the rest is speculation based on dark hints in Scripture and the accumulation of two thousand years of conjecture.

The prefix "anti-" means "against" or "in place of." The Antichrist is thus the opponent of Christ, the false Messiah who tries to take the place of Christ. In the New Testament he is identified by this name only in the letters of St. John (see 1 John 2:18, 22; 4:3; 2 John 7). But Christians have traditionally seen him as well in the biblical references to the beasts of Revelation; the "abomination that makes desolate" (Daniel 11:31; see also 9:27; 12:11); the "desolating sacrilege" (Matthew 24:15); and "the man of lawlessness, . . . the son of perdition" (2 Thessalonians 2:3–10).

Remember that some Catholics (including the preterist and spiritual schools of interpretation) would dispute the claim that the "beast" of Revelation and Daniel refers to the Antichrist to come. But on the common assumption that the references from all these passages do indeed point to the same man, certain conclusions have often been drawn from various Scripture passages:

- There have been other antichrists throughout history in addition to the one who is to come toward the end of history (see 1 John 2:18). For this reason, some have insisted that he is not an individual, but rather a demonic *spirit* that periodically manifests itself in an ungodly *system*. Others say he is both a diabolical system throughout history and a demonic individual to come.

- The Antichrist will derive his great power from the Devil (see Revelation 13:3).

- Before the Antichrist comes, there will be a great "rebellion" or "apostasy" (2 Thessalonians 2:3)—a widespread falling away from the faith (see Matthew 24:10; Luke 18:8).

- The Antichrist is being "restrained" until the time appointed for him to appear (see 2 Thessalonians 2:6–8). Ancient commentators often thought that the presence of the Roman Empire was restraining him; others have concluded that St. Michael the archangel keeps him at bay until God commands otherwise.

- The Antichrist will proclaim himself God, ensconce himself in the "holy place," receive the worship of

the people, and "cause sacrifice and offering to cease"
(2 Thessalonians 2:4; Matthew 24:15; Revelation 13:4;
Daniel 9:27). Some Christians believe the "holy place"
is a rebuilt Jewish temple in Jerusalem where the Old
Testament sacrifices, having been reestablished, will be
suspended. Others think this refers to the Antichrist's
oppression of the Church and outlawing the Most Holy
Sacrifice of the Mass.

- The Antichrist will be haughty and blasphemous, per-
  secuting the Church terribly (see Revelation 13:5–7).
- He will present demonically wrought "wonders" (apparent miracles or diabolical prodigies) and make use
  of a "false prophet" to do the same on his behalf in order to deceive people into worshipping him (Revelation
  13:11–17; 19:20; 20:10; Matthew 24:24).
- He will be publicly opposed by "two witnesses" (or
  "martyrs") to God's truth who work true miracles,
  who are eventually executed by him, and who are finally raised from the dead publicly (Revelation 11:3–
  13). From the earliest centuries of the Church, Christians have speculated that these two witnesses are the
  Old Testament figures Enoch (see Genesis 5:22; Sirach
  44:16; Hebrews 11:5) and Elijah (see 2 Kings 2:1–12),
  both of whom did not die, but were taken up bodily
  from the earth instead. Elijah has been prophesied to
  return "before the great and terrible day of the Lord"
  (Malachi 4:5; Matthew 17:11).

  Others have speculated that they are *Moses* and Elijah, the pair who appeared with Christ on the Mount
  of Transfiguration (see Matthew 17:1–8). This speculation probably arises from the nature of the miracles
  to be worked by the witnesses, which parallel those in
  the Old Testament accounts of Moses and Elijah (see
  Revelation 11:5–6).

- The Antichrist will have extensive political power: to wage war using the armies of several nations (see Revelation 19:19) and to enforce severe economic sanctions against those who refuse to receive his "mark" identifying their allegiance to him, which is related to the number "666" (see Revelation 13:16–18). This last passage especially is extremely difficult to interpret and has lent itself to countless speculations.

- The Antichrist, after his world-ravaging campaign of force and fraud, will at last be vanquished by Christ and thrown into "the lake of fire" (Revelation 19:19–21).

Assorted Speculations About Antichrist

Few biblical figures have received as much speculative attention as Antichrist. Since you are liable to encounter some of the more persistent claims and legends even in contemporary discussions, you may want to acquaint yourself with a few of the more intriguing conjectures. None of the following ideas, we must emphasize, have the status of approved Church teaching.[114]

- For centuries many Christians thought the Roman emperor Nero was Antichrist, who was to come back from the dead to rule the world in the last days.

- Antichrist, St. Hippolytus claimed, will be the Devil incarnate. But later Catholic teaching rules out that possibility, since Satan does not have the power to create a miraculous union of diabolical spirit and human flesh that would be parallel to the incarnation of God's Son. The Devil can only possess a human being, and many Church fathers agreed that he will possess and control his human "host" to an unprecedented degree.

- St. John of Damascus and several other Church fathers

taught that the Antichrist will be the offspring of an illicit sexual union.

- St. Irenaeus, St. Augustine, St. Gregory the Great, and a number of other influential Christian writers concluded that the Antichrist will be a Jew of the tribe of Dan, based on the assumption that Genesis 49:17 and Jeremiah 8:16 are prophecies about him. Sadly, this tradition often provided an excuse for medieval Christians to massacre Jews during times of heightened apocalyptic expectation.

- St. Jerome and others taught that Antichrist will be born in Babylon.

- Some traditions say he will be educated as a child by sorcerers.

- St. Anthony of Padua believed that Antichrist will not be deprived of his guardian angel, but all the angel's labors to do him good will be wasted because of the man's obstinacy in doing evil.

- St. Cyril summed up the view of many Church fathers about the Antichrist when he stated, "His malice will surpass the combined wickedness of all the evil doers gone before him. . . . He will be like an ocean in which all the human and diabolical wickedness shall meet."

- Nevertheless, Antichrist will at first be lavished with honor by those he has deceived. Like the Devil himself, the Antichrist will have at his command considerable natural and supernatural gifts for accomplishing such deception. According to St. Anselm, his wisdom and eloquence will far exceed what any other man has ever possessed or even imagined; he will know all the Bible by heart and possess a perfect knowledge of all the arts.

- At the same time, he will win the affections of many by a pretense of urbane and unbounded humanitarian concern.

- His wealth will be limitless. According to St. Ephraem and St. Anselm, the demons will reveal to him the location of all the riches that have been lost or hidden, even those at the bottom of the sea. They will show him where to find vast new supplies of unmined precious metals and stones. These riches he will use to seduce followers and finance his schemes.

- St. Hippolytus wrote that Antichrist's diabolical prodigies will mimic Christ's divine miracles of healing, exorcism, supernatural knowledge, power over the forces of nature, and even resurrections of the dead. Some of these wonders will be optical illusions or hoaxes, while others will draw upon supernatural diabolical powers.

Conjecture vs. Claims to Inspiration

This sampling of Antichrist lore, along with the debates about interpreting the book of Revelation and the millennium, should illustrate an important truth: The simple, fundamental teaching of the Church about the close of the age can be spelled out in a few short pages. But many volumes could be filled, and have been filled, with the bewildering array of controversies, commentaries, and conjectures that have grown up around the subject across two thousand years.

Much of that massive accumulation of material we can safely leave on the shelf, if we wish. Some of it, perhaps, we might sift through to glean a few useful or fascinating insights. But what if, in the process, we should come across a message about the end times—a prediction, a warning, or even a command—that claims to come straight from heaven?

We come, then, to one last urgent question: Dare we ignore the words of people who say they are speaking for God?

9

On the Trail of the Great Monarch

The Dilemma of Private Revelations

The powerful monarch, who will be sent by God, will up-root every republic. He will submit everything to his authority, and he will show great zeal for the true Church of Christ. The empire of the Muslims will be broken up, and this monarch will reign in the East as well as in the West. All nations will come to worship God in the true Catholic and Roman faith. There will be many saints and Doctors [of the Church] on earth. Peace will reign over the whole earth because God will bind Satan for a number of years until the Son of Perdition. . . . By the grace of God, by the power of the Great Monarch, by the authority of the Holy Pontiff, and by the union of all the most devout princes, atheism and every heresy will be banished from the earth.[115]

This provocative prophecy is attributed to Venerable Bartholomew Holzhauser (died 1658), the German founder of the Apostolic Union of Secular Priests. The title "Venerable" means that he is at the second stage of the canonization process, perhaps destined one day to be fully recognized by the Church as a saint. Surely that designation says something about the man's holiness and integrity.

Are we, then, to believe what he says about the future? Is this truly a message to us from God? Or could even a "venerable" be mistaken in such an important matter?

To answer that question, we must address the dilemma of *private revelations*.

Public vs. Private Revelations

The Catholic Church teaches us that divine revelation is of two kinds. *Public* (or *universal*) revelation is that revelation contained in the Sacred Scripture and Sacred Tradition transmitted by the Church. Together, Scripture and Tradition form the one sacred deposit of the word of God. This deposit was complete with the close of the apostolic age. "No new public revelation," says the *Catechism*, "is to be expected before the glorious manifestation of our Lord Jesus Christ"[116] (66). All Catholics are obliged to believe public revelation as it is authentically interpreted by the Sacred Magisterium.

Certain *private* (or *particular*) revelations, on the other hand, have come to individuals from God down through the ages of the Church. "They do not belong," notes the *Catechism*, "to the deposit of faith. It is not their role to improve or complete Christ's definitive Revelation, but to help live more fully by it in a certain period of history" (67).

Nevertheless, some private revelations have been recognized by the authority of the Church. When the Church approves such revelations, she declares that nothing in them is contrary to faith or good morals and that they may be read without danger or even with profit. Even then, however, Church approval imposes no obligation on Catholics to believe these revelations. With regard to such messages, Pope Benedict XIV has observed: "It is not obligatory nor even possible to give them the assent of Catholic faith, but only of human faith, in conformity with the dictates of prudence, which presents them to us as probable and worthy of pious belief."[117]

The messages of Fatima, for example, are private revelations that have the Church's approval. The Church recommends them to Catholics as encouragements to faith, and millions have been converted or inspired to deeper penance and devotion through reflection on the 1917 apparitions of the Blessed Virgin to three little Portuguese children. Though Catholics are not obliged to accept the apparitions' authenticity, nevertheless, the miracles that took place there, the fruit of holiness that was borne in the lives of the visionaries and others, and the power of the words themselves all combine to urge acceptance of the revelation as true.

On the other hand, some alleged private revelations are obviously not from God and must be rejected. "Christian faith," the *Catechism* declares, "cannot accept 'revelations' that claim to surpass or correct the Revelation of which Christ is the fulfillment" (67). For that reason, the Church rejects, and individual Catholics should avoid reading, the words of "messengers" who say they are inspired by God, but who contradict clear teachings of the Church.

A clear example of such a spurious "revelation" appeared several years ago in an email announcement from a contemporary American who claimed to be a locutionist. ("Locutions" are verbal statements interiorly heard.) The "messenger" was one of a group of no doubt sincere Catholics who regularly distributed the texts of locutions often containing apocalyptic content. On this particular occasion, the locutionist claimed the Blessed Mother had told her that St. Joseph was a second immaculate conception—"conceived without any stain of sin."

The person transcribing the message noted that he had understandable "misgivings" about such a novel doctrine. But he went on to say that while he was transcribing the message, he was "overpowered with a strong scent of roses" for which he could provide no natural explanation. That experience he took as a confirmation that the "revelation" was genuine, and he concluded he could accept the message "without the slightest reservation" (though he did "call for all readers' individual discernment at all times whenever seeing such testimony.")[118]

The problem with this "revelation," of course, is that it blatantly contradicts the clear teaching of the Catholic Church. The dogmatic definition of the Immaculate Conception, issued in 1854 by Pope Pius IX, says explicitly that Mary was "in the first instance of her conception . . . preserved free from all stain of original sin" by "a *singular* grace and privilege granted by Almighty God."[119] That means she was the *only* member of the human race granted this grace and privilege. (Christ was of course free of original sin, but through His own merits, not by a divine conferral of "grace and privilege.")

Interior voices and the scent of roses notwithstanding, then, this message was most certainly not from God. Catholics can confidently reject it as contrary to faith. Perhaps the same alleged locutionist has truly received private revelations from God on other occasions. But on this occasion, she was mistaken, as was her transcriber in accepting it as authentic.

When Discernment Is More Difficult

Discerning the authenticity of these two particular messages should be a no-brainer. On the one hand, the truth of Fatima has been confirmed in numerous ways. The message was in accord with revealed truths of the Catholic faith, and it has been a source of great blessing to millions. Its prophecies have come to pass. The apparition was accompanied by verifiable miracles, witnessed by seventy thousand people—many of whom had come to Fatima as skeptics. The two visionaries who are deceased have been beatified, based on documentation of their personal holiness. Most importantly, the Church has approved the message. What more evidence of its genuineness could we ask for?

On the other hand, the message of St. Joseph's "immaculate conception" clearly fails the test of faithfulness to the revealed truths of the Catholic faith. The same is true for messages from a few other recent alleged locutionists. One "prophet" in particular, for example, has begun making near-Messianic claims for himself and has openly defied the law of the Church. Catholics with even a minimum of religious training should have no difficulties seeing through these charlatans and praying for their correction.

When we are dealing, however, with a more complex body of teaching based on claims of private revelation—teaching that might include traditional Catholic beliefs mixed with error—the involvement of local bishops becomes all the more urgent for our discernment. In one recent case, for example, the bishops of Canada had to act decisively to expose some false claims of a movement based in Quebec and calling itself the "Army of Mary."

This group calls loudly for Catholics to preserve loyalty to the Magisterium, especially the pope. Yet ironically, the private revelations it promotes, some of which have apocalyptic themes, include doctrines that contradict Church teaching. For that reason, the archbishop of Quebec in 1987 formally revoked the decree by which his predecessor had established the group as a pious association of the Catholic faithful. This revocation was made with the full agreement of Rome, after the Congregation for the Doctrine of the Faith had studied the texts of the presumed private revelations promoted by the group and had found them to contain significant errors.

Leaders of the organization appealed the ruling, as was their right, but Church officials have repeatedly confirmed the archbishop's action. Sadly enough, during this time the "Army" has publicly defied episcopal authority and persisted with its teachings and activities. Because of the continuing confusion surrounding the movement, fourteen years after the revocation of the group's approved status, the Canadian bishops issued a doctrinal note warning Catholics of the dangers in the organization's doctrines.

The bishops reported that the group "would have its followers believe, for example, that their 'Immaculate' [Mary] is co-eternal with the Triune God, and that although she was once the historical mother of Jesus, she is now 'reincarnated' and 'dwells' in the very person of the recipient of these presumed private revelations." No wonder, then, that "the Army of Mary [has] forfeited its claim to be a duly recognized Catholic association." "With pastoral charity," the bishops conclude, "we remind all Catholics in Canada to make the revealed Word of God and the teachings of the Church the basis for their life of faith and the central focus of their Christian spirituality."[120] Such wise counsel should be heeded by Catholics everywhere.

Any talk of "reincarnation" should have raised a red flag for Christians who encountered these messages, not to mention the startling notion that Mary has existed from all eternity, as if she were an additional divine person along with the Father, Son, and Holy Spirit of the Blessed Trinity. But claims to private revelation are not always so clearly at odds with the authentic teaching of the Church. In fact, most such claims do not easily lend themselves to a straightforward evaluation. Let's consider, for example, the case of the "Great Monarch" prophecy from Venerable Bartholomew Holzhauser.

First, we should note again that the messenger's life reflected demonstrable holiness in the judgment of the Church; that is why he was declared "Venerable." At the same time, it seems relatively clear that nothing in this particular statement (at least on the surface) is contrary to the faith or morals of revealed truth—though ultimately that evaluation would need to be made by a competent Church authority. So far, so good.

Looking more closely at the text, we note the references to a binding of Satan and to the "Son of Perdition." Both of these apparently allude to apocalyptic biblical passages we have already examined, including the "millennium" passage in the book of Revelation (see Revelation 20:2; 2 Thessalonians 2:3). If we reasonably conclude on the basis of these allusions that this is an end times prophecy of some sort, a few questions arise.

Is this a prediction of an earthly "millennial" kingdom that borders on millenarianism—the end times doctrine rejected by the Church? Those who embrace this prophecy would reply that it is not millenarian in the sense rejected by the Church. Millenarians expect, as the Congregation for the Doctrine of the Faith declared, that "Christ the Lord before the final judgment . . . will come visibly to rule over this world."[121] This particular prediction, on the other hand, insists instead that a "Great Monarch" will rule the kingdom rather than Christ.

Still, at least one significant question remains. If such an important figure as the "Great Monarch" is to appear in the last days, and he figures so prominently in God's plan for the close of the age, why does the Scripture say nothing of him?

The "Great Monarch" of European Legend

When we examine apocalyptic traditions in European history, the issue becomes even more complicated. This particular prophecy actually echoes the predictions of numerous other private revelations from many centuries, all of which speak of a "Great Monarch" who will reign over a golden age of peace and faith before the Antichrist comes. Visions and prophecies of this sort have been attributed to St. Caesar of Arles, Blessed Rabanus Maurus, St. Vincent Ferrer, St. Francis of Paola, St. Hildegard, Venerable Magdalene Porzat, and countless others of wise and holy reputation.

(Not all the attributions, of course, are necessarily accurate, and some are demonstrably inaccurate.)[122]

We can fill in the portrait of this "lion monarch," as he is sometimes called, with dozens of details from these various prophecies. They describe, for example, his French lineage, handsome physical features, glorious attire, and courageous military exploits. During his reign, say the predictions, Christians will live in peace, prosperity, and leisure. A holy pope, the "Pastor Angelicus," will cooperate with him to extend the faith throughout the world and to heal the divisions within Christendom. But the monarch will spend his final days in the Holy Land, where he will lay down his arms and be killed by the Antichrist, who will then be rising to power.

Does the abundance of parallel prophecies from so many centuries seem to be evidence supporting the genuineness of this private revelation? It could certainly seem that way, especially since some of the confirming messages come from canonized saints. On the other hand, it seems just as likely that because these ideas were floating around the culture in medieval Europe, it would be easy for the "prophets" simply to be restating what they had heard from others.

At the same time, many of these prophecies seem to contradict one another, weakening their claim to authenticity. For example, more than a dozen different personal names are attributed to the Great Monarch. And while some say he comes from the East, others say he comes from the West.

The Sibylline Oracles

A more serious problem appears when we look further back in time to discover the circumstances surrounding the earliest known occasions of the "Great Monarch" message. Although some collections of Catholic prophecies on this topic include a passage attributed to the fourth-century bishop and martyr St. Methodius of Patara, this text is actually a seventh-century message apparently written to console Syrian Christians who had come under Muslim rule. But it does draw from a fourth-century book that describes in some detail the "Emperor of the Last Days."

As it turns out, both of these early texts are among the so-called *Sibylline oracles*. These oracles are a collection of utterances that claim to be inspired messages from the Greek Sibyls (ancient pagan prophetesses) in earlier historical periods. But historians have concluded that they were actually written by Jewish and Christian authors in imitation of pagan Sibylline books.

In the *Tiburtina Sibyl*, the earlier of the two texts, the main outlines of the "Great Monarch" legend (for a legend is what it seems to be) are already apparent. The "Emperor of the Last Days" is a Greek monarch who reunites the eastern and western halves of the Roman Empire and reigns in a time of plenty, when oil, wine, and corn are cheap and abundant. He conquers the heathens, destroys their temples, and summons them to be baptized. The Jews also are converted.

When Gog and Magog rise against him (an allusion to Revelation 20:8), with hosts like the sands of the sea, his invincible army annihilates them. Then at last the emperor retires to Jerusalem, lays down the imperial crown and robes at Calvary, and returns the care of Christendom to heaven. The Golden Age closes with Antichrist's appearance; he reigns at the temple in Jerusalem, and the great tribulation begins. Eventually, however, God sends St. Michael to slay the Antichrist so that Christ can return. The later Sibylline oracle largely follows this account, but it expands the story some.

Throughout the Middle Ages, this Sibylline tradition captured the imagination of thousands. The books, of course, were not part of the Bible, and their account of the end times, though overlapping the book of Revelation somewhat, did not fit well with that text's vision. For example, the reference to a millennial kingdom in Revelation comes after, not before, the passages about Antichrist, ending with the unchaining of Satan, who summons Gog and Magog to his aid. And Revelation says nothing of a "Great Monarch"—nor do any biblical references to the last days or the close of the age.

Nevertheless, these stories became extremely influential in the culture of medieval Europe, though they never, of course, entered into the official teaching of the Church. According to some historians, the Sibylline tradition shaped popular religious thinking in the Middle Ages probably more than all other texts except for the Bible and the writings of the Church fathers. These predictions were freely adapted to various situations while keeping the main lines of the ancient story, and by the end of the Middle Ages, they were still widely read and studied.[123]

Are They Trustworthy Predictions?

To be sure, the unusual ancestry of the Great Monarch predictions does not necessarily render them unreliable. Even if they were proven to be straight from a pagan source, we have to remember that God can prophesy through unbelievers, as He did through the pagan prophet Balaam (see Numbers chapters 22–24). Then, too, the oracles may well have been written under the impetus of a political agenda, as some scholars claim. Yet even then, God can speak prophetically through someone whose statement is intended as a political objective rather than a prophecy, just as He spoke through the high priest Caiaphas (see John 11:49–52).

In any case, we are left with numerous age-old prophecies, excerpted and collected in modern volumes, whose claim to be true private revelations from God seems less than compelling. What do we make of them?

Perhaps in the case of the Great Monarch, the best course is simply to wait and see if they come to pass. Even if the words have been spoken by canonized saints, we have no obligation to accept them. Time will prove all things, and there certainly do not seem to be any candidates for an "Emperor of the Last Days" on the horizon just now.

Some who adhere to this prophetic tradition might counter, of course, that belief in a coming golden age can give us hope. But if the hope is false, we will be disappointed. And even if the hope is well-founded, it cannot begin to match the "blessed hope" we already have: "the appearing of the glory of our great God and Savior Jesus Christ" (Titus 2:13).

At most, an assurance that the wonderful era of the Great Monarch must come before the Antichrist—if such expectation does not degenerate into millenarianism—might help Catholics who are obsessively worrying about the latter's imminent arrival. On the other hand, the Antichrist might truly *be* on the horizon. The *Catechism* teaches, after all, that the great tribulation and Christ's second coming "could be accomplished at any moment" (673).

Looking for the Great Monarch, then, who does not appear in Scripture, might lead to overlooking the Antichrist, who does. It might even lead—a more disturbing thought—to mistaking the Antichrist for the Great Monarch. After all, lesser antichrists of the past such as Hitler and Stalin have seduced followers with visions of grand and glorious earthly kingdoms. Surely the Antichrist of the last days will do the same.

For all these reasons, we must exercise careful discernment when placing our confidence in prophetic claims.

An Untidy Reality

The Great Monarch predictions are certainly not the only Catholic prophetic traditions about the end times that we encounter. In fact, messages claiming divine inspiration abound.

The confused Catholic who tries to wade through them

all may at times envy his fundamentalist Protestant brethren. After all—unless they belong to charismatic or Pentecostal circles (and traditional fundamentalists usually shun such groups), their theology does not allow much for private revelations of more than a purely personal nature, such as "God told me to pray for you." For them, the only words of God with which we have to be concerned are in the Bible, and without the help of a Magisterium, they have trouble enough trying to figure out *that*.

As Catholics, however, we know that reality is much less tidy than all that. God did not stop speaking once He had given the Church the apostolic deposit of faith. He continued to explain the full meaning of that deposit through the development of doctrine, which continues down through this present age by the work of the Magisterium, under the guidance of the Holy Spirit. This is how the Church came to understand more clearly, for example, the mystery of the Most Holy Trinity—the truth that God is three Persons in one divine Essence. This most basic of Christian doctrines took several hundred years for the Magisterium to define in a way that would do justice to all the various aspects of the revelation that God had given us in Christ.

Yet there is even more to God's continued communication with the Church than the development of doctrine. He has also continued to give genuine private revelations. How else could St. Catherine of Siena have known the secrets of a pope's heart so she could challenge him to keep a promise he had made to God? How could St. Bernadette have uncovered the hidden spring that has healed thousands? How could three little isolated Portuguese children know, before it happened, that Marxist atheism would gush out of a political revolution in Russia to poison the world—when they did not even know what "Russia" was?

We should have no difficulty believing that God continues

to reveal spiritual and prophetic truths to individual believers. The *real* problem comes in sorting out which claims to revelation are genuine.

Urgent Warnings

A handful of prophetic themes seem to find multiple confirmations in various collections of Catholic prophecies, some of them dating back centuries. We can read about the expected catastrophic collision of a comet with the earth; three days of perilous worldwide darkness; a global warning to repent followed by a chastisement; a heightened role for the Blessed Mother in the affairs of earth; and, as we have already noted, an "era of peace" with millennial overtones.

To complicate the matter even further, contemporary "messengers" have sprung up and multiplied as fast as wild mushrooms, and some of them may be just as poisonous. Their messages sometimes agree with one another, sometimes not. Meanwhile, anyone who wants to stay up on the latest alleged locutions has to invest considerable time reading through the stacks of visionary emails that fly around the world daily via the Internet.

A number of these messengers call for concrete, immediate actions from their listeners. Some insist, for example, that Catholics must procure a supply of blessed candles (a few sources even dictate that they must be *beeswax* candles), because only these will be capable of providing light in homes during the "three days of darkness." Others call for the creation of hidden sites of refuge, well stocked for survival, to be used soon when the great persecution of the Church arrives. Still others urge the faithful to move away from coastal areas, because the coming comet will cause tidal waves that will wipe out the populations of coastlines around the world.

Here the stakes are considerably higher than with the Great Monarch prophecies. If heaven is truly warning us to buy candles or build a refuge against the dangers of darkness or persecution, then by all means we had better respond— if not to protect ourselves, then at least for the sake of our families and others who may depend on us in such terrible crises. In fact, even aside from the issue of personal safety, obedience to God is essential. So whatever it is He genuinely tells us through a messenger, we had better take action.

On the other hand, if these messengers are mistaken, then following them could lead to costly mistakes. Having a stockpile of dusty (but blessedly dusty) candles is no problem. You can always use them sooner or later. Yet imagine pulling up your personal roots from a lovely beach community on the Florida Gulf Coast because an alleged locutionist has warned repeatedly and urgently that the comet strike and subsequent tidal wave are imminent—a few months away at most. So you sell your home quickly at a loss; leave a fine job, extended family, and friends; and start all over again in a strange place hundreds of miles inland.

Now imagine how it feels to have the slow realization creep up on you, as the years go by uneventfully, that you have paid that steep price for nothing. The comet never came.

Year after year you had told yourself, "*It's still coming. It's just been delayed. Aren't most prophecies conditional? Maybe the disaster has been delayed by prayers and sacrifices.*"

Or maybe the alleged locutionist was deluded.

In any case, the comet never came. And you are too old now for all those morning jogs on the beach that you have missed so terribly. The kids (who never learned to swim) have grown up and moved off to southern California beaches anyway. The older extended family members you used to see every day, and who refused to come with you, have all gone on to their reward. And the price of Florida real estate has risen so sharply that the most you could afford there now is to rent a shed for your lawnmower.

That is a high price to pay for misplaced confidence. No doubt, since you acted in good faith, God may still reward you for trying to obey Him and to protect the family He gave you. Surely He can bring good out of your mistake. But don't you think He would have been more pleased if you had seen through the false message in the first place?

Guidelines for Discernment

The above scenario is not exaggerated. Some Catholics have paid even more dearly for being deceived by false claims to private revelations from God. In light of these situations, we can see why the Church wisely refuses to demand belief in private revelations.

Catholics can steer a course safely toward heaven without them, trusting instead in God's grace as He pours it out through the Sacraments, the Scripture, and all the ministries of the Holy Spirit. Those are His primary and essential means in the present age of drawing us closer to Himself and restoring His image in us so we can be fit to live with Him forever.

Even so, we certainly do not want to miss out on any extra graces our Lord may want to give us through private revelations. How much poorer we would be if our Lord had never asked St. Margaret Mary Alacoque to spread devotion to His Sacred Heart! How many souls have been drawn to God because that revelation has spurred them to make use of the more ordinary means of grace! If God has truly spoken, and His words have meaning—perhaps even urgency—for us, we are wise to want to hear and obey them.

Given that desire for obedience, a few guidelines for discernment when the Church's approval of a message has not been forthcoming may help us in dealing with a claim to private revelation. There are of course no foolproof methods for sorting out the wheat from the chaff. Sometimes we cannot recognize the chaff until the fire comes along to burn it up. But several questions can help us look for the truth in the meantime.

The pertinent issues center not just on the *message*, but also on the *messenger*. Since people most often encounter claims to private revelations through reading a message rather than personally meeting the messenger, we will start with queries about the text of the message itself.[124] Consider these:

- Do you have some assurance that the version of the message you have available is an accurate copy of the original, with nothing later added, suppressed, or corrected? Editorial revisions may be an indication that the original message had problems in content that had to be masked before it could be made public.

- Does the message contradict clear teaching of the Church with regard to faith or morals? If so, reject it. If you are not sure, find someone—a priest, or a lay person better trained than you in such matters—who can help you determine whether it does.

- Does the message agree with the commonly recognized facts of history and science? Again, you may need the advice of someone more knowledgeable about the pertinent information.

- Does the message have the goal of bringing its hearers to salvation? Messages that seem intended only to satisfy curiosity or to entertain an audience are suspect. When occultists, for example, claim to be receiving communications from God or angels, they often tend in such directions.

- Does the message attempt to pronounce authoritatively on an issue that can be legitimately disputed, such as the timing of the Second Coming or the proper approach to the book of Revelation? If it claims to settle such an issue definitively, without an official pronouncement of the Magisterium, then in effect it is claiming the status of public revelation. Reject it.

- Does the message attempt to pronounce authoritatively on some disputed issue of history or science, such as the identity of an ancient book's author or the true age of the universe? If so, be suspicious of it. Those are not usually the kinds of questions the Holy Spirit is interested in answering through special revelations.

- Is the message just a collection of simplistic spiritual platitudes? If so, it is more likely that the messenger is only repeating unwittingly some common thoughts from other sources.

- Does the message sound self-serving? Are words of praise for the messenger reported as coming from heaven? Does the message claim a special, privileged, or exalted role for the messenger? If so, the message might have its source in vanity rather than the Holy Spirit.

- Is the tone of the message fit for a communication from God? We are not talking here about stylistic qualities; God often speaks through messengers with little eloquence or training in the fundamentals of composition. We mean instead whether the words reflect the dignity and seriousness of a revelation from heaven. Again, in occult circles, the messages conveyed are often trivial and pedestrian.

- If the message extends a call to particular exterior works —certain charitable acts, the founding of a new organization, the establishment of a new devotion, preparations for the future—are these works reasonable? Are they good in themselves? Do they fill a need? On the other hand, would they be somehow injurious to other good works the listeners should be performing? Would they tend primarily to the benefit of the messenger (such as a call for donations)?

- Have the messages been subjected to the tests of time and examination?
- If a work has been started because of the revelation, has it produced good spiritual fruit?
- Has the messenger's local ordinary (the bishop administering his diocese) offered a public evaluation of the message or the messenger? No doubt this is not always the final test of its authenticity; bishops must be extremely cautious about such matters, given the history of fraudulent or misguided visionaries. Sometimes the ordinary will grant approval only long after the message has been given. But we should view such caution and delays as being, in general, to our benefit.

Questions About the Messenger

Next we come to questions about the messenger. It is not always possible to know much about the life of the person claiming private revelations unless the Church has already conducted an official investigation into the matter. But if you can learn the answers to at least some of the following questions, you will be in a better position to discern the genuineness of the *person* making the claims that are in question —an important context for the genuineness of the message.

- What personal qualities or conditions of the messenger might be relevant to an evaluation of the message? Is there any history of mental, emotional, social, spiritual, or even medical problems that might affect the trustworthiness of the messenger?

- What kind of theological training does the messenger have? Could the message simply be a rehash of knowledge gleaned from prior education, reading, or conversations?

- What virtues has the messenger displayed before and after the messages were received and published? Has there been a growth in personal holiness, especially in humility?

- Does the messenger have a healthy fear of being deceived by self or by the Devil?

- Does the messenger *crave* or *pursue* private revelations? If so, he is more vulnerable to deception, and the messages are more likely to be the result of either wishful thinking or demonic influence.

- Does the messenger submit gladly and regularly to the counsel of a competent spiritual director?

- Does the messenger claim to have received revelations other than the one you have examined? If so, and you can examine them, do they meet the criteria laid out above?

- If the messenger has previously made specific predictions, have those predictions come to pass? Or has the messenger had to rely on the suspicious explanation (or later "revelations") that the unfulfilled prophecy was either misunderstood by listeners or else delayed or canceled by God?

- Has the messenger received any extraordinary graces of union with God? Are there any verifiable supernatural signs? Neither of these, of course, guarantees that God has approved what a messenger says; but such phenomena, if occurring, should be taken into consideration.

- Has the messenger had great hardships to bear? Extraordinary trials often accompany extraordinary favors.

The Rapture Trap

Heroic endurance of adversity can be a clear sign of friendship with God, though again, this is no guarantee that the messages are of divine origin.

- Is the messenger typically characterized by a spirit of peace or a spirit of agitation? Does he seem to be motivated by charity or driven by anger or a desire for attention?
- Will the messenger gain wealth or accolades because of the revelations?
- If someone challenges the messenger, how do the messenger and his followers respond? Is their response humble and charitable or arrogant and hostile? Do they shun those who doubt the authenticity of the message? Sadly enough, some close friendships and even marriages have been shattered over disagreements about a claim to private revelation.

Growing in Discernment

Discernment is a lifelong process. It takes time and effort. You have to make use of the abundant resources available for continually educating yourself about the Faith. You have to become better acquainted with the God who grants genuine revelations. Only then can you recognize error or deception when it comes your way.

We should repeat here the important truth that Christians can spend a lifetime without ever delving into private revelations and still find all the grace they need to gain eternal life with God in heaven. But if you choose nevertheless to investigate such messages, perhaps the best rule of thumb for growing in discernment is this: *For every hour you spend reading, thinking about, and talking about private revelations, spend at least three hours reading, thinking about, and talking about Scripture and the Catechism.* Read the lives of the saints as well.

Private revelations, no matter how improbable on first sight, have a way of appearing plausible if you immerse yourself in them long enough. They lose their strangeness. They seep down in subtle ways into the cracks of your mind. Before long, you have lost your objectivity toward them. Anyone skilled in the techniques of propaganda or brainwashing can tell you that immersion is the key to persuasion.

If you plan to dive into private revelations, then, stay "underwater" for only brief periods of time. Come up often to breathe normally again by returning to the fresh air of Sacred Scripture, Tradition, and the Magisterium—and stay there for a while.

You may never discover the deep secrets of the Great Monarch. But you will draw much, much closer to the King of Kings.

Left Behind or Left Out?

A Final Word

We have taken a dizzying tour in nine chapters: from Bethlehem to Babylon, Mount Olivet to Muenster, the Old Jerusalem to the New. From the Lamb's throne to the lake of fire. From the camps of rebel German peasants to the palace of the Great Monarch. On the way, we have had a few eye-opening detours down roads that lead to nowhere: the treacherous paths of secret rapture theorists, zealous millenarians, and alleged locutionists.

What have we learned on our tour?

Some Important Lessons

The Big Picture

First, by stepping back to get the big picture of Christ's mission on earth, we have seen how His first advent, His ministry through the Church in the present age, and His second advent all fit together. This world is broken. But the Son of God came to the world, remains present in the world, and will come again to the world so that "the world might be saved through Him" (John 3:17).

That is why we celebrate Christmas and Easter, Good Friday and Pentecost. That is why we receive the Sacraments and meditate on Scripture. That is why we discipline ourselves in Advent and Lent. And that is why we pray, "Thy kingdom come!"

Christ has died. Christ is risen. Christ will come again.

The "Plain Sense" of Scripture

Second, we have examined Scripture to see what it plainly tells us about Christ's return to earth. It says nothing of a secret rapture. It promises no escape from the persecution of the Antichrist.

Instead, Scripture predicts that Christ's coming will be a glorious event of such grandeur that it could never be kept a secret. It warns Christians that until He comes, they will suffer tribulation; and if they are living on earth when the Antichrist comes, they will suffer *great* tribulation. But it promises that if they endure to the end by God's grace, they will be saved.

These straightforward interpretations of Scripture, we found, have been held consistently throughout the history of the Church by Catholic teachers, Eastern Orthodox teachers, and many Protestants as well.

The Rapture Trap

Third, we saw the unbiblical origins of the secret rapture teaching. We observed how interpreters must twist the Scriptures to try to read this peculiar scenario into the text. And we also saw how much trouble Christians can get into when they fail to recognize the Sacred Magisterium. Believers desperately need this authoritative interpreter of the Bible, which God in His mercy has given to the Church.

At the same time, we uncovered the dangers of the quirky theological system that usually surrounds the invisible "third" coming idea. We traced its inadequate vision of the Church and the present age. And we learned how many rapture promoters are both subtly and not-so-subtly attacking the Catholic Church.

What the Church Teaches

Fourth, we summarized the teachings of the Catholic Church with regard to the close of the age. We found the *Catechism* to be a "sure guide" in clear language, presenting the essentials that Catholics everywhere are obliged to believe. Meanwhile, we discovered that God has left us with a number of mysteries about the end times that are yet unsolved.

Within the boundaries the Church has laid out, a lively debate continues about matters on which the Church has remained silent. Unless God should happen to reveal more light to the Church on these issues, they will probably be disputed until Judgment Day.

Private Revelations

Finally, we took a look at the confusing world of private revelations. Noting the critical difference between these and public revelation, we saw how Catholics are not obliged to accept the former, even when the Church has approved them. But we also observed that private revelations have enriched the life of the Church immeasurably, and if God is speaking to us through them, we should want to listen.

Volumes of Catholic prophecies have been collected, insisting we pay attention to the chorus of voices they present— not all of which are singing in harmony with one another or with revealed Catholic truth. So we ended with a few guidelines for discerning claims to private revelation, helping us wisely examine both the messages and the messengers.

Some Friendly Advice

It is time now to close with a few words of friendly advice.

If you are a Catholic who has been invited by a friend or relative to explore the *Left Behind* books or tapes, one thing should be crystal clear by now: They are not worth your time. And if you have been a Catholic consumer of the *Left Behind* products or similar materials, no matter how entertaining they might seem, you should lay them aside. They are spiritual poison.

Strong words, yes. But true words. Sadly enough, however sincere their intentions may or may not be, the people behind *Left Behind* will deceive you. They will fill your head with flawed history, faulty theology, and twisted interpretations of Scripture. They will lead you astray in matters of eternal importance.

These people continue to repeat age-old falsehoods about the Catholic Church, the Church that Jesus Christ Himself founded through His Apostles. And they want to persuade you to leave that Church. They want you to trade all its rich spiritual feast for a pot of half-baked, spoiled leftovers they call the "true" faith.

Don't fall into their trap. Instead, take the time to learn more about what the Church teaches so you can avoid that sort of trouble.

Of course, Catholics who are well-grounded in the Faith and capable of debating theology with non-Catholics might do well to study the *Left Behind* novels and related texts so they can better understand the flaws in these books. With Bible and *Catechism* in hand, they could help others to identify the problems of the rapture teaching. But if you are not yet prepared to be a skilled defender of the Faith in this way, your time will be much better spent with solid Catholic literature that will nourish your mind and heart on the truth.

This book is not intended to offer a full-fledged defense of Catholic truth. There are countless books, magazines, tapes, and websites out there already that provide all the biblically based, theologically sound evidence and arguments you need for such a task. (See some recommended books in the list at the end of this volume.) If you make use of these resources, you can be firmly established in your faith and learn to discern the errors of those who attack the Catholic Church. A wise and holy spiritual director would also be invaluable.

The purpose of this book has been much more specific: to show how one particularly popular religious idea in America right now, the secret rapture notion, is a dangerous deception and part of a larger web of false ideas. If you have read carefully, you should be convinced by now from Scripture and Tradition, reason and history, that the *Left Behind* theology leads to trouble—just as deception *always* leads to trouble.

Recently some Catholics have tried to wrench the rapture idea from its Dispensationalist context and graft it into orthodox Catholic theology. Usually this hybrid notion is buttressed by appeals to unapproved private revelations. But even when the "third" coming doctrine has been severed from its anti-Catholic roots, it remains unorthodox. It simply cannot be fit into the Church's clear teaching that Christians will suffer at the hands of Antichrist before our Lord's single, glorious return to earth.

If you are eager to learn more in depth what we can truly know about the end of the world, that information is readily available. Meditate deeply on the relevant scriptural passages we have noted. Reflect carefully on what the *Catechism of the Catholic Church* has to say about the subject as a context for the scriptural texts.[125]

If you feel up to it, you might even try tackling such thought-provoking texts as Venerable John Cardinal Newman's "Advent Sermons of Antichrist" or the twentieth book of St. Augustine's *City of God* (and the fifty-third chapter of the eighteenth book as well). Other books by Catholics of lesser reputation (and sometimes lesser wisdom as well) abound, hoping to fill in more apocalyptic details. As you read all these, keep in mind that in matters on which the

Church has remained silent, Catholics are free to speculate within the bounds of revealed truth, and many of them have.

Nevertheless, their speculations do not all agree. So they cannot all be right, and they certainly do not carry the weight of official Church teaching. Remember: The Magisterium of the Catholic Church is your unerring guide to understanding Scripture, not whatever ideas might be tossed about by individual Catholics.

If you have discovered some of the books out there by Catholics with private revelations, or books promoting such revelations, read cautiously and with discernment. Compare what they say, and especially what they predict for the future, with what the Church clearly teaches. As we have seen, some contemporary alleged locutionists are openly contradicting established Catholic doctrine. Remember that Catholics are not obliged to accept any private revelations, even those that the Church has approved.

Meanwhile, keep in mind the old story (perhaps only a legend, but nonetheless instructive) about a question once posed to St. Francis of Assisi. As the humble saint was weeding a garden, a visitor asked him, "What would you do if you knew that tomorrow the world would end?"

His reply was quick: "I would finish weeding the garden."

Those are the words of a man who was so confident he was serving God's purposes, he had no fear of the end of the world. Should Jesus come back to earth, St. Francis hoped simply to hear the words, "Well done, good and faithful servant" (Matthew 25:21). He intended to be found doing what God had called him to do at that moment—even if it was only weeding a garden.

If we can cultivate the same kind of attitude toward the close of the age, we too can be busy "gardening"—weeding out mistaken apocalyptic notions and planting instead seeds of a vibrant faith, hope, and charity.

Marana tha!

Finally, *pray*. Ask the Holy Spirit to give you wisdom and discernment. Ask Him for boldness with the people you know—boldness to tell them the truth about the future He has planned. Pray that He will draw you close to His heart, that He will make you more like Himself, that He will grow you into a mature, holy son or daughter fit to live with Him eternally.

Intercede for the Church as well. Ask our Father in heaven to strengthen it, to heal its divisions, to warm the hearts of those within it who are cold and indifferent. Pray that He will protect it from the attacks of its enemies, both within and without—especially those who shamelessly assault it or seek to undermine it while claiming to speak in His name. Ask the Holy Spirit to urge pastors and other Catholic educators to preach and teach courageously and clearly what God has revealed to the Church about the close of the age. As long as there is a vacuum of correct catechesis on the subject, Catholics will continue to be seduced by fundamentalist errors and spurious claims to private revelation.

Pray for the Church's enemies. Ask God to enlighten and convert them. Pray that He will reveal to them all the glorious riches of the fullness of Catholic faith. Call on Him to help our separated brethren over all the obstacles they must overcome to return to the peace of His Church. Pray that they will avoid, not being left behind, but being left out—outside the door of that magnificent spiritual mansion, the Catholic Church, to which their Father and ours patiently calls them home.

Ask the Blessed Virgin Mary for her intercession and help in all these concerns. Keep in mind St. John's dazzling vision in the book of Revelation: a Woman, piercing the darkness of catastrophes and diabolical assaults, a Lady "clothed with the sun, with the moon under her feet, and on her head a crown of twelve stars" (Revelation 12:1). As the *Catechism* affirms, when we look to the close of the age, we find that "the Church is awaited by the one she venerates as Mother of her Lord and as her own mother. 'In the meantime the Mother of Jesus, in the glory which she possesses in body and soul in heaven, is the image and beginning of the Church as it is to be perfected in the world to come. Likewise she shines forth on earth, until the day of the Lord shall come, a sign of certain hope and comfort to the pilgrim People of God'" (972).[126]

Above all, pray for the coming of the Lord. Jesus taught us to pray this way in the Our Father: "Thy kingdom come!" (Matthew 6:10). In Aramaic—the language Jesus spoke—the early Christians begged fervently: *"Marana tha!* [Our Lord, come!]"* (1 Corinthians 16:22, NAB). It is one of the Church's most ancient petitions, ringing down the centuries of the present age.

In this prayer, we join with the saints of all time, "all who have longed for his appearance" (2 Timothy 4:8, NAB). Today and every day, then, until the close of the age, let every faithful heart echo the cry with which the Scripture itself draws to a close (Revelation 22:20):

"Amen! Come, Lord Jesus!"

Notes

INTRODUCTION

[1] The second title, targeting a popular rather than scholarly audience, gives "Bob Gundry" as the author's name. A similar response from a Catholic viewpoint, giving more attention to the confusing array of allegedly "biblical" arguments offered by secret rapture believers, is now in manuscript stage. The author of that forthcoming work is Carl Olson, a Catholic convert from a Protestant fundamentalist background. His book should prove to be quite valuable for Catholic apologists who wish to engage in extended debates with rapture believers.

CHAPTER ONE

[2] Tim LaHaye and Jerry Jenkins, *Left Behind: A Novel of the Earth's Last Days* (Wheaton, Ill.: Tyndale, 1995), is the first book in the series; the opening scenario of this chapter comes from that book.

[3] See, for example, Tim LaHaye and Jerry Jenkins, *Are We Living in the End Times? Current Events Foretold in Scripture . . . and What They Mean* (Wheaton, Ill.: Tyndale, 1999), 98.

[4] Robert H. Gundry, *The Church and the Tribulation: A Biblical Examination of Posttribulationism* (Grand Rapids, Mich.: Zondervan, 1973), 161.

[5] An attempt to clarify my use of the terms "evangelical Protestant" and "fundamentalist Protestant" may be helpful here. These labels are admittedly fluid; their meanings have varied over the course of American religious history, and their application depends to a great extent on the religious or cultural assumptions of the person using the words. In this book, when I write "evangelical Protestants" (or more briefly, "evangelicals"), I will mean this: those Protestants who (1) see themselves as adhering to the "classical" theologies of the Reformation, especially the teaching of Martin Luther and John Calvin; and (2) also emphasize a personal experience of divine grace in conversion, as found in the teaching of John Wesley. In practice, of course, evangelical belief often differs considerably from the teachings of Luther, Calvin, and Wesley—

as we shall see, for example, with regard to the "secret rapture" notion itself.

In this setting, when I write of "fundamentalist Protestants" (or more briefly, "fundamentalists"), I refer to a particularly strident type of evangelical whose religious attitudes are more militant in defense of their faith against all threats, both real and perceived. These fundamentalists typically (1) stand in opposition to major aspects of modern culture, especially its secularizing tendencies; (2) take a more hostile stance with regard to the Catholic Church, whose teaching they clearly recognize as a challenge to many of the traditional Protestant dogmas they hold dear; and (3) are distinguished by a rather peculiar system of interpreting Scripture called "dispensationalism"—a system that has adopted the "rapture" teaching as its own. (More about this in chapter six). Not all fundamentalists are strict dispensationalists, but in America, the two traditions nearly coincide, and dispensational notions such as the rapture have found their way into the larger evangelical community.

Though many fundamentalists still accept the label "evangelical" for themselves, many (perhaps most) contemporary evangelicals reject the label "fundamentalist" for themselves. Despite a shared theological conservativism, those who prefer to be called "evangelicals" typically desire to be more open than fundamentalists to positive (or at least redeemable) elements in modern culture. They also are more likely to recognize sincere Christians of other traditions—such as Catholics—as spiritual brothers and sisters.

Ironically, many of the "fundamental" Christian doctrines that the fundamentalists affirm are also embraced by traditional Catholics. Both groups stand in opposition to modernist tendencies to abandon age-old doctrines such as Christ's virgin birth, miracles, bodily resurrection, ascension, and second coming. As many traditional Catholics and fundamentalist Protestants joining hands in the pro-life movement have discovered, despite important differences, these two Christian traditions actually have many theological and moral essentials in common. But the secret rapture doctrine is certainly not one of them.

For a history of these groups in America, see B. L. Shelley, "Evangelicalism," and T. P. Weber, "Fundamentalism," in *Dictionary of Christianity in America*, Daniel G. Reid, ed. (Downer's Grove, Ill.: InterVarsity Press, 1990), 413–16; 461–65.

⁶ For more on these martyrs, see Robert Royal, *The Catholic Martyrs of the Twentieth Century: A Comprehensive World History* (New York: Crossroad, 2000).

⁷ See LaHaye and Jenkins, *End Times*, 171–77; similar teaching can

be found in Tim LaHaye, *Revelation Unveiled* (Grand Rapids, Mich.: Zondervan, 1999), 65–71; 260–77.

CHAPTER THREE

[8] St. Ignatius of Antioch, *Epistle to the Ephesians*, 20, 2; see also *Catechism of the Catholic Church*, English translation, 2nd ed. (Washington, D.C.: United States Catholic Conference, Inc., 1997), 1402–5; hereafter cited as "CCC."

[9] See the *Dogmatic Constitution on Divine Revelation (Dei Verbum)*, 2, 10.

[10] See, for example, the claims about four judgments in the commentary on Matthew 25:32 by C. I. Scofield, whose *Scofield Reference Bible* (New York: Oxford, 1st ed., 1909) has influenced the beliefs of countless American fundamentalists for nearly a century.

CHAPTER FIVE

[11] For more on this and related movements, see R. L. Numbers and J. M. Butler, eds., *The Disappointed: Millerism and Millenarianism in the Nineteenth Century* (Bloomington, Ind.: Indiana University Press, 1987).

[12] In the disciples' question, the biblical Greek word translated as "coming" (*parousia*) is often used by St. Paul and other biblical writers to refer to Christ's second advent (see, for example, 1 Corinthians 15:23; 2 Thessalonians 2:8; 2 Peter 3:4; 1 John 2:28). But the word can also be translated "appearance." A few biblical scholars adopt that alternative translation here and conclude that the disciples were not asking about Christ's return to earth at all. Rather, they say, these men were expecting Christ to "appear" or "manifest" Himself as judge through the terrible event He had just predicted.

Some interpreters go even further to insist that all our Lord's predictions in reply to their question refer only to the temple's destruction, not to His second coming. So they would view the Olivet discourse as actually having little to do with the end of the world. At most, they conclude, the destruction of the temple serves to foreshadow the cosmic disturbances that will come at the close of the age.

Nevertheless, the claim that Jesus was only talking about first-century events has found little support since the days of the early Church. For example, the *Teaching of the Twelve Apostles* (or the *Didache*), a text of the first or second century, alluded to this passage in its chapter on the Antichrist and the end of the world. A number of Church fathers also understood Jesus' reply on this occasion to be a prophecy of *both* the temple's demise *and* the close of the age. Among these, to name a few, were such highly respected writers as St. Irenaeus (c. 125–c. 203), St. Victorinus (died c. 304), Origen (c. 185–c. 254), St. Hippolytus (died c. 235), St. John Chrysostom (c. 347–407), and St. Augustine (354–430), all of whom quote verses from this passage to talk about Christ's second coming at the close of the age. See the *Didache*, 16; 2–7; St. Irenaeus, *Against Heresies*, IV, 33, 12–13; St. Victorinus, *Commentary on the Apocalypse*, 13, 13; Origen, *De Principiis*, I, 5, 5; *Against Celsus*, II, 49; VI, 45–46; St. Hippolytus, *Fragments From the Commentary on Daniel*, 39–43; *Treatise on Christ and Antichrist*, 62–64; St. John Chrysostom, *Homilies on the Gospel of St. Matthew*, X; LIII, 23; LXXV; LXXVII; St. Augustine, *Epistles*, XCIII, 8, 34.

St. Augustine comments in a letter to Hesychius (LXXX) that we cannot be sure which of the "signs" of Christ's coming (such as wars, earthquakes, famines, and so on) apply to the destruction of the temple, which to Christ's second advent, and which to His ceaseless visiting of His Church in the present age. But he refers the ambiguity to the signs, not to the event of Christ's return itself, which he assumes is indeed described in this passage. In discussing the Second Coming (with reference to St. Augustine's letter), St. Thomas Aquinas (c. 1225–1274) reveals that he too believes that the Olivet discourse (including the parallel passages in the other Gospels) refers in part to the Second Advent (*Summa Theologica*, III, Suppl., Q. 73, Art. 1; see especially "Reply to Objection 1"; Q. 74, Art. 2, "Reply to Objection 3").

The view of all these writers—that in the Olivet discourse, Jesus was referring to both events—is reflected in the *Catechism of the Catholic Church*, which repeatedly cites His words on this occasion to teach about events still to come at the close of the age. (See the footnotes referring to Matthew chapter 24 and parallel passages for paragraphs 671–675, 697, 2612.) Even believers in the secret rapture agree with this perspective.

For all these reasons, in this discussion we can safely adopt this view as our own. Yet even if it should be the case that our Lord was speaking on this occasion only of first-century events, the critique of the secret rapture notion based on other biblical texts can stand on its own.

[13] See CCC, 697.

[14] Bob Gundry, *First the Antichrist: A Book for Lay Christians Approaching the Third Millennium and Inquiring Whether Jesus Will Come to Take the Church Out of the World Before the Tribulation* (Grand Rapids, Mich.: Baker, 1997), 15–16.

[15] For more on these unconvincing distinctions, see Gundry, *The Church and the Tribulation*, 89–99.

¹⁶ Douglas J. Moo, "Response [to Feinberg]," in Gleason L. Archer, et al., *The Rapture: Pre-, Mid-, or Post-Tribulational?* (Grand Rapids, Mich.: Zondervan, 1984), 99–100.

¹⁷ *End Times*, 104.

¹⁸ See Marilyn J. Agee's "Projected Chronology of End-Time Events," at home.pe.net/~mjagee/endtime_chron.html (August 5, 2001). Material was accessed on August 28, 2001.

¹⁹ J. Alberto Soggin, *Introduction to the Old Testament: From Its Origins to the Closing of the Alexandrian Canon* (Louisville, Ky.: Westminster/John Knox Press), 368–71.

²⁰ The song was Larry Norman's "I Wish We'd All Been Ready." The *Left Behind* series takes its title from this same biblical passage.

²¹ For a sample of the ensuing debates (of the more charitable sort), see Archer, et al., *The Rapture*.

CHAPTER SIX

²² *Dialogue With Trypho*, 110. The texts of all the documents cited from the Fathers can be found in *The Ante-Nicene Fathers: Translations of the Writings of the Fathers Down to A.D. 325*, Alexander Roberts and James Donaldson, eds. (Grand Rapids, Mich.: Eerdmans, 1987 reprint), 10 volumes; and *A Select Library of the Nicene and Post-Nicene Fathers of the Christian Church*, Philip Schaff, ed. (Grand Rapids, Mich.: Eerdmans, 1988, reprint), First and Second Series, 28 vols. Some quotes have been modernized.

²³ *Against Heresies*, V, 26, 1; 35, 1.

²⁴ *Scholia on Daniel 12:1*.

²⁵ *Treatise on Christ and Antichrist*, 64.

²⁶ St. Jerome, Letter XIV.

²⁷ St. Augustine of Hippo, *City of God*, XX, 8, 11, 14.

²⁸ *City of God*, XX, 20.

²⁹ St. John Chrysostom, *Homilies on Romans*, XIV.

³⁰ St. John Chrysostom, *Homilies on Thessalonians*, VIII.

³¹ Quoted in Gundry, *First the Antichrist*, 162–63. For more about this text, see this author's discussion in his "Postscript," 161–88. Catholics should keep in mind that Gundry's book is a thoroughly Protestant view. But as a whole it is helpful in showing how even an evangelical Protestant might argue against the secret rapture teaching. See also Gundry, *The Church and the Tribulation*.

³² St. Thomas Aquinas, *Summa Theologica*, Suppl. Q. 77, Art. 2.

³³ St. Bernard of Clairvaux, *Sermon on the Song of Songs*, 33, 16.

[34] Martin Luther, *Preface to the Revelation of St. John*, II; see also his *Sermon on John 16:13*.

[35] John Calvin, *Institutes of the Christian Religion*, IV, vii, 25; III, xx, 42.

[36] Calvin, *Commentary on First Corinthians*, 52.

[37] Mather is quoted in Paul Boyer, *When Time Shall Be No More: Prophecy Belief in Modern American Culture* (Cambridge, Mass.: Harvard, 1992), 75. Morgan Edwards' book was entitled *Two Academical Exercises on Subjects Bearing the Following Titles; Millennium, Last. Novelties* (Philadelphia: Dobson and Lang, 1788).

[38] For a recent edition of the original Spanish version, see Manuel Lacunza, *Venida de Mesías en gloria y majestad* (Puebla: Cladie, 1994).

[39] Some who have written about the nineteenth-century British promoters of the secret rapture idea claim that these teachers were influenced by the visions of a young girl, Margaret McDonald. But the historical evidence for this particular claim seems to me to be less than compelling.

[40] For a further sampling of Dispensational ideas, see the ubiquitous notes in *The New Scofield Reference Bible*, edited by C. I. Scofield (New York: Oxford, 1969). For more on the story of Dispensationalism and its apocalyptic views in America, see Boyer.

[41] For more on Darby's teaching and influence, see Ernest R. Sandeen, *The Roots of Fundamentalism: British and American Millenarianism, 1800–1930* (Chicago: University of Chicago Press, 1970).

CHAPTER SEVEN

[42] Quoted in Robert Cameron, "Notes by the Way," *Watchword & Truth* 35 (December 1913): 337, which in turn is quoted in Archer, et al., *The Rapture*, 26. Emphasis in the original.

[43] David L. Cooper, quoted in LaHaye and Jenkins, *End Times*, 5.

[44] LaHaye and Jenkins, *End Times*, 33–34.

[45] See, for example, LaHaye and Jenkins' statements in *End Times*, 174.

[46] See W. H. Lampe, ed., *The Cambridge History of the Bible*, v. 2, *The West from the Fathers to the Reformation* (Cambridge: Cambridge University Press, 1969), 391. For a summary of early Bible translations, see A. J. Maas, "Versions of the Bible," in *The Catholic Encyclopedia* (New York: Robert Appleton, 1912), v. 15, available online at www.newadvent.org/cathen/15367a.htm.

[47] For an English translation of pronouncements by this and other

ecumenical councils, see Norman P. Tanner, ed., *Decrees of the Ecumenical Councils* (Washington, D.C.: Georgetown University Press, 1990), in two volumes. The texts of the Fifth Lateran Council are also available online at www.pax-et-veritas.org/Councils/lateran5.htm.

[48] More on these and other medieval and Reformation apocalyptic movements can be found in Norman Cohn, *The Pursuit of the Millennium: Revolutionary Millenarians and Mystical Anarchists of the Middle Ages* (New York: Oxford, 1961, rev. ed.), and Boyer, chapter two, "Rhythms of Prophecy Belief," 46–79.

[49] Quoted in Cohn, *The Pursuit of the Millennium*, 213.

[50] See Luther's tracts against the peasants in J. M. Porter, ed., *Luther: Selected Political Writings* (Philadelphia: Fortress Press, 1974), 71–88. For more on his attitude toward the book of Revelation, see his *Preface to the Book of Revelation* (1522) in volume 6 of *Works of Martin Luther*, C. M. Jacobs, trans. (Philadelphia: Muhlenberg, 1932).

[51] Hal Lindsey with C. C. Carlson, *The Late Great Planet Earth* (Grand Rapids, Mich.: Zondervan, 1970), 127.

[52] CCC, 760. Sources cited in the *Catechism:* J. P. Migne, ed., *Pastor Hermae*, Vision 2, 4, 1: *Patrologia Graeca* (hereafter "PG") (Paris: 1857–1866) 2, 899; cf. Aristides, *Apol.* 16, 6; St. Justin, *Apol.* 27: PG 6, 456; Tertullian, *Apol.* 31, 3; 32, 1: PG 1, 508–09.

[53] From Darby's collected letters, quoted in Sandeen, *Roots of Fundamentalism*, 63.

[54] Quoted in William G. McLoughlin, *Revivals, Awakenings, and Reform* (Chicago: University of Chicago, 1978), 144.

[55] Tim LaHaye, *Revelation Unveiled* (Grand Rapids, Mich.: Zondervan, 1999), 30–31.

[56] CCC, 849.

[57] *Gaudium et spes*, 40, 2; quoted in CCC, 854.

[58] John F. Walvoord, *The Thessalonian Epistles* (Findlay, Ohio: Dunham, 1957), 83.

[59] Gundry, *Antichrist*, 15.

[60] Carl E. Olson, "Waiting to Be Raptured: Dispensationalist Thought in America," accessed online August 29, 2001, at www.nativityukr.org/various_files/Waiting_for_the_Rapture.html.

CHAPTER EIGHT

[61] Tim LaHaye, *No Fear of the Storm* (Sisters, Ore.: Multnomah, 1992), 14, quoted in Gundry, *Antichrist*, 17.

[62] Gundry, *Antichrist*, 15.

[63] Tim LaHaye and Jerry Jenkins, *Tribulation Force: The Continuing Drama of Those Left Behind* (Wheaton, Ill.: Tyndale, 1996), 53.

[64] *Tribulation*, 53–55. The apparent confusion about the words "Apocrypha" and "Apocalypse" is found on page 54. This astonishing mistake is not easily explained as a mere typographical error. These are such basic, commonly used terms in biblical studies that no serious scholar of the Bible could confuse them.

[65] *Tribulation*, 269, 271.

[66] *Tribulation*, 273, 279.

[67] LaHaye and Jenkins, *End Times*, xi.

[68] LaHaye and Jenkins, *End Times*, 171.

[69] LaHaye and Jenkins, *End Times*, 172.

[70] As a sample of evangelical texts on world religions, see George W. Braswell, *Understanding World Religions*, rev. (Nashville: Broadman & Holman, 1994); Norman Anderson, ed., *The World's Religions*, 4th ed. (Grand Rapids, Mich.: Eerdmans, 1975); for a broader treatment, see John F. Wilson and W. Royce Clark, *Religion: A Preface*, 2nd ed. (Upper Saddle River, N.J.: Prentice Hall, 1997).

[71] LaHaye and Jenkins, *End Times*, 173–74.

[72] Numerous books, tapes, and magazine articles are available to help Catholics respond to the kind of accusations against their faith typically offered by fundamentalists. A good book to start with is Albert J. Nevins, *Answering a Fundamentalist* (Huntington, Ind.: Our Sunday Visitor, 1990). Also helpful in this regard are the numerous apologetics tracts available from Catholic Answers; on this particular issue, see "Is Catholicism Pagan?"

[73] Ralph Woodrow, *Babylon Connection?* (Riverside, Calif.: Ralph Woodrow Evangelistic Association, 1997); Alexander Hislop, *Two Babylons; or, papal worship proved to be the worship of Nimrod* ([n.p.], 1858). See Woodrow's website at www.ralphwoodrow.org/books/babylon.htm. This material was accessed on August 29, 2001.

[74] LaHaye and Jenkins, *End Times*, 174.

[75] LaHaye and Jenkins, *End Times*, 174; see also 4–6.

[76] For further reading about the Protestant Reformers' use of St. Augustine, see Jaroslav Pelikan, *The Christian Tradition: A History of the Development of Doctrine*, vol. 4, *Reformation of Church and Dogma, 1300–1700* (Chicago: University of Chicago Press, 1984); see references in the index under "Augustine—relation to," 411.

[77] LaHaye and Jenkins, *End Times*, 174.

[78] LaHaye and Jenkins, *End Times*, 174–175.

⁷⁹ See Albert J. Nevins, *Answering a Fundamentalist*, 117.

⁸⁰ LaHaye and Jenkins, *End Times*, 176–77.

⁸¹ "The Catholic Origins of Futurism and Preterism" at www.aloha. net/~mikesch/antichrist.htm; Alan Campbell, "The Secret Rapture—Is It Scriptural?" at www.1335.com/secrapt.html; both sites were accessed on August 30, 2001.

⁸² Keep in mind that the broader field of eschatology also includes the "last things" with regard to the human individual: death, individual (or "particular") judgment, heaven, purgatory, and hell. But these other subjects are of course beyond the scope of our discussion.

⁸³ Numbers in parentheses refer to the relevant item in the text of the *Catechism*. The notes appearing in the *Catechism* are referenced in the endnotes of this chapter.

⁸⁴ Luke 21:27; cf. Matthew 25:31.

⁸⁵ Matthew 24:44; 1 Thessalonians 5:2; 2 Thessalonians 2:3–12.

⁸⁶ Cf. 2 Thessalonians 2:4–12; 1 Thessalonians 5:2–3; 2 John 7; 1 John 2:18, 22.

⁸⁷ Cf. Luke 18:8; Matthew 24:12.

⁸⁸ Cf. Revelation 19:1–9.

⁸⁹ Cf. Revelation 13:8; 20:7–10; 21:2–4.

⁹⁰ Cf. Denzinger-Schönmetzer, *Enchiridion Symbolorum, definitionum et declarationum de rebus fidei et morum* (1965), 3839. Hereafter cited as "*DS*."

⁹¹ Romans 11:20–26; cf. Matthew 23:39.

⁹² Romans 11:12, 25; cf. Luke 21:24.

⁹³ Ephesians 4:13; 1 Corinthians 15:28.

⁹⁴ Lateran Council IV (1215); *DS* 801; Philippians 3:21; 1 Corinthians 15:44.

⁹⁵ John 6:39–40, 44, 54; 11:24; *Lumen Gentium* 48 §3.

⁹⁶ Cf. Revelation 20:12; 2 Peter 3:12–13.

⁹⁷ Matthew 13:41–42.

⁹⁸ Matthew 25:41.

⁹⁹ 2 Peter 3:13; cf. Revelation 21:1.

¹⁰⁰ Ephesians 1:10.

¹⁰¹ Vatican II, *Gaudium et spes* 39 §2.

¹⁰² Cf. Ephesians 1:14; 2 Corinthians 1:22.

¹⁰³ 2 Peter 3:13.

¹⁰⁴ See William Hendriksen, *More Than Conquerors* (Grand Rapids, Mich.: Baker, 1939), 11–64.

¹⁰⁵ See *City of God*, XX, 6–9.

[106] Bible scholar Scott Hahn, for example, suggests this possibility in *The Lamb's Supper: The Mass As Heaven on Earth* (New York: Doubleday, 1999), 73.

[107] Lactantius, *Epitome of the Divine Institutes*, 72.

[108] St. Justin Martyr, *Dialog With Trypho*, 80. St. Irenaeus thought that the first-century teacher Papias had received his millenarian teaching personally from the Apostle John—a conviction that would no doubt have influenced him and others to accept this doctrine (see St. Irenaeus, *Against Heresies*, V, 33, 4). But the early church historian Eusebius insisted that Irenaeus was mistaken, and that "Papias himself, in the preface to his discourses, by no means declared that he was himself a hearer and eyewitness of the holy Apostles; instead, he shows by the words he uses that he received the doctrines of the faith from those who were their acquaintances" (Eusebius, *Church History*, III, 39, 1–3). Eusebius implied that Papias' information was closer to misunderstood hearsay than reliable testimony. He concluded: "I suppose that Papias got these ideas [of an earthly millennial kingdom] through a misunderstanding of the apostolic accounts, not perceiving that the things said by them were spoken mystically in figures" (12).

We should note, however, that some Catholics dispute Eusebius' position and interpret the seemingly millenarian statements of these early Christian writers as figurative language, insisting that the Church fathers were not truly millenarian, but rather expected a future "era of peace" in which Christ will reign invisibly and spiritually rather than visibly and in the flesh. See, for example, Joseph Iannuzzi, *The Triumph of God's Kingdom in the Millennium and End Times: A Proper Belief From the Truth in Scripture and Church Teachings* (Havertown, Penn.: St. John the Evangelist, 1999), 9–43.

[109] Congregation for the Doctrine of the Faith, Decree of 19 July 1944, *DS*, 3839.

[110] Cf. *DS*, 3839.

[111] For examples of this "spiritual millenarianism" in a variety of forms, see Iannuzzi, *Triumph*; Desmond A. Birch, *Trial, Tribulation & Triumph: Before, During and After Antichrist* (Santa Barbara, Calif.: Queenship, 1996); Ted and Maureen Flynn, *The Thunder of Justice: The Warning, the Miracle, the Chastisement, the Era of Peace* (Sterling, Va: MaxKol Communications, 1993); The Marian Movement of Priests, *To the Priests: Our Lady's Beloved Sons* (Milan, Italy: Movimento Sacerdotale Mariano, n.d.). Bud Macfarlane, Jr., presents similar ideas through fiction; see his novel *Pierced by a Sword* (Fairview Park, Ohio: Saint Jude Media, 1995).

112 Cf. Revelation 13:8; 20:7–10; 21:2–4.

113 *City of God*, XX, 7–9.

114 Most of these and other speculations of this sort are described in P. Huechedé, *History of Antichrist* (Rockford, Ill.: TAN, 1968, reprint).

CHAPTER NINE

115 Yves Dupont, *Catholic Prophecy* (Rockford, Ill.: TAN, 1970, reprint), 40.

116 *Dei verbum*, 4; cf. 1 Timothy 6:14; Titus 2:13.

117 Pope Benedict XIV, *De canon.*, III, liii, xxii, II.

118 Email from Joseph Hunt, "Messages Via Louise Tomkiel, October 29, 1998," received November 3, 1998.

119 Pope Pius IX, *Ineffabilis Deus*, 1854, emphasis added.

120 "Doctrinal Note of the Catholic Bishops of Canada Concerning the Army of Mary," Canadian Conference of Catholic Bishops, June 29, 2001. This Doctrinal Note received the *recognitio* of the Congregation for the Doctrine of the Faith on August 10, 2001 (Prot. N. 216/74-13501), and was subsequently published by the Canadian Conference of Catholic Bishops on August 15, 2001. For an overview of the creed of the Army of Mary, see *Le Royaume* 143 (July 1, 2000): 8. The full text of the bishops' document is available at the website of the Canadian Conference of Catholic Bishops, www.cccb.ca. This material was accessed September 1, 2001.

121 Congregation for the Doctrine of the Faith, Decree of July 19, 1944.

122 Most of the prophecies in this tradition can be found in R. Gerald Culleton, *The Prophets and Our Times* (Rockford, Ill.: TAN, 1974, reprint); see also Birch, *Trial, Tribulation & Triumph*, chapter five, "Chronological Prophecies of a Great King, His Relationship to a Chastisement," 241–82.

123 See Cohn, *Pursuit of the Millennium*, 30–36.

124 For an excellent essay on these and other considerations, see Augustine Poulain's article on "Private Revelations" in the 1912 edition of the *Catholic Encyclopedia* (New York: Robert Appleton, 1912), available online at newadvent.org/cathen/13005a.htm.

LEFT BEHIND OR LEFT OUT?

[125] In the *Catechism*, see especially paragraphs 668–82; 972; 988–1004; 1015–17; 1186; 2771–72; 2776.

[126] The *Catechism* quotes here from *Lumen Gentium* 68; cf. 2 Peter 3:10.

For Further Reading

By Catholic authors about the close of the age, the book of Revelation, and related subjects, from a variety of viewpoints:

Birch, Desmond A. *Trial, Tribulation & Triumph: Before, During and After Antichrist*. Santa Barbara, Calif.: Queenship, 1996.

Fanzaga, Livio. *Wrath of God: The Days of the Antichrist*. A. J. O'Brien, trans. Fort Collins, Colo.: Roman Catholic Books, 1997.

Féret, H. M. *The Apocalypse Explained*. Elizabethe Corathiel, trans. Fort Collins, Colo.: Roman Catholic Books, [n.d.], reprint.

Hahn, Scott. *The Lamb's Supper: The Mass As Heaven on Earth*. New York: Doubleday, 1999.

Iannuzzi, Joseph. *The Triumph of God's Kingdom in the Millennium and End Times: A Proper Belief From the Truth in Scripture and Church Teachings*. Havertown, Penn.: St. John the Evangelist, 1999.

Kramer, Herman Bernard F. Leonard. *The Book of Destiny: An Open Statement of the Authentic and Inspired Prophecies of the Old and New Testament*. Rockford, Ill.: TAN, 1975, reprint.

Miceli, Vincent P. *The Antichrist*. Fort Collins, Colo.: Roman Catholic Books, 1981.

Montague, George T. *The Apocalypse and the Third Millennium: Today's Guide to the Book of Revelation*. Ann Arbor, Mich.: Servant, 1998.

By non-Catholic authors who reject the secret rapture doctrine:

Frazier, T. L. *A Second Look at the Second Coming: Sorting Through the Speculations*. Ben Lomond, Calif.: The Conciliar Press, 1999.

Gundry, Robert H. *The Church and the Tribulation: A Biblical Examination of Posttribulationism*. Grand Rapids, Mich.: Zondervan, 1973.

———. *First the Antichrist: A Book for Lay Christians Approaching the Third Millennium and Inquiring Whether Jesus Will Come to Take the Church Out of the World Before the Tribulation*. Grand Rapids, Mich.: Baker Books, 1997.

MacPherson, Dave. *The Rapture Plot*. N.p., 2000.

Moo, Douglas. "The Case for Posttribulationism." In *The Rapture: Pre-, Mid-, or Post-Tribulational?* Gleason L. Archer, Jr., et al., ed. Grand Rapids, Mich.: Zondervan, 1984, 169–211. See also Moo's responses to the other essays.

On the historical background of the secret rapture doctrine and apocalyptic movements:

Boyer, Paul. *When Time Shall Be No More: Prophecy Belief in Modern American Culture*. Cambridge, Mass.: Harvard, 1992.

Cohn, Norman. *The Pursuit of the Millennium: Revolutionary Millenarians and Mystical Anarchists of the Middle Ages*. New York: Oxford, 1961, rev. ed.

McLoughlin, William G. *Revivals, Awakenings, and Reform*. Chicago: University of Chicago Press, 1978.

Numbers, R. L., and J. M. Butler, eds. *The Disappointed:*

Millerism and Millenarianism in the Nineteenth Century. Bloomington, Ind.: Indiana University Press, 1987.

Sandeen, Ernest R. *The Roots of Fundamentalism: British and American Millenarianism, 1800–1930.* Grand Rapids, Mich.: Baker, 1970.

Resources for deepening and defending your faith as a Catholic:

Abbott, Walter M., ed. *The Documents of Vatican II.* New York: America Press/Association Press, 1966.

The Catechism of the Catholic Church, English translation, 2nd ed. Washington, D.C.: United States Catholic Conference, Inc., 1997.

Catholic Answers. *Tract Sampler.* Available from Catholic Answers, P. O. Box 199000, San Diego, CA 92159.

Hardon, John. *The Catholic Catechism.* Garden City, New York: Doubleday, 1975.

Keating, Karl. *Catholicism and Fundamentalism: The Attack on "Romanism" by "Bible Christians."* San Francisco: Ignatius, 1988.

———. *What Catholics Really Believe: 52 Answers to Common Misconceptions About the Catholic Faith.* San Francisco: Ignatius, 1992.

Kreeft, Peter. *Catholic Christianity: A Complete Catechism of Catholic Beliefs Based on the Catechism of the Catholic Church.* San Francisco: Ignatius, 2001.

———. *Fundamentals of the Faith: Essays in Christian Apologetics.* San Francisco: Ignatius, 1988.

Madrid, Patrick, ed. *Surprised by Truth: Eleven Converts Give the Biblical and Historical Reasons for Becoming Catholic.* San Diego, Calif.: Basilica, 1994.

————. *Surprised by Truth 2: Fifteen Men and Women Give the Biblical and Historical Reasons for Becoming Catholic*. Manchester, N.H.: Sophia Institute Press, 2001.

Nevins, Albert J. *Answering a Fundamentalist*. Huntington, Ind.: Our Sunday Visitor, 1990.

Shea, Mark P. *By What Authority? An Evangelical Discovers Catholic Tradition*. Huntington, Ind.: Our Sunday Visitor, 1996.

Schreck, Alan. *Catholic and Christian: An Explanation of Commonly Misunderstood Catholic Beliefs*. Ann Arbor, Mich.: Servant, 1984.

Sheed, Frank. *A Map of Life: A Simple Study of the Catholic Faith*. San Francisco: Ignatius, 1994.

Stravinskas, Peter M. J. *Our Sunday Visitor's Catholic Dictionary*. Huntington, Ind.: Our Sunday Visitor, 1993.

————. *The Catholic Response*. Huntington, Ind.: Our Sunday Visitor, 2001, rev. ed.

Thigpen, Paul. *Blood of the Martyrs, Seed of the Church: Stories of Catholics Who Died for Their Faith*. Ann Arbor, Mich.: Servant, 2001.

————. *A Dictionary of Quotes From the Saints*. Ann Arbor, Mich.: Servant, 2001.

About the Author

Paul Thigpen, Ph.D., is a senior editor for Servant Publications and associate editor of *Envoy* magazine. He began his study of "end times" movements and beliefs at Yale University, where he received a B.A. *summa cum laude* with distinction in the major of Religious Studies. He was awarded the prestigious Woodruff Fellowship at Emory University in Atlanta, where he earned an M.A. and Ph.D. in historical theology. Thigpen has served as assistant professor of American religion at Southwest Missouri State University in Springfield; as a fellow in theology at The College of Saint Thomas More in Fort Worth, Texas; and on the adjunct faculty of Saint Leo University in Savannah, Georgia. His abiding interest in apocalyptic and millenarian movements has prompted him to continue research, writing, and teaching on the subject.

An award-winning journalist, Thigpen has published more than five hundred articles for national and international audiences. He is also a best-selling author, having published twenty-five books, including most recently *A Dictionary of Quotes From the Saints* (Servant, 2001) and *Blood of the Martyrs, Seed of the Church: Stories of Catholics Who Died for Their Faith* (Servant, 2001). *The Rapture Trap* draws not only from his study of "end times" fervor, but also from his personal experience: He is a former evangelical Protestant pastor who entered the Catholic Church in 1993. Thigpen lives with his wife, Leisa, and their two children in Savannah, Georgia.

To order additional copies of
The Rapture Trap,
or for bulk discounts,
please call Ascension Press
(800) 376-0520.

Please visit
www.AscensionPress.com
for information about
other Ascension Press titles.